Rhetoric, Women a
in Early Modern E

Rhetoric has long been a powerful and pervasive force in political and cultural life, yet in the early modern period rhetorical training was generally reserved as a masculine privilege. This volume argues, however, that women found a variety of ways to represent their interests persuasively, and that by looking more closely at the importance of rhetoric for early modern women, and their representation within rhetorical culture, we also gain a better understanding of their capacity for political action.

Offering a fascinating overview of women and rhetoric in early modern culture, the contributors to this book:

- examine constructions of female speech in a range of male-authored texts from Shakespeare to Milton and Marvell;
- trace how women interceded on behalf of clients or family members, proclaimed their spiritual beliefs and sought to influence public opinion;
- explore the most significant forms of female rhetorical self-representation in the period, including supplication, complaint and preaching;
- demonstrate how these forms enabled women from across the social spectrum, from Elizabeth I to the Quaker Dorothy Waugh, to intervene in political life.

Drawing upon incisive analysis of a wide range of literary texts including poetry, drama, prose polemics, letters and speeches, *Rhetoric, Women and Politics in Early Modern England* offers an important new perspective on the early modern world, forms of rhetoric and the role of women in the culture and politics of the time.

Jennifer Richards is Reader in English at the University of Newcastle upon Tyne and **Alison Thorne** is Senior Lecturer in English at the University of Strathclyde. They have each published several books and articles on rhetoric and the early modern period.

Contributors:
Danielle Clarke, James Daybell, Martin Dzelzainis, Huw Griffiths, Helen Hackett, Rachel Heard, Hilary Hinds, Patricia Parker, Neil Rhodes, Susan Wiseman

Rhetoric, Women and Politics in Early Modern England

Edited by
Jennifer Richards and Alison Thorne

Routledge
Taylor & Francis Group

LONDON AND NEW YORK

First published 2007
by Routledge
2 Park Square, Milton Park, Abingdon OX14 4RN

Simultaneously published in the USA and Canada
by Routledge
270 Madison Avenue, New York, NY 10016

Routledge is an imprint of the Taylor & Francis Group, an informa business

Typeset in Baskerville by Laserwords Private Limited,
Chennai, India
Printed and bound in Great Britain by Antony Rowe Ltd,
Chippenham, Wiltshire

British Library Cataloguing in Publication Data
A catalogue record for this book is available
from the British Library

Library of Congress Cataloging-in-Publication Data
A catalog record for this book has been requested

ISBN 10: 0–415–38526–1 (hbk)
ISBN 10: 0–415–38527–X (pbk)

ISBN 13: 978–0–415–38526–8 (hbk)
ISBN 13: 978–0–415–38527–5 (pbk)
ISBN 13: 978–0–203–96590–0 (ebk)

Contents

Acknowledgements

This collection has been a long time in the making. It originated in a conference held at the University of Strathclyde in 2003, Renaissance Rhetoric, Gender and Politics. First of all we would like to thank all of those who contributed in various ways to its success and, especially, Robert Maslen, Katherine Eisaman Maus, Margaret Philips, Ceri Sullivan and James Thain as well as the Department of English Studies at Strathclyde who generously helped to fund it. We have been very privileged in our contributors, both those who participated in the conference and those who joined the project at a later stage, all of whom have helped to shape the scope and purpose of this book. In particular, we should thank them for their conscientiousness, good humour and staying power in responding to our suggestions. Special thanks go to Neil Rhodes for exemplary patience. Not only was he one of our keynote speakers but he agreed to undertake the difficult task of writing the afterword and did so with characteristic kindness and good grace. We are also grateful to Mariangela Palladino and Patrick Hart for cheerfully lending their computing expertise in the last stages of the project. Finally, thanks must go to our long-suffering partners, George Biddlecombe and Dermot Cavanagh and, of course, to Perdy, for keeping us entertained along the way and making us jelly.

Alison would like to dedicate this book to her mother, Beryl Thorne, whose untiring support has sustained her through every research project. And Jennifer would like to dedicate it to her sisters, Helen and Rosie.

Contributors

Danielle Clarke is Senior Lecturer in the School of English and Drama Studies at University College Dublin. She is the author of *The Politics of Early Modern Women's Writing* (Longman, 2001) and editor of the poems of Whitney, Sidney and Lanyer for Penguin Classics. She has published widely on gender and writing, textual editing, language and sexuality in the early modern period and is currently working on a book-length study of relationships between gender and discourse in the Renaissance.

James Daybell is Senior Lecturer in History at Plymouth University. He has also taught at the University of Reading and Central Michigan University. He is author of *Women Letter-Writers in Tudor England* (Oxford University Press, 2006), editor of *Early Modern Women's Letter-Writing, 1450–1700* (Palgrave, 2001; Winner of the Society for the Study of Early Modern Women award for best collaborative project, 2002), and *Women and Politics in Early Modern England, 1450–1700* (Ashgate, 2004) and has written numerous articles and essays on early modern gender, social and cultural history.

Martin Dzelzainis is Professor of Early Modern Literature and Thought at Royal Holloway, University of London. He has written many articles on John Milton, Andrew Marvell and Civil War culture and politics. He has edited Andrew Marvell, *The Rehearsal Transpos'd* and (with Annabel Patterson) *The Rehearsal Transpos'd: The Second Part*, in *The Prose Works of Andrew Marvell* (Yale University Press, 2003). He is also editor of *John Milton: Political Writings* (Cambridge University Press, 1991) and, with Warren Chernaik, *Marvell and Liberty* (Macmillan, 1999). With Paul Seaward, he is general editor of *The Works of Edward Hyde, Earl of Clarendon* and editor of Volume

X: The Histories for *The Complete Works of John Milton* (both forth-coming from Oxford University Press). Currently, he is completing *The Flower in the Panther: Truth-telling, Print and Censorship in England, 1662–1695*, also for Oxford University Press.

Huw Griffiths is Lecturer in Early Modern English Literature at the University of Canterbury, Christchurch, New Zealand. He has published a number of articles on national geographies in early modern England and a book on *Hamlet: A Reader's Guide to Essential Criticism* (Palgrave Macmillan, 2005). He is currently working on a monograph entitled 'A Nation in Ruins'.

Helen Hackett is Reader in English at University College London. Her publications include an Introduction to *A Midsummer Night's Dream* for the Penguin Shakespeare edition, *Women and Romance Fiction in the English Renaissance* (Cambridge University Press, 2000), *Writers and Their Work: 'A Midsummer Night's Dream'* (Northcote, 1997) and *Virgin Mother, Maiden Queen: Elizabeth I and the Cult of the Virgin Mary* (Macmillan, 1995).

Rachel Heard completed her Ph.D. at the University of St Andrews. She has written a series of biographies for Volume III of the *Oxford History of Literary Translation in English* (forthcoming), and she is working on a book provisionally entitled 'Shakespeare, Gender and Rhetoric'. She has taught medieval and Renaissance literature at the Universities of St Andrews and East Anglia.

Hilary Hinds is Senior Lecturer in English at Lancaster University. She is the author of *God's Englishwomen: Seventeenth-Century Radical Sectarian Writing and Feminist Criticism* (Manchester University Press, 1996), editor of Anna Trapnel's *The Cry of a Stone* (1654) (MRTS, Arizona Center for Medieval and Renaissance Studies 2000) and co-editor of *Her Own Life: Autobiographical Writings by Seventeenth-Century Englishwomen* (Routledge, 1989). She has also published a number of articles on early modern sectarian writing in *Literature and History, Renaissance and Reformation* and *Quaker Studies.*

Patricia Parker is Professor of Comparative Literature at the University of Stanford. She is the author of *Literary Fat Ladies: Rhetoric, Gender, Property* (Methuen, 1987) and *Shakespeare from the Margins: Language, Culture, Context* (University of Chicago Press, 1996). She is the co-editor, with Geoffrey Hartman, of *Shakespeare and the Question of Theory* (Methuen, 1985), with David Quint, of *Literary Theory/Renaissance Texts* (Johns Hopkins University Press, 1986) and, with Margo Hendricks, of *Women, 'Race' and Writing in the Early Modern Period* (Routledge, 1994). She is currently editing the Arden III *Midsummer Night's Dream*.

Neil Rhodes is Professor of English Literature and Cultural History at the University of St Andrews. His publications include *The Power of Eloquence and English Renaissance Literature* (Harvester, 1992) and *Shakespeare and the Origins of English* (Oxford University Press, 2004). He has also co-edited, with Jonathan Sawday, *The Renaissance Computer: Knowledge Technology in the First Age of Print* (Routledge, 2000) and, with Stuart Gillespie, *Shakespeare and Elizabethan Popular Culture* (Arden Shakespeare, 2006).

Jennifer Richards is Reader in English at the University of Newcastle. She is the author of *Rhetoric and Courtliness in Early Modern Literature* (Cambridge University Press, 2003), the editor of *Early Modern Civil Discourses* (Palgrave Macmillan, 2003) and co-editor, with James Knowles, of *Shakespeare's Late Plays: New Readings* (Edinburgh University Press, 1999). *Rhetoric: The New Critical Idiom* is forthcoming with Routledge.

Alison Thorne is Senior Lecturer in English at the University of Strathclyde. She is the author of *Vision and Rhetoric in Shakespeare: Looking through Language* (Palgrave Macmillan, 2000) and the editor of the *New Casebooks: Shakespeare's Romances* (Palgrave Macmillan, 2003). She is the author of various articles and essays on Shakespeare, rhetoric, aesthetics and other aspects of early modern culture and is currently writing a book on 'Female Supplication in Early Modern Drama and Culture'.

Susan Wiseman is Reader in English at Birkbeck College, the University of London. She is the author of *Aphra Behn* (Northcote House, 1996), *Politics and Drama in the English Civil War* (Cambridge University Press, 1998) and *Conspiracy and Virtue: Women, Writing and Politics in Seventeenth-Century England* (forthcoming from Oxford University Press).

1   Introduction

Jennifer Richards and Alison Thorne

[Women] whom nature hath made to keep home and nourish the
family [. . .] [are] not to meddle with matters abroad, not to bear
an office in the city or commonwealth, no more than children and
infants.

(Smith 1583: 20)

In what ways can we conceive of early modern women as politically
active? We are not the first to ask this question, or to struggle to
answer it positively. Remarkably, in England two women held supreme
power from 1553–1603, but despite this extraordinary state of affairs
women were largely excluded from the early modern public sphere.
They could not serve as jurors, lawyers, magistrates, counsellors or as
members of parliament. They did not study in the universities or at the
inns of court; nor did they write treatises about, or debate publicly,
constitutional or theological matters. As the painstaking efforts of
many feminist scholars have established, in this period women of
aristocratic and middling rank did write prolifically. Yet this often
took the form of 'private' devotional works as well as poems and plays
intended for circulation among family and friends. When women did
venture to publicise their thoughts through the medium of print,
they risked infamy (Krontiris 1992: 17–18). A notable exception to
women's removal from public life, of course, is the interventions
made by female religious radicals and political activists in the 1640s
and 1650s, figures such as Elizabeth Poole who related her visions
to the Army Council in 1648 and 1649, the Fifth Monarchist Anna
Trapnel who spoke out against the 'pomp of Cromwell and the rulers
of England' in 1654 (Crawford 1996: 137) and the leveller women
who petitioned Parliament in the 1640s about a range of issues
(Higgins 1973: 200–18). However, female petitioning was frequently

met with ridicule and hostility. Ann Hughes describes the response to the leveller women who petitioned parliament on 23 April and 7 May of 1649, initially to secure the release of leveller men from prison, the second time for the 'right' to petition and to represent their grievances. Contemporary newsbooks record that the Speaker responded belatedly to the first petition to the effect that he had already made his answer to their husbands and that they should go home and manage their domestic affairs (Hughes 1995: 163). In this case, such an injunction was not successful because, as Hughes notes, the leveller women 'considered themselves as citizens as well as wives, mothers and widows' (1995: 164); hence the second and stronger petition in May.

We should remember, however, that such examples constitute an important exception to the rule, although this time from the opposite end of the social, not to speak of the political, spectrum to Mary I and Elizabeth I. Undoubtedly, the upheavals of the mid-seventeenth century did favour 'unorthodox behaviour', as Lois G. Schwoerer has noted; we could say that 'religion animated and empowered women, giving them confidence and a sense of responsibility for their church and society', though without advancing sexual equality (Schwoerer 1998: 61–2). In general, though, early modern women did not *usually* intervene quite so openly, not least because of the cultural prohibition against women's speaking in public and also, and in relation to this, because they had not received the formal education that would have prepared them to do so.

Religion empowered women in a way that the humanist educational curriculum did not. Indeed, the different content and aims of male and female education have been emphasised and worried over in feminist histories, not least because of the close association perceived to exist between training in rhetoric and political action in this period. In contrast to their sisters, wives and mothers, for instance, men of middle rank and above who attended grammar school or were tutored at home would have received at least a rudimentary introduction to the classical art of persuasion, and this training was envisaged as preparing them to make some contribution to public life. Rhetoric can be understood, in the first place, as a body of rules, a list of devices that rationalise the act of 'speaking well' or persuasively; in early modern England, it also constituted a programme of reading, supplying boys and university students with linguistic resources that they could deploy, as the need arose, in their own speech or written compositions.

The study of rhetoric was closely associated with the study of Latin which was, again, unavailable to all but a few women. Schoolboys were first given elementary sentences, usually moral phrases, to enable them to grasp the rules of Latin syntax. After using these to master 'accidence', they would then read dialogues, later Latin letters and plays, excerpting from these texts phrases which they could adapt grammatically in their conversations and writings, but which they could also imitate for 'rhetorical' effect (Mack 2005: 6–7). Boys were encouraged to spot stylistic devices as they read and to collect these as well as any 'commonplaces' that they discovered: that is, proverbs, maxims or pithy sayings, ready-made phrases which were excerpted and stored in 'commonplace books' under headings ('places') so as to facilitate their easy retrieval for future use. Underpinning this programme was the pragmatic philosophy of the Roman technical manuals, perhaps especially Quintilian's encyclopaedic *Institutio oratoria* (*On the Training of the Orator*), the complete manuscript of which had been rediscovered in 1416. From these sources, Tudor schoolboys and their masters gained a new confidence in the possibility of arriving at a 'socially useful, pragmatic truth' (Kahn 1985: 376), and beyond this, they found what we would term a role model, the *vir civilis* (the civil man) 'who knows how to plead in the law courts for justice and to deliberate in the councils and public assemblies of the *res publica* in such a way as to promote policies at once advantageous and honorable' (Skinner 1996: 69). Rhetorical training created resourceful and flexible minds. It produced a generation of public servants, counsellors and 'intelligencers' who were skilled in the art of deliberative oratory, that is, men who were linguistically equipped to move others to act. Arguably, it also produced the *male* polemicists of the religious sects in the mid-seventeenth century, many of whom had received and used this training, even if they made a show of rejecting it in their own writing.

Historians and literary critics largely agree that this male education was dreary but enabling; by contrast, female education is viewed primarily in restrictive terms as inhibiting intellectual development. The same pragmatic philosophy that promoted rhetorical training for men as a necessary prerequisite for a life of public service also served to justify women's debarment from such training on the grounds that they could not hold civic office. Instead of aiming to produce articulate female subjects, women's education was, notoriously, geared to the shaping and management of women's moral character and conduct and to preparing them for their domestic roles as wives, mothers and household managers. In practice, this meant that women were usually expected to confine themselves to acquiring housewifery skills and a level of literacy sufficient to enable them to discharge their domestic duties and to read the religious and homiletic texts that would fortify them against the perceived weaknesses of their sex. That women were at a notable disadvantage in this respect is well documented and understood, and any number of humanist educationalists can be mustered to support and explain the reasoning behind the rarely qualified refusal to extend formal tuition in the arts of speaking to women.[1] One early contributor to the debate on female education was Italian humanist, Lionardo Bruni. Despite his willingness to open up certain areas of the new curriculum to women, including poetry, history, moral philosophy and the study of the 'great Orators of antiquity', Bruni used the vocational argument in his *De studiis et literis* (*c*.1405) to refute any suggestion that they should strive to become proficient in rhetoric themselves:

> My chief reason is the obvious one, that I have in view the culti-vation most fitting to a woman. To her neither the intricacies of debate nor the oratorical artifices of action and delivery are of the least practical use, if indeed they are not positively unbecoming. Rhetoric in all its forms, – public discussion, forensic argument, logical fence, and the like – lies absolutely outside the province of woman.
>
> (Bruni, cited in Woodward 1905: 126)

Another highly influential voice in defining the parameters of female learning was that of the Spanish humanist and tutor to Mary Tudor, Juan Luis Vives, whose *De institutione foeminae Christianae* (1523), translated by Richard Hyrde under the title *Instruction of a Christian Woman* (*c*.1529), would appear in five English editions before the end of the century (Henderson and McManus 1985: 82). Vives opposed formal training in rhetoric for women not only on account of its lack of practical utility, but also, and more crucially, because its 'public' nature jeopardised women's reputation for chastity which, he insisted, it was the purpose of their upbringing and education to safeguard. Whereas 'it is meet that the man have knowledge of many and divers things, that may profit both himself and the commonwealth', Vives argues that a woman should be mindful only of preserving her modesty by staying at home and 'hold[ing] her tongue demurely' (Watson 1912: 55). Hence his tart pronouncement, much quoted since, that 'As for eloquence, I have no great care, nor a woman needeth it not, but she needeth goodness and wisdom' (Watson 1912: 54). The belief that erudition is acceptable in a woman only in so far as it is commensurate with her 'honesty' and makes her a better 'helpmeet' or mother was widely echoed in the period, even by those writers such as Hyrde and Thomas More who put a more liberal gloss on this position. More, for example, who came closest to acknowledging the intellectual parity of the sexes, commended the retiring modesty of his studious daughter, Margaret Roper, who 'never hunt[ed] after vulgar praises' for her scholarly accomplishments, 'nor receive[d] them willingly', but contented herself with a readership of two: her father and husband (cited in Watson 1912: 189).

Unsurprisingly, then, feminist historians have concluded that women's education in the period served primarily to close off the possibility of women achieving a public voice and to reinforce the ideological imperatives that confined them to the domestic sphere. However, it is not just a problem of the segregation of male and female education. Rhetorical handbooks have also been seen to contribute to the elaboration of a negative and highly circumscribed model of female speech. As the ground-breaking work of Patricia Parker established in the 1980s, the rhetorical manuals inscribe an unflattering discrepancy between male and female speech forms through their gendered taxonomy of linguistic styles, a classification in which verbal excesses were codified as feminine in relation to a prevailing ideal of 'virile' eloquence that was constructed as pure, orderly, concise, vigorous and, above all, spare (Parker 1996). Thus, Parker argues, Desiderius Erasmus's *Lingua* (1525), a treatise on 'the use and abuse of the tongue', draws on proverbial notions of female loquacity in its disparagement of verbal over-abundance as a feminine 'disease' even as Erasmus acknowledges its affinities with a 'Ciceronian copiousness' that was widely emulated in male writings of the period including his own (Parker 1989). More broadly, Parker sets out, in *Literary Fat Ladies* (1987), to show that popular handbooks on rhetoric or poetics, such as George Puttenham's *Arte of English Poesie* (1598), conceive of rhetoric as an ideologically 'motivated' discourse, 'an instrument of civil order', its function being not only to regulate instances of verbal and social indecorum but also, and by extension, to maintain the 'natural' hierarchical ordering of the household and commonwealth which language should reflect. If women feature prominently in such discussions of rhetoric, it is not as practitioners of this art, but through their long-standing association with 'unruly tropes' and other linguistic 'abuses' as analogously disruptive 'figures' needing to be brought under control. This connection rested, in turn, upon classical and biblical commonplaces which elided verbal fluency in women with uncontrollable sexual desire and the abandonment of their 'proper' place in the social order, as exemplified by the 'moovable' harlot of

Proverbs 7, who is 'full of babling and loude woordes' and 'whose feete can not abyde in her house' (Parker 1987: 104–7).

A similar agenda is discernible in the constraints imposed on female speech by the conduct literature (homilies, marriage sermons, household manuals) of the period which recycled the familiar derogatory stereotypes of the railing wife, scolding shrew and garrulous gossip. But the key difference is that women's failure to govern their 'glibbery member', here too understood as a by-word for unbridled wantonness and disruption of male authority, is opposed not to manly eloquence, but to an ideal of female reticence. That silence is a woman's 'best ornament' was tirelessly reiterated. Making explicit the double standard underpinning this dictum, Dod and Cleaver affirm that 'the dutie of man is, to be skilfull in talke: and of the wife, to boast of silence' (Dod and Cleaver 1612: 43). But, in a tacit admission that it was neither feasible, nor indeed desirable, for women to observe this ideal in all circumstances, conduct-book writers devoted most of their energies to laying down ground rules as to what is, or is not, a socially acceptable manner of speaking for wives and maids. As a counterpoise to the cautionary anti-type of the verbally (and sexually) incontinent whore or shrew, they promote a normative model of reserved female speech exuding humility, mildness and deference that signifies the wife's acceptance of her subjugation as a divinely ordained state. Thus William Whately argues that 'the wives tongue toward her husband must be neither keene nor loose; neither such as argues rage nor neglect: but savouring of all lowlinesse and quietnesse of affection' (Whately 1619: 196).

Similarly, in *Of Domesticall Duties* (1622), William Gouge advises that when in the company of her husband, a wife's 'words must be few, reverend and meeke', for silence 'implieth a reverend subjection, as on the other side too much speech implieth a usurpation of authoritie' (Gouge 1976: 281–2). Gouge reinforces this message by citing the Pauline edict against women speaking out in church (1 *Timothy* 2: 12), a prohibition which, like other conduct writers, he extends to the domestic sphere. Meanwhile, Richard Brathwait advises a young gentlewoman who finds herself in social situations where she is compelled to talk to pick her topics of conversation carefully:

> It suites not with her honour, for a young woman to be prolocutor. But especially, when either men are in presence, or ancient Matrons, to whom shee owes a civill reverence, it will become her to tip her tongue with silence. Touching the subject of your discourse, when opportunity shall exact it of you, and without

touch of immodesty expect it from you; make choyce of such arguments as may best improve your knowledge in houshold affaires, and other private employments. To discourse of State-matters, will not become your auditory: nor to dispute of high poynts of Divinity, will it sort well with *women* of your quality [. . .] In one word, as modesty gives the best grace to your behaviour, so moderation of *Speech* to your discourse.

(Brathwait 1631: 89–90)

If staying silent is not an option, women must still strive to ap-proximate this condition by practising a decorous 'moderation' in their 'discourse'; above all, they are enjoined to confine their talk to 'houshold affaires' and not presume to discuss 'State-matters' and other topics that lay outside their natural capacity and province.

This model of female speech has served as the basis for much feminist critical analysis of women's talk. Taking their cue from moralists such as Gouge and Brathwait, some critics have suggested that early modern women were caught in an impossible double bind: if they expressed themselves too volubly, they were liable to be branded as harlots, shrews or scolds; if they refrained from doing so, they were reduced to a state of mute impotence, leav-ing them no valid position from which to speak (Jardine 1983, Belsey 1985, Newman 1991). Yet, there are risks in reading pre-scriptive writings as though they were uncomplicatedly indicative of women's actual experience and of the limited discursive opportu-nities available to them. Despite the prescriptions of the conduct books, historians have noted that the behaviour of women inside and outside the home often 'diverged from prescribed patterns' quite dramatically (Capp 1996: 120). For instance, it is hard to reconcile the image of the tongue-tied and submissive woman ide-alised in the conduct literature with examples that abound in other sources of women haranguing their menfolk or publicly accusing their female neighbours of sexual misconduct (Capp 1996, Gowing 1996). Susan Amussen notes that in practice even the most pro-saic activities required of the housewife made 'the expectation of silence [. . .] virtually impossible to meet'; women could not man-age a busy household 'without talking themselves [. . .] nor did one succeed in the market[place] if one was too meek or obedient' (1999: 87). While, as literary critics have observed, the Elizabethan and Jacobean theatre produced more than its fair share of strikingly articulate female characters who prove themselves to be not a jot less adept or versatile in their choice of ripostes than their male counterparts, without necessarily exercising their 'wit' in obviously transgressive ways.

Yet, for all the reasons noted above, scholars who are interested in recovering the political significance of women in early modernity have chosen to focus, not on reclaiming for women a rhetorical culture to which they allegedly did not belong, but on expanding our conception of 'politics'. Thanks in large measure to their efforts, politics is no longer narrowly conceived as debate about constitutional issues or restricted to the institutions of government. Indeed, in an essay that appeared in Hilda L. Smith's landmark collection, *Women Writers and the Early Modern British Political Tradition* (1998), Lois G. Schwoerer notes that the idea of 'political culture' rather than 'politics' is particularly useful to feminist historians because it provides a framework for a conception of participation that could involve women of different social ranks and take different forms: 'dispensing patronage, influencing decision makers and elections, petitioning, demonstrating, gift-giving, entertaining, haranguing, reporting seditious conduct, writing and disseminating ideas in printed form' (Schwoerer 1998: 57–8). That our conception of the early modern 'public sphere' needs extending to take account of female activity is now widely granted, though this is subject to differing interpretations. On the one hand, as David Norbrook has noted, in the mid-seventeenth century 'it was not unambiguously clear to the authorities that women could not form part of' the commonwealth, of the 'new public' that was being formed; he cites as examples the petitioning of the leveller women in the 1640s and the reception of the work of the Dutch humanist Anna Maria van Schurman, who was 'strongly admired' by the Parliamentarians (Norbrook 2004). Nonetheless, he recognises the limitations of this activism: 'Agitation by women did not, however, include a demand for female suffrage' (Norbrook 2004: 232). On the other hand, as Smith cautions, to 'focus too narrowly on issues of rights, and voting, as constituting political standing' is to misrepresent a culture that had a 'broader and more inclusive understanding of politics' (Smith 1998: 10, 4), one that is concerned with duties and obligations rather than rights and a more flexible sense of the 'public' sphere.

Indeed, despite Thomas Smith's strict demarcation of the public sphere as masculine and the private sphere as feminine, cited in the epigraph to this chapter, the boundary between these domains was in fact blurred (Capp 1996: 317, Gowing 1996: 26). The domestic idiom of political language compromises our sense of the household as a purely 'domestic' space. Women's domestic roles were generally recognised as already possessing an inherently political dimension.

Thus, Gouge argues in the early seventeenth century that although the overwhelming majority of women 'are not admitted to any publike function in Church or commonwealth', their 'conscionable performance of houshold duties', inasmuch as it ministers to the good of both, 'may be accounted a publike worke' (Gouge 1976: 18). The assumption that the civic and domestic realms were interconnected – that the family was a 'little commonwealth', as Gouge puts it, 'wherein the first principles and grounds of government and subjection are learned' (Gouge 1976: 18) – informed the language of household manuals and political tracts in both restrictive and enabling ways (Amussen 1988: 54–64). It could reinforce patriarchal values, most famously in Robert Filmer's defence of absolutism, *Patriarcha; or the Natural Power of Kings* (1680). However, an emphasis on women's 'houshold duties' could also be enlisted to authorise women's entry into the 'public' sphere in ways that Gouge never envisaged. For instance, in their collective petitioning of Parliament in 1649 and 1653, leveller women protested against the violation of their 'honest households' by government troops, arguing that they could not be expected to 'sit in silence' at home while such atrocities were being perpetrated but were forced by the enormity of these 'publick Calamit[ies]' to take a stand in defence of their families and, by extension, of the 'Nations ancient Rights and Liberties'. Despite conceding that 'it is not our custom to address ourselves to this House in the publick behalf', these women held that the political crisis created by parliamentary 'tyranny' left them no option but to quit their normal sphere: 'we are so over-prest, so over-whelmed with affliction, that we are not able to keep in our compass, to be bounded in the custom of our sex'. Familial obligations are pressed into service here in order to argue for women's 'undoubted right to petition', but also, and more boldly still, to stake out a claim for their right to 'an equal interest with the Men of this Nation in those liberties and securities contained in [. . .] the good Laws of the Land'.[2] This example demonstrates just how problematic the division of the public and private spheres along gendered lines is for this period. Our conception of the meaning of the term 'public', however, also needs fresh consideration; it should be extended to encompass 'all that was "common, open, abroad"', while public space was deemed to include markets, streets, neighbourhoods, playhouses, taverns; anywhere, in fact, where men *and* women were on show and negotiated and conducted business with one another' (Withington 2005: 199–200). In this redefined 'public' of markets, streets and neighbourhoods, 'female' speech – gossip, slander, conversation – can be seen to take on a new political significance.

For example, the status of men in the community depended on their reputation as 'honest' householders; this rested on the behaviour of their dependants, but also on their own reputations, of which women were often 'the brokers' (Gowing 1996: 123). Women's talk could make or break reputations, and although their own were extremely vulnerable in turn, proferred sexual slurs and insults also gave them 'surpassing scope for action'; indeed, women took to the courts in increasing numbers to defend their reputations (Gowing 1996: 137).

Given this development of feminist political history, a collection of essays such as this, which explores the relationship between women, politics *and* rhetoric, might seem an unpromising move. But we think that it is important to recover this term and its close synonym 'eloquence', not least because the conception of rhetoric against which feminised political talk – gossip, slander, conversation, etc. – is implicitly opposed, is oversimplified, and this leaves in place the very gendered division that historians and literary critics have attempted to trouble and contest: men orate; women gossip. Obviously, we do not dispute that men and women had different opportunities to influence others or used different modes of speech or literary forms for that purpose. We do not want to argue that women were 'orators' like men, although women in positions of unusual power, such as Elizabeth I, had been trained in formal rhetoric and were persuasive public speakers (Orlin 1995). But there is a need, we argue, to expand our understanding of the terms 'rhetoric' and 'rhetorical' in just the same way that has been done for the concepts 'politics' and 'political' in order to make visible, on the one hand, the varieties and effectiveness of women's eloquence in a range of contexts and, on the other hand, and just as importantly, how female eloquence was already conceived as being fraught with political meaning. Eloquence is a crucial term for us because it provides a vocabulary and a way of thinking that bring into view the often untutored persuasiveness of women's speech and its capacity for critical engagement with received ideas and structures of authority. Moreover, it can encompass many different sorts of speech, including gossip and conversation, but also more structured rhetorical forms concerned with the traditional oratorical aims of exhortation and dissuasion, accusation and defence. Indeed, rhetoric can help us to understand the intrinsic eloquence of much female speech which seems troublingly self-negating, that is, speech or writing that emphasises the weakness of the speaker or seeks to influence indirectly.

On the current model, as we have seen, rhetorical skill is understood as dependent on the kind of formal training available, usually, only to boys and young men, while our conception of early modern rhetoric follows closely its definition in early modern technical handbooks, which did inscribe a gendered hierarchy. However, it is important to remember that rhetoric has never been just a system, a body of rules. The ancient theoreticians already understood that 'eloquence' – the force, fluency or expressiveness of speech or writing – pre-exists its codification as 'rhetoric'. The handbooks do indeed advise on the organisation of a speech and its content, and classify linguistic 'ornaments'. But these represent only one aspect of rhetorical education. Just as important to the development of persuasiveness is 'practice'. Cicero argued in *De oratore* (*On the Ideal Orator*), that it is not the study of rules that makes one eloquent, but the practice of writing for and speaking to a variety of social occasions and contexts. This idea underpins the rhetorical training of boys in the sixteenth century implicitly and sometimes more explicitly. The collection and analysis of linguistic devices and commonplaces supports the classroom practice of 'declamation', arguing pro and contra (Rhodes 2004, Mack 2005). However, humanists could also appeal to Cicero's endorsement of practice-based rather than technical training in order to challenge the traditional authority of the schoolmaster. In his Cambridge lectures, published as *Rhetor* in 1577, Gabriel Harvey followed Cicero in rejecting the dead theorisation of persuasive speech and argued instead that eloquence depends on 'reading, praising, criticizing, correcting, refuting, and irritating' the best rhetoricians, and by joining 'in discussions, disputes, and dialogues' (Harvey 1577: 75–6; Richards 2007).

This allows for an important change of emphasis. Harvey may be describing a community of university-educated male disputants, but the importance he attaches to 'practice' can be extended to include other kinds of speaker, other kinds of disputational context. Arguably, this is already recognised in many of the handbooks and treatises that 'theorise' restrictions on female speech, for these also reveal a more complex engagement with the practice of women's talk than is often taken account of in critical discussion. For example, there is a danger that excerpting prescriptive advice from *On Domesticall Duties* (1622) obscures the caveats that Gouge is repeatedly prompted to offer his female readers, and also the reflexive engagement with the issue of how women should speak that this text encourages. In his preface, Gouge records the objections raised by his female parishioners when his directives were 'first uttered out of the pulpit'. In particular, these women rejected 'the application of the wives subjection to her restraining of the common goods of the family without, or against her husbands consent', but failed to notice, he adds, the 'Cautions and Limitations' that he had also given them on this subject (Gouge 1976: ¶3v). Tellingly, this text is full of such cautions and limitations which acknowledge the impracticality of restrictive advice applied to *all* women and which stress the importance of negotiation within the household. For instance, Gouge may recall that 'the Apostle enjoyneth *silence* to wives in their husbands presence', but it should be noted that this is almost immediately qualified as he warns that St Paul's command is not to be taken too literally: 'for silence in that place is not opposed to speech, as if she should not speake at all, but to loquacitie, to talkativenesse, to over-much tatling: her husbands presence must somewhat restraine her tongue, and so will her verie silence testifie a reverend respect'. But on the latter point he is again forced to concede that silence is a far from unambiguous signifier of female submission and may indeed 'imply' its opposite: 'stoutnesse of stomacke, and stubbornnesse of heart' (Gouge 1976: 281–2) (Luckyj 2002: 58–62). We could argue that Gouge is being forced to compromise the rigid rules that he is offering wives, except that his advice is also self-consciously structured to initiate negotiation of these norms. Key to this is the rhetorical reading that Gouge's text invites: the reader is asked to follow the process of its composition, taking note of its 'disposition' (arrangement), for example, of the fact that the elaboration of the 'wives duetie' is meant to 'answer' her husband's, but also vice versa (¶4r). In this regard *On Domesticall Duties* is by no means exceptional; many conduct books of the period incorporate 'objections' to their own prescriptions and even, in some cases, adopt a more overtly dialectical structure.[3]

This is, of course, a small 'gain': the redoubtable Gouge is not quite so unyielding on the subject of women's speech as we initially thought. However, there are other reasons why emphasising rhetoric as 'practice' is helpful in making visible women's rhetorical activities. Once rhetoric is conceived as the study of 'eloquence', the development of which depends on 'practice' in a variety of contexts rather than technical training and scholarly regimens, then it is possible to begin to extend its exercise to women of all ranks, not merely the small classically educated and privately tutored female elite (Queen Elizabeth, Lady Jane Grey, More's daughters, the Cooke sisters) that has tended to monopolise critical attention. Indeed, we should bear in mind that rhetorical skills could be acquired by women through a variety of channels, formal or informal, direct or indirect. Attending a play, reading a letter or listening to a sermon, to cite but a few examples, would all have offered opportunities to develop an awareness of a range of rhetorical forms. As James Daybell remarks in this collection, the sophisticated mastery of the structure and stylistic conventions of different epistolary genres displayed by upper-class female suitors was probably acquired 'less from formal tuition, than from vernacular letter-writing manuals that transmitted classical epistolary models to a wider non-Latinate audience', or through 'practical contact' with everyday correspondence (see p. 173). Lower down the social scale, female sectaries, many of them from the middling or 'meaner' sort, were not deterred by their lack of instruction in formal disputation from speaking out on matters of ecclesiastical doctrine or arguing with ministers. On the contrary, they often made a point of contrasting their own untutored yet divinely inspired eloquence favourably with the sophistries of a university-educated clergy. Patricia Crawford notes how in her debates with the Presbyterian minister Thomas Edward, the separatist and later leveller, Katherine Chidley deployed 'the standard rhetorical ploys about lack of scholarly training, but in such a way that this became a strength: her answers were "not laid downe in a Schollerick way, but by the plaine truth of Holy Scripture"' (Crawford 1996: 133). Equally, Laura Gowing and Tim Stretton have shown how the testimony of female witnesses and litigants who flocked to the consistory and equity courts in unprecedented numbers in this period often demonstrated an intuitive grasp of the persuasive efficacy of particular narrative strategies that owed more to popular oral culture than to knowledge of forensic discourse (Gowing 1996, Stretton 1998).

All of this sounds very positive, but crucial questions remain. What forms did women's eloquence take? How did women negotiate the cultural constraints imposed on female speech and behaviour? And, perhaps most importantly of all, given the meagre credibility ascribed to women's words relative to those of men (Gowing 1996: 50–2), how did they establish their *ethos*, that is, an authoritative and trustworthy rhetorical persona from which they could persuasively intervene in 'public' debate? These are tricky issues. For while there is abundant evidence to suggest that women's lack of formal rhetorical training did not prevent them from speaking effectively in a variety of contexts, it is still necessary to recognise that their interventions *were* restricted. An important source of female authority, as we have already noted, lay in the household, and this informed how women represented and probably conceived of their rhetorical interventions: as a natural extension of their established roles as wives, mothers, mistresses of households, patrons and godly women, prompted by the various duties and responsibilities that were associated with these functions. Many early modern women used their familial or domestic identities to speak or write of matters that exceeded the confines of domestic life. For example, women of gentry or aristocratic stock took advantage of their extensive family, local and court connections as a means of participating informally in the patronage system (Harris 1990). Their recognised duty to promote the interests and standing of their family, through the use of their epistolary skills, licensed them to solicit political favours of one kind or another from government officials on behalf of kin, clients, neighbours, 'friends' and other dependants. Moreover, when interceding for close family members, they projected themselves as exemplary spouses and mothers driven to act purely from maternal solicitude or wifely devotion, secure in the knowledge that 'familial responsibility provided a firm moral justification for women's intervention in business matters beyond the strictly defined domain of the household' (Daybell 2006a: 16). Other factors, notably socioeconomic status, could contribute to the fashioning of a confident rhetorical persona capable of transacting 'business' of various sorts within the public sphere. Thus, James Daybell attributes the remarkable self-assurance with which elite female suitors deployed a Senecan language of political friendship in their correspondence – an idiom normally reserved for men – to consciousness of their elevated rank and the considerable sources of political influence and patronage at their disposal (see p. 179, also Magnusson 2004).

Inevitably, early modern women's tendency to speak and write in terms of a traditional understanding of their place, identities and roles within the social order often steered them towards rhetorical forms which it is difficult for us nowadays properly to appreciate or, indeed, accept. Nowhere is this more evidently the case than with such apparently disabling yet pervasively used speech forms as supplication and complaint, which accentuated the speaker's lowliness, weakness and incapacity. In their different ways, both these already-feminised modes of utterance suggest a speech situation in which the speaker typically assumes a stance of humble and grief-ridden self-abnegation that declares their helpless dependency on more powerful others (usually the male interlocutor or absent addressee) to redress the wrongs they have endured. Examples of female speakers pleading and 'complaining' abound in classical and scriptural texts and were carried over into, and popularised by, the vernacular literary tradition (see Heard in this collection, p. 51). Ovid's *Heroides* – a collection of verse epistles purportedly authored by mythical heroines such as Penelope, Dido, Ariadne and Medea and addressed to the lovers who have abandoned them in subtly modulated accents of lamentation, entreaty, accusation, vituperation and reproach – offered early modern readers perhaps the richest illustration of the infinitely flexible uses to which these overlapping modes of persuasion could be put. As Ovid's text became more widely accessible as a result of the numerous translations and 'imitations' published in the late sixteenth and seventeenth centuries – including those of George Turbeville (1567), Michael Drayton (1597) and Wye Saltonstall (1636) – it was increasingly appropriated and adapted to a range of expressive purposes by female poets, notably Isabella Whitney, Mary Wroth and Aphra Behn. Indeed, although the lamenting or beseeching female voice was of course a rhetorical 'fiction' initially scripted, interpreted and printed by and for men, women were not slow to recognise its potential value as a linguistic resource that could be mobilised in a range of contexts beyond the literary and that was amenable to being manipulated to their advantage as well as in their disfavour.

Nevertheless, it remains hard for us to understand why female speakers and writers of the period were attracted to such overtly disempowering forms of self-presentation. From a feminist critical perspective the representation of a female voice that emphasises the speaker's passivity and vulnerability obviously makes for uncomfortable reading. Neglect of these speech forms, though, is compounded by the inattention of political historians to supplication and complaint in favour of more traditional forms of rhetoric, especially the deliberative oration. This is despite the fact that their connections with the mainstream rhetorical tradition were well recognised by influential rhetoricians in this period. Thus Erasmus and Thomas Wilson categorise the language of entreaty as a form of deliberative speech that seeks to persuade or dissuade an audience from taking a specific course of action (Wilson 1982: 76, 144, Erasmus 1985: 71, 172–81). Originally denoting a 'bill' of grievances submitted by a plaintiff, 'complaint' was also understood to have strong affinities with forensic rhetoric, a link that was sustained by the use of legal terminology and the adoption of postures of accusation, defence and self-exculpation which were constitutive features of this 'genre' (Kerrigan 1991: 7). Even so, the preference for 'milder', less agonistic types of persuasion that characterise such 'genres' as supplication and complaint increases the difficulty of thinking of them as a form of political *action*. In order to address the relationship between women, rhetoric *and* politics, however, it is essential that we recover their significance as a moral and affective force within early modern political culture.

Supplication and complaint could provide a highly effective vehicle for social and moral protest, often ventriloquised through female speakers in texts authored by both men and women. The suffering (*pathos*) on which these speech forms are predicated may invest the speaker's accusations, pleas or laments with a compelling moral authority and affective eloquence (*pathos* in its other sense) that serves, ironically, to restore the very agency they seemed to erase. Isabella Whitney, for example, marshals both Ovidian and Christian strains of 'moral complaint' in order to denounce the treachery of men in *The Copy of a Letter* (1567) and to express social dissatisfaction through her identification with the hardships suffered by the urban poor in her 'WYLL and Testament' (1573) (Beilin 1990). Moreover, in a culture where social relations were governed by the principle of reciprocal obligation, the articulation of such grievances could exert considerable political pressure by appealing to the moral duty of the strong to come to the aid of the weak. We should not be surprised, then, to find women drawing upon these 'literary' modes of expression in more public contexts: for example, when writing suitors' letters, giving legal testimony or, during the Commonwealth, in their petitioning and printed 'complaints' protesting against government policy (Kerrigan 1991: 60). It was not uncommon for female suitors who found themselves in desperate straits – in cases, for instance, where they or their spouses had fallen from political grace – to adopt an excessively deferential posture and sorrowful language of entreaty, reminiscent of that employed by Ovid's forlorn heroines, in their written pleas for succour. These women typically highlighted their feminine frailty and dramatised the afflictions laid upon them in ways that were designed to elicit the pity and favourable intercession of state officials (Thorne 2006). In his study of women's dealings with the Court of Requests during Elizabeth's reign, Tim Stretton documents the strategic use of a similar rhetorical ploy by female litigants. In a bid to gain judicial sympathy, single women and widows were apt to play upon their own poverty or 'simplicity' and consequent vulnerability to sharp practices, aligning themselves with such scriptural types as the 'importunate widow' of Luke 18 as objects deserving of equitable treatment (Stretton 1998: 49–51, 180–7). These examples show how such rhetorical practices could work to 'put women in relation to politics' (to borrow Susan Wiseman's useful phrase in her essay in this collection, p. 132), albeit in more oblique, complex and mediated ways than were available to their male coevals. Moreover, we would argue that these distinctive forms of eloquence facilitated women's attempts to influence the course of political (or legal) action and debate, in part *because* they were so finely adapted to their social and ideological environment.

Supplication and complaint were not the only forms that female persuasion might take. During the turbulent decades of the mid-seventeenth century, women from across the social spectrum began to assert their right to meddle more directly in 'State-matters' and 'high poynts of Divinity'. A small, but disproportionately significant, group of sectarian women defied the Pauline prohibition on female teaching in church so as to assume the task of testifying to their beliefs through their preaching, prophesying and published writings in the conviction that they were being called upon to do so by God. Inevitably, their high-profile activities exposed them to accusations of witchcraft and whoredom as well as the threat of physical punishment and often set them on a collision course with civic and church authorities, as the story of the brutal treatment meted out to the Quaker preacher Dorothy Waugh illustrates (Hinds in this collection, p. 195). In their printed 'pleas' and 'vindications', female Nonconformists resorted to a common repertoire of rhetorical strategies in order to justify their controversial incursions into the public domain. In particular, they appealed to the established Protestant principle of the spiritual equality of the sexes in the sight of God, which laid on them the responsibility to pursue not only their own individual salvation but, as they saw it, that of the community at large. Adapting the humanist and exegetical practice of arguing from 'example' and 'authority' for their own purposes, they also enlisted biblical precedents in order to prove that female preaching had divine warrant. Citing scriptural texts, notably Joel 2:28 ('I will pour out my spirit on all flesh; and your sons and your daughters shall prophesy'), alongside a plethora of exemplars including Deborah, Hannah and Judith, Quaker leader Margaret Fell inveighed in her tract, *Women's Speaking Justified, Proved and Allowed of by the Scripture* (1666) against 'the blind priests' who 'preach sermons upon women's words; and still cry out, "Women must not speak. Women must be silent"' (cited in Donawerth 2002: 69).

For all their militancy, however, these sectarian women did not abandon the practice of invoking, revising and manipulating conventional models of womanhood as a means of shoring up their precarious position. In startling contrast to the general assertiveness of their speech and actions, many of them still insisted on foregrounding their own worthlessness, in their textual self-presentations at least. Disclaiming any active desire or personal fitness to undertake the work of bearing witness to God's word, female dissenters tended to define themselves as abject creatures no better than worms or, at best, as a passive medium, a 'contemptible instrument', for the divine spirit that spoke through them (Hinds 1996: 87–107). Recounting her troubled mission to Cornwall in her *Report and Plea* (1654), the Fifth Monarchist prophet Anna Trapnel refuses any credit for her skilful answers under cross-examination at the Sessions House in Truro, on the grounds that 'in all that was said by me, I was nothing, the Lord put all in my mouth, and told me what I should say [. . .]. So that I will have nothing ascribed to me, but all honor and praise given to him whose right it is' (Trapnel 1654: 24). However, just as with the other 'lowly' forms of rhetorical *ethos* we have discussed, so with these expressions of self-abasement it is important to take a more nuanced view. For, as Hilary Hinds argues, such extreme acts of self-denial amount to more than an expression of the traditional Christian abhorrence of pride or a way of deflecting the usual 'charges of impropriety or immodesty' levelled at publicly vocal women. Crucially, the dissolution of the self created space for the emergence of a powerful new authorial voice grounded in the unassailable, transcendent authority of divine truth (Hinds 1996: 106). What we encounter here, then, is an inversionary logic not unlike that which translates female self-abnegation and submission to a higher (male) power in the act of supplicating into an enhanced moral authority. Only in this case the paradoxical equation of physical weakness with spiritual strength was grounded in biblical authority, as summed up in a passage that carried a special resonance for Trapnel as for other female sectaries: 'God hath chosen the weak things of the world, to confound the things that are mighty, and base things of the world, and things which are despised hath God chosen; yea, and things that are not, to bring to nought things that are' (1 Cor. 1:27–8; cited in Trapnel 1654: 17).

This collection has two broad aims, first, to reflect on the many different ways in which female eloquence is represented in this period and, second, to explore some of the forms that it took in practice. Several contributors consider the varying constructions of female speech in male-authored texts written either with a view to inhibiting or disrupting their speaking out, or indeed to offer differently nuanced ways of reflecting on familiar political problems. Other contributors are interested in the ways in which women adapted, circumvented or, in some cases, defied linguistic prohibitions in order to intercede with government officials on behalf of clients or family members, to proclaim their spiritual beliefs or to influence public opinion on a range of issues. That is, they are concerned specifically with the diverse ways in which women's rhetoric did contribute to and often reconstituted the terms of political debate.

This collection opens with Patricia Parker's study of 'backward spelling' which builds upon her ground-breaking work of the 1980s. Parker argues that in the early modern period all forms of writing (or reading) in a backwards or 'sinister' direction were freighted with negative connotations, evoking the backwards spells of witchcraft, the effeminising retrogression of men to the imperfect state of women or boys along with other 'inversions' of the natural teleological order. Unorthodox graphic forms such as the backwards-sloping *italics* or the reversal of alphabetic letters and numerals, she contends, carried 'a sexual as well as discursive import' for early modern readers; in particular they were linked with the preposterous 'sin' of sodomy (p. 29). Parker suggests, however, that we need to be equally attentive to the submerged religious and 'geopolitical' meanings encoded in these various 'overdetermined' forms of 'false writing'. Thus, John Bale used the palindrome 'Roma/Amor' as a basis for attacking the 'preposterous amor' closely associated with the Roman Catholic Church in Protestant polemics, just as the Hebrew and Arabic systems of writing or notation in a reverse direction were seen as indicative not only of the sexual perversions of 'eastern' peoples but of the heretical practices of the infidel. Drawing upon a broad range of textual sources, she shows how the 'threat of reversibility' inhabits all these forms of 'preposterous inversion': a fear that Englishmen will 'turn Turk', Jew or Papist through a process of backsliding conversion to false forms of worship and sexual practice (p. 37).

Chapters 2 and 3 offer different approaches to the anxious treatment of female eloquence in prescriptive and literary writings. In her study of the representation of female pleaders in the so-called 'Tradition of Women Worthies', Rachel Heard considers the rhetorical strategies used by a variety of male writers to deal with the perceived potency of female eloquence. Contempt for female pleaders, she notes, could manifest itself in different ways. Primarily, though, anxious male writers took refuge in well-worn commonplaces, such as association of the female public speaker with the whore. Some male writers do champion the virtue of female pleaders, Heard acknowledges, but tend to do so by 'domesticating' their speech. For example, John Shirley's *Illustrious History of Women* defends the 'virtuous Roman Lady' Amasia from accusations of androgyny by emphasising her modesty, the traditional marker of female virtue. Yet, paradoxically, it is these very qualities of moderation and regulation that are also valued in male petitioning, leaving authors such as Shirley with a curious problem: a recognition of the fact that virtuous women already possess the very qualities prized in 'mild oratory'. It is perhaps discreet recognition of this, alongside the increase in the number of women participating in court action, which explains attempts to contain female eloquence.

Meanwhile, Danielle Clarke suggests that the preoccupation of feminist readings with notions of voice and articulation is in turn complicit with early modern anxieties about female speech. In fact, rhetoric and the rhetorically inflected reading of classical and Christian texts bequeathed an alternative set of values and practices to early modern women. This structured not only how women's language was viewed, but also how women viewed language and its potential for individuation and political intervention. A gap exists between the familiar moral insistence on the desirability of women's silence and the evident awareness in the period of the power and agency of female speech in specific situations and contexts. Clarke's chapter explores the complex ways in which women were included and excluded in early modern rhetorical culture by focusing on the reception of Ovidian 'echo' (construed as both a character and a figure). Ovid is famous, of course, for his profound interest in the self-cancelling 'power' of female speech, and this paradox is embodied in the figure of 'echo'. In the early modern period, 'echo' represents garrulous, empty female speech; however, there is always a suspicion that this may also represent rhetorical agency: 'echo' repeats selectively. Clarke explores how the allusion to the figure of Echo in Milton's *Paradise Lost* figures the exclusion of women from rhetorical culture but also admits the potential for their inclusion. She also considers how other writers – notably Shakespeare and Mary Wroth – use the Ovidian myth to represent female subjectivity in a more nuanced way.

In contrast, Chapters 4 and 5 are interested in how the imagining of extreme examples of female speech, and its failure, can enable male authors to offer caustic political advice in contexts uncongenial to free and open debate. Huw Griffiths' chapter traces Shakespeare's use of *adynaton* – the figure that represents the impossibility of expression – in his narrative poem, *The Rape of Lucrece*, and he explores the poem's use of frustrated female speech to reflect on the impossibility of political debate in England in the 1590s. The rape of Lucretia, the founding myth of the Roman republic, is recognised as informing the masculinism of the republican tradition. So often the retelling of this story is used to define a masculine public sphere over and against a private sphere of female suffering. Not so in Shakespeare's narrative poem, argues Griffiths. Indeed, the emphasis on Lucrece's broken communication in this text offers ironic commentary on the absence of just such a masculine public sphere in the 1590s. Shakespeare is renegotiating the lessons that can be learned from Ovid's *Heroides*, a source for his representation of female lament and a standard textbook for rhetorical imitation in the Tudor classroom. As Griffiths argues, Shakespeare seems to be more attuned than humanists such as Erasmus to the 'ironic critique of the idea of transparent and equitable communication' presented by Ovid.

Martin Dzelzainis is also interested in the association of a particular figure with a fictional female speaker. This time, the figure is *parrhesia*, a term which, despite the fact that it connotes the speaking of unadorned truth to power, is itself a rhetorical device, while the fictional speaker who represents it is the (low-born) Duchess of Albemarle in Andrew Marvell's *The Third Advice to a Painter*. This poem has long perplexed Marvell critics who are uncertain as to why an opposition satire, written at the height of the second Anglo-Dutch war of 1665–7, should be given to a female speaker and, moreover, one who is figured as a garrulous, lewd 'Half witch, half prophet'. To address this problem, Dzelzainis recalls the complexity of the figure *parrhesia*, the fact that its promise of unvarnished truth-telling can easily be seen as a refined form of rhetorical duplicity. This begins to explain why Marvell may have chosen the Duchess to voice his criticisms. While this negative view of *parrhesia* coincides with gendered concerns about the relationship between 'truth' and 'ornament', in Marvell's poem its use by the figure of the Duchess of Albermarle is also called upon to represent the problem of speaking the truth.

Susan Wiseman's chapter argues for a radical extension and reinter-pretation of the field of evidence that reveals the relation of women to politics in the seventeenth century; this involves exploring the ways in which classical and biblical precedents might be made to work politi-cally. This relationship is still obscured, she argues, even by the newly expanded canon of male political writing. As an alternative to these approaches, Wiseman draws attention to the role of female exem-plarity and its widespread use in various modes of political argument. She considers how 'affective' examples work politically, contributing to a conception of female political virtue. Wiseman analyses how speech forms typically seen as expressing female vulnerability, such as 'supplication' and 'petition', need to be understood as elaborating forms of female political action. In the early seventeenth century, such examples provided an important means of placing women in relation to politics. However, these examples were not uniform in their effect; they could be coded in such a way that they were open to diverse forms of politicised reading. Wiseman demonstrates this by exploring two classical examples, Lucretia and Arria, and one biblical example, Esther, all of whom are called upon in different ways in a range of seventeenth-century writings, but also by focusing on the diverse use and representation of the possibilities of example in one text, Aemelia Lanyer's *Salve deus rex judaeorum.*

By contrast, the following chapters focus on the rhetorical strategies used by women of differing social status to enhance their personal 'credit' and authority and thereby enable them to intervene more effectively in matters of political and religious consequence. Thus, Helen Hackett's chapter explores the shifting use of maternal imagery as a persuasive device in Elizabethan political discourse. She argues that the figuration of Elizabeth I as 'symbolic mother' of the nation and church was, at best, a double-edged strategy that could be used to challenge as well as bolster her authority. At first, this image was enlisted to persuade the people of England to accept a female ruler. But it quickly became a site of contestation in the 1560s and early 1570s as Elizabeth I's counsellors sought to convince her of the need to marry and produce an heir. On the other side, the Queen employed her figurative maternity as a self-defensive strategy to 'deflect attention away from her reluctance to become an actual mother' (p. 152). This imaginary parent–child relationship between the Queen and her subjects was also invoked on both sides in the struggle over freedom of speech. During the Anjou courtship, Elizabeth's capacity for motherhood, both literal and emblematic, was again placed at the centre of a heated 'rhetorical contest', though now the positions in this debate were reversed, with the Queen actively pressing for the marriage. Once the possibility of her bearing a child had evaporated, Hackett detects a marked shift in the ways and contexts in which maternal imagery was invoked: from its use as a tool of deliberative rhetoric to put the case for and against marriage to its 'epideictic' use as a means of praising the monarch. In the cornucopian iconography of late Elizabethan panegyric, the Queen's virginity is represented, paradoxically, as bestowing a 'mystical' fecundity on her realm, in an attempt to both mask and compensate for the fact of her childlessness. Hackett argues, however, that this hyperbolic language was accompanied by an 'undertow of dissent' which figured Elizabeth's infertility as the source not of the nation's prosperity, but of its political stasis and decay.

James Daybell is also concerned with the capacity of early modern women to exercise political influence through their mastery of rhetorical forms, in this case via the letter of recommendation. Daybell argues that elite women's 'conversance with the formal conventions of [this] epistolary genre' calls into question the long-held assumption that women were wholly excluded from the classical rhetorical tradition (p. 173). These women display a sophisticated understanding of stylistic conventions that can be said to bridge the 'apparent division' between 'formal, institutional, and professional' training in rhetoric and the 'innate, yet untrained' persuasive qualities that characterise the verbal formulations of less privileged women (p. 173). Concomitantly, their letters bear witness to the crucial role played by upper-class women within the patronage system, a role directly comparable to that performed by men. Indeed, he finds the 'easy familiarity' with which many of these women employed a Senecan language of 'political friendship' in their correspondence with government officials 'suggestive of the high degree of confidence and authority with which they [. . .] intervened in the political arena' (p. 174).

Hilary Hinds is interested in the peculiarities of Quaker rhetoric and its complex intersection with questions of gender and class, as exemplified by Dorothy Waugh's account of her preaching in the Carlisle marketplace and consequent imprisonment (published in 1656). She seeks to explain the intensely hostile response to the early Quaker movement by isolating what was uniquely troubling about its forms of public speaking. Despite continuities between their conception of sacred rhetoric and that underlying more orthodox modes of preaching, Hinds argues that the Quakers were throwing down a radical challenge to conventional understandings of preaching, rhetoric and gender. Their speech acts constituted 'a literal enfleshment of Quaker doctrine' congruent with their foundational belief in the 'indwelling Christ', a belief that, contentiously, erased distinctions between the literal and figurative, the spiritual and material. In keeping with their search for 'lived modes of signification' *beyond* the linguistic, the Quakers also gave concrete and practical expression to the traditional preacherly reliance on metaphor and theatricality by enacting 'the drama of their theology in the streets, gaols, marketplaces and steeplehouses' (p. 206). It was this 'insistence on the physical and spatial as well as linguistic dimension' of their rhetorical performances, Hinds suggests, that brought Quaker preachers into direct conflict with the civic and religious authorities (p. 206). Hinds uses Waugh's struggle with the mayor of Carlisle over the interpretation of her actions to reflect on the inherent limitations of the Quakers' 'embodied rhetoric' and its attempts to contest and transform social meanings.

Notes

1 As Catherine Eskin notes, there was some variation in the degree to which early modern educationalists countenanced the teaching of rhetoric to women (1999: 102), but the fundamental position remained the same.

2 Quotations are from 'To the Supream authority of this Nation [. . .] The humble PETITION of divers wel-affected WOMEN' (24 April 1649); 'To the supreme authority of England [. . .] The Humble Petition of divers well-affected WOMEN' (5 May 1649) and 'Unto every individual Member of Parliament: The Humble Representation of divers afflicted Women-Petitioners' (29 July 1653). On the absence of a 'clear sense of a public-private split paralleling gender divisions' in leveller discourse, see Hughes (1995: 181), and Gillespie (2004: 85–92).

3 For examples of popular conduct books structured as a dialectical debate about women, see Elyot 1940; Castiglione [1561] 1994; and Tilney 1573.

2   Spelling backwards

Patricia Parker

I never yet saw man [. . .]
But she would spell him backward [. . .]
        Much Ado About Nothing

From the time of *Literary Fat Ladies: Rhetoric, Gender, Politics* (1987),
I have been focusing on the ways in which what might appear to be
purely rhetorical or linguistic structures or concerns are implicated in
questions of gender, property and politics. In 'Virile Style' (published
in *Premodern Sexualities* in 1996) I turned from the *dilation* or *amplifi-
catio* associated with female bodies to the Roman and early modern
tradition of the *nervosus*, sinewy or 'virile' style, contrasted in Quintilian to the *cinaedus*, effeminate or pathic male – a tradition reflected
in Montaigne, in Jonson's *Discoveries* and in the sinewy or 'plain' style
of early modern science. My current work in progress is focused on
the geopolitics of 'Asiatic' style, both as it appears in contrast to 'Attic'
style in Roman writing and as it figures in early modern descriptions
of 'the Stile 'a the big Turkes' (Dekker, *Satiromastix*), an updating
of 'Asiatic' style to representations of the Ottoman Turk as the new
power of the East. This is in turn part of a larger project that will
include not only the ways in which grammar, rhetoric, sexuality and
gender are interrelated in the period, but also the association of 'ink-
horn' terms with blackface and the implications of apparently merely
verbal or rhetorical forms for the study of early modern racial and
religious interconnections. This chapter, which looks at the ways in
which Hebrew and Arabic numbers, as well as witchcraft and sodomy,
were implicated in what was understood as spelling 'backwards', is
part of this new work.
    In *Much Ado about Nothing*, Beatrice is described as spelling men
backward ('I never yet saw man, / How wise, how noble, young,

how rarely featur'd, / But she would spell him backward'), in lines that go on to observe 'So turns she every man the wrong side out' (Shakespeare 1974: 3.1.59–70). Spelling backwards here conjures not only the familiar spells of witchcraft – as witches say prayers backwards to raise the Devil – but also the threat of unmanning by a witch's spellbinding 'ligatures' ('weakening the nature of some men, to make them unable for women', as King James put it in the *Daemonologie*) (James VI and I 1597: 3), and so spelling a man 'backward' from male to female ('If fair-fac'd,/She would swear the gentleman should be her sister' (*Much Ado*, 3.1.61–2)). In a play filled with allusions to turning or conversion (including a reference to turning Turk) as well as with emblems of effeminated men (regressing to the female but also to beardless 'boys'), spelling backwards in *Much Ado* simultaneously connects different forms of conversion or inversion to deformations in the order of writing, parodied in Dogberry's 'Write God first', contradicted by his inability to order a discourse in the proper sequence. The lines on the Beatrice who 'would spell him backward' thus evoke the multiple possibilities within *spelling* itself, from reading, writing, and the backward spells of witches to inversions in the hierarchy of gender, including the teleology of progression from 'imperfect' to 'perfect'.

Within the discourse of witchcraft, the backward spells of witches were repeatedly associated with the sinister or left as well as with the inverted or reversed, with 'sinistral or devilish acts' (kissing the backside, reversing the course of rivers, and making the sign of the cross with the left rather than the right hand), making everything 'preposterous and done in wrong way', as Pierre de Lancre observed (Clark 1997: 14). Turning everything in 'a retrograde and preposterous way' is a sign of the witchcraft that turns an entire household 'topsie turvy' in *The Late Lancashire Witches* (1634). A 'lusty' man is also effeminated or made impotent by a 'ligatory point' and the 'hare' that (like the 'hyena') figured alternations of 'male' and 'female' is compared to a 'Hermaphrodite' (Heywood and Brome 1979: 145, 148, 153, 190–2). Clark observes that the 'Eve' seduced by Lucifer was frequently represented as the first 'witch'. Created second, she came preposterously 'first' in sin: a backward spelling that had as its righting the familiar palindrome of 'Eva' and the 'Ave' described as undoing the spellbinding 'charmes' that had led to the preposterous inversion of the Fall itself: 'Spell *Eva* backe and *Ave* shall you find, / The first began, the last reverst our harmes, / An Angel's witching wordes did *Eva* blinde, / An Angel's *Ave* disinchants the charmes'.[1] In these and other earlier modern instances, various forms of 'spelling' in reversible directions

connected not only the graphic and the bewitching but both with the
direction of providential history itself.

   Spelling in its multiple senses – rerighting and rewriting a 'retrograde and preposterous way' – underwrites the regal counterpart of
this crucial conversion or turning in Ben Jonson's *Masque of Queenes*,
whose anti-masque of witches involves 'a magicall Daunce, full of
praeposterous change, and gesticulation, but most applying to theyr
property: who, at theyr meetings, do all thinges contrary to the custome of Men, dauncing, back to back, hip to hip, theyr handes ioyn'd,
and making theyr circles backward, to the left hand' (Jonson 1925–52:
VII, 278–319). Jonson's marginal notes invoke an entire range of female furies, enchantresses and witches, from Medea to Virgil's Allecto,
Lucan's Erictho, and Horace's Canidia, suggesting the unruly female
as what will be ultimately converted or transformed by its 'turning'
machine. But in a masque whose 'praeposterous' witches were played
by male players and whose notes include Pliny's description of the
castrated male 'Priests of Cybele', the backwards or 'praeposterous'
associated with the witches may at the same time suggest (as the term
'preposterous' does elsewhere in Jonson himself) the unmanning or
effeminising of men, including the castrated Attis, who is turned from
male into female, 'he' to 'she'.[2] Among the 'sinister births' recorded
in Jonson's learned margins is the hyena, which (along with the hare)
figured 'preposterous' inversions or changes of gender in a 'contrary'
direction (alluded to in the context of a 'Ganymede', for example, in
Shakespeare's *As You Like It*).[3]

   The queens who replace these 'sinister' witches both right and
rewrite the anti-masque by turning instead in the direction of 'masculine' virtue, in a masque whose conclusion celebrates the power of
James (author of the *Daemonologie* that traced witchcraft back to 'Eve')
to counter the witches' 'praeposterous' or 'backwards' spells. The
third dance of these queens enacts a graphic spelling that reverses
the witches' leftward or 'sinister' direction by enacting the writing of
the name of the King's own son: '*graphically* dispos'd into *letters*, and
honoring the Name of the most sweete, and ingenious *Prince, Charles,
Duke of Yorke*' (Jonson 1925–52: VII, 313–14). The masque as a whole
thus appears to progress definitively from 'left' to 'right', moving
teleologically 'forward' to this simultaneous writing and rerighting. In
a masque that complexly inscribes the power of Queen Anna herself
within a structure that is ultimately ruled by the King, James's own position as *paterfamilias* is stressed in the writing out of the name of a son,
not the unproductive sexuality associated with witchcraft and witches

but towards a telos that is simultaneously patriarchal and familial, contrasted with the 'praeposterous', 'sinister' and bewitching.

As with the contraries of contemporary witchcraft treatises, however, which (as Clark observes) never successfully exorcise the threat of a reversible 'turning' (Clark 1997: 136–7, 128), the progression of Jonson's *Masque* towards the 'right' simultaneously evokes the possibility of conversion in the opposite direction. Though the masque appears to move in one direction only – from left to right, female (or castrated, 'imperfect' male) to the perfection of 'heroicall, and masculine Vertue' – its inclusion of the 'hyena' among nature's 'sinister' births invokes the familiar threat of 'praeposterous' inversion, backwards not only to the unruly (or Eve-like) female but to the less than 'perfect' male. Stephen Orgel's analysis in *The Jonsonian Masque* of its sudden turn from 'darkness' to 'light' stressed the absolute separation of its two worlds; but the masque's own 'turning Machine' – together with the 'hyena' and internal echoings across the masque's ostensibly separated parts – keeps open the possibility of 'turning' in both directions, including the reversion, suggested in Orgel's own subsequent essay, 'Nobody's Perfect: Or Why Did the English Stage Take Boys for Women?', to 'imperfect' male (see Orgel 1965 and 1989).

James himself – male successor to Elizabeth (or the 'monstrous regiment' of women) and the king whose subordination of female 'furies' included turning away from his own more 'sinister' maternal inheritance as well as promoting patriarchal models in family and state – might thus be not simply the telos or endpoint of this masque's apparently unidirectional progression but a figure whose relations with male favourites complexly associated him with the 'preposterous amor' traditionally figured by the 'hyena' cited in the masque's notes as one of nature's 'sinister births'. In relation to *The Masque of Queenes*, such a subtext must remain in the realm of subtlety and speculation – even (or perhaps especially) in the work of a writer such as Jonson, whose familiarity with this other sense of the 'praeposterous' is clear – like the relation to this same reigning king of the multiple figures of preposterous inversion in *Macbeth*, where the witches' 'charm' is 'wound up' in reverse and the 'weyard' of these 'weyard sisters' evokes yet another contemporary synonym of the preposterous, or reversed.

Graphic forms of spelling backwards – including the reversal of alphabetical letters – figured in early modern texts not only as counterparts of the backward spells of witches but as an index of 'preposterous amor' itself. To this we now turn.

If ye spell Roma backwarde [. . .] it is preposterous *amor*, a
love out of order or a love against kynde.

Bale, *Englysh Votaryes*

What is *a*, *b*, spell'd backward, with the horn on his head?

Shakespeare, *Love's Labour's Lost*

All in *Italica*, your backward blows.
All in *Italica*, you Hermaphrodite [. . .]

Fletcher, *Nice Valour*

Spelling backwards as the inversion of 'right writing' in every sense –
evoked in *Much Ado*'s lines on spelling a 'man backwards' – repeatedly
figured in early modern texts in the context of the sexually 'praeposterous'. Orthography (or 'right writing') shares its *orthos* with *orthodox*:
the straight or erect contrasted to the crooked, leaning or curving
in the inverse of the 'right' direction. What the title of Richard
Mulcaster's *Elementarie* (1582) called the 'right writing of our English
tung' thus readily lent itself to the homophonic association of 'writing'
with 'righting' ('can reading be right before writing be righted [. . .]?
or can writing seme right, being challenged for wrong?'). Writing
from left to right as well as observing the proper 'order in writing'
(unlike discourses that 'preposterously [. . .] begin at the latter end',
as John Hart's *Orthographie* put it) came with a sexual as well as discursive import in early modern texts (Mulcaster 1970: [iv, v]; Hart
1569: A1). Jonson invokes multiple figures of the 'preposterous' or
'backward' in *Discoveries*, for example, a text whose very title is bound
up with its claim that 'language most *shows* a man'. Insisting that a
man's 'reason' cannot be 'in frame' if his 'sentence is preposterous',
it opposes a 'masculine' or 'virile' style to the 'preposterous' habits of
contemporary 'Gallants', signs of the degeneracy of an age in which
'wits grow downe-ward, and Eloquence growes back-ward' (Jonson
1925–52: VIII, 581, 588, 591–2, 607).

'Preposterous' in this early modern sense denoted not just the sexual reversal of back for front but the 'unnatural' inversion of the 'right
writing' of Nature, both *contra naturam* and contrary to the orthodoxy
of 'right writing' that observed the proper order of recto and verso,
before and behind. As the 'right' writing associated with the *orthos*
as the straight opposite of crooked or curved, 'orthography' is contrasted in sexual as well as graphic contexts with the 'sinister' or 'left'.
Alexander Hume's unpublished *Of the Orthographie of the Britan Tongue*
(*c*.1617) makes the connection explicitly: 'The printers and wryteres

of this age, caring for no more arte then may win the pennie, will not paen them selfes to knau wither it be orthographie or skaiographie that does the turne'. As Jeffrey Masten observes of this passage, Hume coins the term 'skaiographie' (from *skaios*, 'left, left-handed, awkward, crooked') as the opposite of the rectitude of orthography.[4] The analogy between writing and sexual practices – reflected in Nashe's complaint that 'posterior Italian and Germane cornugraphers sticke not to applaude and cannonize vnnaturall sodomitrie' (where 'cornugraphers' combines the 'posterior' use of a sexual 'horn' with the schoolmaster's 'hornbook' or 'ABC') – continues graphic metaphors familiar from medieval writers such as Alain de Lille, where the 'orthography' of Nature is contrasted to 'falsigraphie' or 'false writing', associated not only with the witchcraft of Venus whose 'femaleness dooms her to falsigraphia from the start', but with turning backwards from 'male' to 'female' rather than in the direction of 'perfection', replacing 'right writing' with movement in the direction of the lame or 'limping' left hand.[5]

Claudio in *Much Ado* – whose very name evokes lameness or limping – is described as turning 'orthography' when he leaves behind the world of male–male relations linked with Saturn (the planet whose effect is traditionally queering) for heterosexual marriage. But the fact that his marriage is to a 'Hero' who is also a transvestite boy continues, at an end that ambiguously alludes to 'double dealing' as well as the uncertain order of 'after' and 'before', to suggest the deformations figured by the purely verbal character 'Deformed', spelling 'men' backwards to 'boys' as well as 'women'.[6] In Alain de Lille, where the writing 'pen' is assimilated to the role of the penis in generation, the perversion of right writing described as the way of 'nature' occurs when men take the role of passive 'anvil' rather than active 'hammer'. This unmanning is explicitly associated with the witchcraft or black magic of Venus, which turns a 'he' into a 'she', a leftwards turning simultaneously described as a *denigrating* or blackening: 'The active sex shudders in disgrace as it sees itself degenerate into the passive sex. A man turned woman (*femina vir factus*) blackens (*denigrat*) the fair name of his sex. The witchcraft of Venus (*ars magice Veneris*) turns him into a hermaphrodite'.[7]

The retrograde and preposterous in early modern writing (which continued to be influenced by such paradigms) repeatedly identified the spells of witches with other forms of spelling backwards. The description of backward or 'arsy-versy' turning as conversion in a 'retrograde and preposterous way' in *The Late Lancashire Witches* evokes the retrograde that was not only a synonym for the preposterous (as in the tradition of reading, writing, or spelling in a 'retrograde order, beginning with the last'),[8] but also the astrological term for a movement that reversed the order of the signs, i.e., from east to west. The 'signe retrogradant' evoked by 'Southward Sol doth retrograde, / Goes (Crab-like) backward' in Sylvester's *Du Bartas* (1598) was the 'Signe of Cancer which is cleped the Crabbe'.[9] The 'arseward' or backward movement of the 'retrograde crab' made the crab itself a familiar figure for the 'preposterous', including for the contrary or unruly female. The preposterous inversion of witches is compared to the backward movement of 'crabs' in influential treatises of demonology (including one where witches are described as approaching the Devil 'with their backs towards him like crabs'), while the 'backward' pleasures of a female shrew are compared by Richard Brathwait to 'a very Crab'.[10]

Influenced by both classical and medieval traditions of spelling backwards, early modern texts frequently exploit the link between sexual and graphic. 'Retro' or 'retrograde' verses – which could be read backwards – were part of a long-standing tradition known to early modern writers. Florio's *Worlde of Wordes* (1598) gives 'retrograde' as 'Retrogrado, that goeth backward. Also that which is to be *read* backward', alluding to 'retrograde' verses that could be read in both directions.[11] Palindromes themselves could summon the sexually 'retrograde' or backwards. Martial has a famous *Epigram* (2.86) which begins 'I don't pride myself on palindromes or read pathic Sotades backwards' ('Quod nec carmine glorior supino/nec retro lego Sotaden cinaedum'), associating verses capable of being read 'backwards' with the castrated or emasculated 'Attis' (transformed from 'he' to 'she') and the 'Greekling' ('Graecula') that would become a favourite denigrating synonym for sodomite in humanist invective.[12] The commentary on Martial's epigram on writing and reading 'retro' or backwards provided by Farnaby (whom Jonson himself consulted) makes the link between 'retrograde' verses, Ovid's influential lines on a witch's spells and the 'retrograde' or 'backward course' of 'rivers' and the palindrome '*Roma/Amor*', reversible letters to which John Bale and other early modern writers gave an explicitly sodomitical sense. Reading 'backwards' or towards the 'left' (as in the 'praeposterous' dance of Jonson's witches) is described in Farnaby's *Martial* as 'ennervating', 'emasculating' or 'unmanning'.

The 'retrograde' movement shared by witches and crabs was also used for the reverse reading of the letters of the alphabet, whose backward spelling was given a sodomitical inflection. 'Say these letters B, C, D, E, F, G, H, I, K, and retrograde them from K to B', counsels one seventeenth-century text, using 'retrograde' as a verb meaning to 'turn back, reverse, revert'.[13] Modern readers are accustomed to the sexual import of reversals such as 'cuff' and 'fuck', '(k)noc(k)' and 'con', the palindrome lurking within the Porter Scene of *Macbeth*. But other reversals of alphabetical position may not immediately strike us as related to the 'preposterous' in the sexual sense. In *Love's Labour's Lost*, for example, a play filled with alphabetical as well as other kinds of letters, what seems a simple discussion of 'orthography' yields a form of reverse spelling when the 'Moth' once thought to be a backward-turning anagram of 'Thom' Nashe (or 'an ass') asks 'What is a, b, spell'd backward, with the horn on his head' (5.1.47–8). The lines invoke the schoolboy's hornbook, the thin plate of translucent horn used for spelling the 'ABC'. But in ways akin to Nashe's 'posterior cornugraphers', it also suggests – at the level of bodily writing – not only the horns of 'cuckoldry' but the 'horn' that (in *Much Ado about Nothing* or 'noting' as 'writing') is another word for penis and, hence, the sexual subtext of this entire exchange: Latin 'Quis quis' here is a familiar homophone of 'kiss kiss', while the tutor who 'teaches boys the hornbook' comes with the sense of 'tutor' that long associated the *pedagogus* (or schoolmaster) with 'pedicare', or backwards entry. The schoolmaster's tutoring is already sexualised in the scene where Sir Nathaniel says, 'their sons are well tutored by you, and their daughters profit very greatly under you' and Holofernes responds 'if their sons be ingenuous, they shall want no instruction; if their daughters be capable, I will put it to them' (4.2.77). The reversal of alphabetical position (in 'a, b, spell'd backward') occurs in a scene of 'arts men' or 'ars-men' that includes reference to a 'dunghill' ('I smell false Latin'), the 'well culled', and 'some show in the posteriour of this day'. *Love's Labour's Lost* (whose end reflects the absence of comedy's traditional union of 'Jack' and 'Jill') begins with pointed reference to the 'obscene and most preposterous event' of a man whose name evokes Adam, following a woman who is both a 'maculate' Eve and a transvestite boy and proceeds to the reversible Moth's address to the 'eyes' (or I's) of boy players who act the parts of 'Ladies', turning their 'backs' to him on stage, in scenes whose 'Muscovites' (and Moors) may summon links with both witchcraft and sodomy. Spelling backwards thus extends the 'preposterous' introduced at the beginning of this play not only to letters and alphabetical position, or a tutoring linked with 'preposterous amor', but to multiple forms of preposterous inversion.

Even *Hamlet* – which we are still not accustomed to thinking of in this way, almost two decades after Terence Hawkes' 'Telmah' or *Hamlet* spelled backwards – connects writing and righting in the description of boy players 'whose writers do them wrong', proclaiming against their own 'succession', in lines that evoke (in little 'eye-asses') the familiar use of boy players as Ganymedes or catamites, or the inversion of right writing. *Hamlet* repeatedly stresses the link between writing (including handwriting) and the linearity of righting as 'succession' or teleological sequence. But it is also filled with backwards reversals, explicitly invoking the crab cited by *Hamlet* himself as the figure of reversal ('Yourself, sir, shall grow old as I am, if like a crab you could go backwards'). And even its famous tropical turning (in the punning lines on the 'tropically' named *Mousetrap* which looks both 'before' and 'after') evokes a tropic that may simultaneously suggest the Tropic of Cancer (or the Crab) and its own 'arseward' or backward turning.[14]

Perhaps the most striking instance of spelling backwards is the palindrome '*Roma/Amor*', long associated with witchcraft's backward spells but also applied to the 'sodometrye' or 'preposterous amor' of the 'Roman' Church and the reversed (or west-to-east) turning of imperial Rome to Byzantine (and Islamic) Constantinople. The 'sinister' inversion of orthography or right writing is linked in this case not only to 'preposterous venery' but to other forms of backwards conversion. 'Roma' spelled backwards was part of the famous ninth-century *Versus Romae*, where the palindrome '*Roma/Amor*' functions as the turning point of the entire text, the pivot or reverse *translatio* represented by Constantinople or the 'New Rome on the Bosphorus' (Kantorowicz 1957: 82). In early modern English usage, 'Rome backwards' (or 'Arsey-versey Love') was a familiar euphemism for backwards sexual entry, associated in Barry's *Ram-Alley* (which juxtaposes 'hole backwards' with 'Rome backwards') with the 'Termagant' who was simultaneously a tyrant, an idol said to be worshipped by Saracens and 'Turks' and a familiar term for a domineering or shrewish woman (Barry 1952: 36). In the work of Roman convert John Bale, *Roma* spelled 'backwarde' (or 'preposterous *amor*') is 'a love out of order or a love agaynst kynde', sign of both preposterous venery and the witchcraft and idolatry associated in Protestant polemics with the Roman Church, a 'backwards' spelling inseparable from Rome's 'preposteration' of Christian 'truth' to Hebrew ceremonies and the 'Synagogue of Satan' figured by Papist, Turk, and Jew.[15]

Other apparently only graphic forms bore a similar cultural weight – linking italics, for example, to what was known as sexual entry 'the preposterous Italian way'. Sexual entry by the 'posterne' or 'back door' according to the supposed 'Italian fashion' was one of the most common figures for the 'arsy versy', 'assbackwards', or 'preposterous' in the sexual sense, evoked in the 'back-door'd Italian' of Dekker's *1 Honest Whore*, in Middleton's "'tis such an Italian world, many men know not before from behind' in *Michaelmas Term* and the sexually suggestive 'key given after the Italian fashion, backward' in *A Mad World, My Masters*. 'In Italy', according to Lacy's *Dumb Lady*, 'both women and boys have their before behind, behind before, as well as your horses have here'. In Mason's *The Turk*, a gentleman usher whose office is normally to come 'before' remarks that his 'office' (a standard sexual term) has been 'italianated, I am faine to come behinde' (5.1.2156). 'Italian' and 'Italian fashion' continued to have these associations in English writing throughout the early modern period. William Webbe writes that 'the filthy lust of the deuillish *Pederastice*', alluded to in Spenser's *Shepheards Calender* (Eclogue 6), 'is skant allowable to English eares, and might well haue beene left for the Italian defenders of loathsome beastlines, of whom perhappes he learned it' (Arber 1870: XII, 54). A page in Fletcher's *Honest Man's Fortune* notes that 'since our French Lords learned of the Neapolitans, to make their Pages their Bedfellows, [it] doth more hurt to the "Suburb Ladies" than twenty dead vacations' (3.3.219–21). One of the many texts linking William III with sodomy asserts that 'Billy with Benting does play the Italian', while a 'Ladies Complaint' from the 1690s claims that King William 'Makes love like an *Italian* and Rules like a *Turk* [. . .] who would ha' thought that a Low Country *Stallion* [. . .] should prove an *Italian*'. The 'preposterous Italian way' was at the same time associated with reversing the normative direction in multiple senses. In Fletcher's *Lovers' Progress* a steward declares that 'Love's a terrible Clyster, / And if some Cordial of her favours help not, / I shall like an Italian, dye backward, / And breathe my last the wrong way' (1.1.19–22). Neville's *News from the New Exchange* observes that sexual orthodoxy will 'make the Italian Knight lose all his Custome, for going the wrong way to worke with our English Ladies'. In a sodomitical context, an 'Italian fault' figures the error in 'grammar' described by Alain de Lille, turning 'male' into 'female' in the inverse direction of right writing: Dallington's *View of Fraunce*, for example, proclaims it 'an Italian fault [. . .] to take the Masculine for the Feminine', in both the sexual and the grammatical sense.[16]

In a context in which letters themselves were assimilated to bodily orifices and positions, even type fonts could be 'preposterous'. The graphic counterpart of the sexually 'backward' or 'preposterous Italian fashion' was thus '*Italica*' or italic, which slopes 'instead of being erect as in the Roman' (a 'type' that Swift as late as 1733 associated with printing 'Letters' in 'vulgar Shapes').[17] In an essay whose title ('Spellbound') suggests the multiple forms of spelling involved, Randall

McLeod describes the problems of 'ligatures' and 'back-kerns' which are prone to 'foul', including 'typesetting problems in typical italic faces of the day' ('where alone the fouling potential exists', since italic has 'more kerned sorts than black-letter or roman fonts'). The word he identifies as most readily defining 'the oddity of this design characteristic of old italic' is '*assbackwards*' itself (McLeod 1984: 82–3). 'Ligatures' – familiar from the spellbinding ligatory points of witchcraft invoked in *The Late Lancashire Witches* and the lines of *Much Ado* on spelling a man backward – thus linked both kinds of spelling, including the sodomitical forms of italic as spelling backwards evoked in Fletcher's *Nice Valour* (*c.*1616), where sexually double-meaning lines on a 'Printer' include not only 'Pica Roman' but '*Italica*', and 'backward blows' and coming 'behinde' ('come behinde, 'tis in *Italica* too') are explicitly associated with the '*Italica*' of a 'Hermaphrodite' ('All in *Italica*, your backward blows / All in *Italica*, you Hermaphrodite') (Beaumont and Fletcher 1966–96: VII, 4.1.235–7, 4.1.300–19 and 5.3.29).

***

men do with him as they would with Hebrew letters,
spell him backwards and read him. [. . .]
John Earle, *Microcosmography*

Italica this! [. . .]
They put their pens the Hebrew way methinks.
Middleton, *A Game at Chess*

The association of spelling backwards with both witchcraft and 'preposterous amor' was further extended to Hebrew and other languages that were read or written in a 'left' or 'sinister' direction. The Egyptians were said to 'write their letters aukelie' (i.e., awkwardly) from right to left, the reverse direction of the 'awk-ward' and 'gauche' sounded in *Henry V*, in the speech on Henry's claim as neither 'awkward' nor 'sinister'.[18] In Middleton's *Game at Chess*, the fine for 'Sodomy, sixpence' (the 6 that inverts 9 in the backwards system of 'Arabic' numbering to which we will return) is said to be a 'sum' that should be placed on the 'backside' of the book of a 'Bishop', in lines whose association of sodomy (or preposterous amor) with the church of Rome includes the Bishop's acknowledgment that 'There's few on's very *forward*, sir' (4.2.106). In an earlier scene (1.1.304–5), in the midst of a discussion of letters ('Anglica', 'Gallica', 'Germanica' and 'Hispanica') and Jesuits already associated with both sodomy and the danger that Protestant England might be converted 'backwards' to Rome, an Italian letter in '*Italica*' or backward-leaning script is described as putting the sexual 'pen' the reverse or 'Hebrew way' ('*Italica* this! [. . .] They put their pens the Hebrew way methinks').

Hebrew – written backwards or to the left – was compounded in early modern writing with the associations surrounding witchcraft and sodomy as forms of spelling backwards (including the 'left' rather than orthographical 'right' hand), just as circumcision was associated with 'the sinstre rooted persuasion of the Jewes', in Coverdale's translation of Erasmus' commentary on Galatians (3:1), the biblical text that describes Christians as bewitched 'backwards' to the Hebrew scriptures (Coverdale 1549: chap. 5, fol. 18r). Joshua Trachtenberg's *The Devil and the Jews* and other more recent work cite representations of a Jew riding backwards and other figures of inversion, in relation to various Pauline texts on turning 'back' to idolatry, sodomy, and circumcision (Trachtenberg 1943, Mellinkoff 1973). The hyena associated with 'sinister' births and with turning backwards from 'male' to 'female' was associated with the 'Jew' in bestiary and other traditions.[19] In Drayton's 'Moone-calfe', a figure characterised as 'Nor man, nor woman, scarse Hermophradite' is described as looking 'like one for the preposterous sin, / Put by the wicked and rebellious Jewes, / To be a Pathique in their Malekind Stewes' (Drayton 1931–41: III, 170). As with the association of Jews with Esau and Ishmael rather than Isaac and Jacob (understood as figuring the Hebrew scriptures' 'rightful' Christian heir), the description links the 'preposterous sin' that is condemned in Hebrew scriptures with the 'wicked and rebellious Jewes' themselves, just as the text of Romans, Chapter 1, on those who 'turn' back to 'idolatry' (and a sexual 'use' described as *contra naturam*) is applied to Jews as backwards-turning or backsliding worshippers of the golden calf.

The connection between spelling, reading or writing 'like a Jew' and the inversion of sodomy understood as 'the preposterous sin' is underlined by the language that identifies the 'arsy-versy' with both. Witchcraft, sodomy and putting the 'pen' sexually 'the Hebrew way' are associated as forms of inversion or spelling backwards, including sexual practices seen as turning men into women – just as Hebrew was associated with witchcraft and its backward spells.[20] The backward spelling of 'Hebrew letters' (as in the epigraph from Earle's *Microcosmographie*, 'men do with him as they would Hebrew letters, spell him backwards and read him') was repeatedly conflated with its sexual counterpart (Earle 1628: C13v–D2). Jonson associates the Roman Sejanus – a 'noted pathic of the time' (1.213–16) – with sexual forms of inverted writing, when Sejanus (described as having 'prostituted his abused body') imagines that 'Egyptian slaves' and Hebrew 'print [his] body full of injuries' (2.140, 142), marking him with 'the backward ensigns of a slave' (3.262).[21] In an episode of Matthew Paris's *Chronica Majora* (1244), a crucified boy is found with Hebrew letters written on his flesh, and Jewish converts or *conversos* are summoned from the 'Domus conversorum' to read the script, in a context that (like the later alphabets of Mandeville's *Travels*) suggests a link not only between sodomy and a carnal 'Hebrew' writing but also with the threat of reversible 'conversion' posed by the *conversos* themselves. This recalls the 'bewitching' of the Galatians 'backwards' to circumcision by 'Jewish Christians or Christian Jews', a description whose chiasmic formulation suggests the threat of reversibility unsettling to any unidirectional teleology of conversion in the 'right' direction (Shapiro 1996). It is even possible that in the reversible 'ab' (or 'abba') of *Love's Labour's Lost* ('What is *a*, *b*, spell'd backward, with the horn on his head?') this 'horn' on the head (combined with a backwards spelling) evokes not only the associations of 'hornbook' and 'horn' with the alphabetic 'ABC', the writing 'pen' and cuckoldry, but also the 'horned hat' (*pileum cornutum*) and horns associated with the Mosaic scriptures and the 'arsy versy' (as well as carnal) Jew, especially since the Geneva gloss on Galatians represented the Hebrew testament itself as an 'ABC' that needed to be read in the 'right' direction.[22]

Thomas Palmer cites reading backwards 'like a Jue' among examples of the 'arsy-versy' in his emblem on 'Preposterous or overthwart doings', a term ('doings') itself compounded with sexual resonances. Though Palmer's emblem makes no explicit reference to sodomy, Mario DiGangi does, in a brilliant reading of the sodomitical resonances of 'Hebrew' in Chapman's *Bussy D'Ambois*, a play whose plot appears to operate only on the 'hetero' side of the 'homo/hetero divide'. DiGangi writes of Bussy's end:

> Monsieur's assassination of Bussy from behind represents a sodomitical punishment for Bussy's refusal to remain properly, submissively, open. To Bussy, the very word 'murder' is 'Hebrew' (5.3.76), a language he cannot understand because it is read in the same 'back-wards' direction that corrupt clergymen 'vent' their bowels of luxurious meals (3.2.46) [. . .] Penetrated from behind, Bussy regards his murder as an 'arse varse' violation of his great spirit: 'Guise and Monsieur, Death and Destiny / Come behind D'Ambois: is my body then / But penetrable flesh?' (5.3.124–6).[23]

There is even more to the preposterous or backwards associations of Bussy's rise and fall than DiGangi's brief treatment suggests. 'Falling star' (5.3.191–3) is one of the play's multiple comparisons to Lucifer, identified with preposterous inversions of all kinds, including sodomy, witchcraft and bewitching 'backwards' by Jews. In the opening scene (which evokes both sexual 'service' – including the backwards or sodomitical – and the Luciferic *non serviam*) there is an even more striking reminder of the plot's Luciferic original: 'Many will say, that cannot rise at all, / Man's first hour's rise, is first step to his fall: / I'll venture that; men that fall low must die, / As well as men cast headlong from the sky' (1.1.136–9).

In a play that opens with Bussy's 'Fortune, not Reason, rules the state of things,/Reward goes backwards, Honour on his head' (1.1.1–2), the iterated emphasis on 'backwards' (both coupled and contrasted with 'forwards'), which DiGangi reads as part of its sodomitical counter-discourse, is explicitly linked to witchcraft and its backward spellings, conjurings that will later summon Behemoth himself: 'To gain being forward, though you break for haste / All the Commandments ere you break your fast: / But believe backwards, make your period / And Creed's last article, I believe in God' (1.1.98–101). The last two lines allude to the witches' 'inversion of parts of the liturgy' that 'was an accepted technique for conjuring devils',[24] placing at the end or 'period' the Creed's 'I believe in God', which belongs at the beginning. Such backward spelling is simultaneously assimilated in *Bussy D'Ambois* to 'Hebrew', and sodomitical inversion. The affinity between the sodomitical subtext of Chapman's play, witchcraft and Hebrew (or 'backwards') writing is underscored by the iterated references to handwriting and 'hands' capable of moving not just from 'left' to 'right' but in the reverse direction, to 'clock finger turning the wrong way' (2.1.57) and to 'conjuring' in the sexual sense as well as the summoning of demons such as 'Cartophylax'.

Jews are explicitly introduced in lines on 'jewels' (distinguishing signs of the 'Hebrew', along with the horned hat and sumptuary 'O') in Bussy's response to King Henry's 'Truth's words like jewels hang in th'ears of Kings' (3.2.6): 'Would I might live to see no Jews hang there instead of jewels; sycophants I mean, / Who use Truth like the Devil, his true foe, / Cast by the Angel to the pit of fears, / And bound in chains; Truth seldom decks Kings' ears' (3.2.7–11), a response that combines 'Jews' with 'sycophants' (preposterous risers whose upstart history may not differ from his own) and the Lucifer whose rise and fall or reversal of fortune had already been associated with upstarts such as Bussy.[25] The anti-Semitism continues in Bussy's speech here in the comparison of the 'Slave Flattery' to a poisoning 'red-hair'd man', a figure whose red hair (like Shylock's) may summon, with Judas, yet another reminder of the Jews (3.2.15–18).[26] Soon after, in this same scene, Bussy invokes the 'Hebrew' read backwards for the bodily 'venting' (from the backside) of the 'Clergyman' ('Turning the rents of his superfluous Cures / Into your pheasants and your partridges; / Venting their Quintessence as men read Hebrew', 3.2.44–6), in a speech devoted to the 'turning' world in which a 'Great Man' who 'affects royalty, rising from a clapdish', 'rules so much more than his suffering king' (3.2.28–9), lines whose inversion of the relation between subject and king illustrate DiGangi's remark that in Chapman's court plays those higher up vie for the attention of the favourite rather than the other way around.

'Right' and 'left' are repeatedly stressed in Chapman's play. But what is most remarkable, in relation to the threat of reversibility posed by witchcraft, preposterous amor, backwards or 'Hebrew' writing and the reverse conversion associated with turning (or returning) 'Jew' is the exploitation of the 'Ambo' (or 'both' directions) within the name of Bussy d'Ambois himself. Much is made of this name in a play that will finally conclude with 'Ill plays on both sides' or the 'both sides' of the 'ambodexter'. When D'Ambois is asked his name, it is with an emphasis on the double-meaning 'serve' that suggests sexual service as well as subservience ('Is your name D'Ambois? [. . .] serve you the Monsieur? [. . .] I serve the Monsieur'). When Bussy's name is repeated in the shortened form of 'Ambo', the 'B' text includes lines that highlight not only the link between 'Ambo' and 'Ambois' but the variable spelling of 'Ambois' as 'Amboys', containing within it the 'boy' (catamite or Ganymede) that underwrites the sense of going 'both' ways:

Maff.: [. . .] Here sir Ambo.
D'Amb.: How, Ambo, sir?
Maff.: Is is not your name Ambo?
D'Amb.: You call'd me lately D'Amboys, has your Worship
      So short a head?
Maff.: I cry thee mercy D'Amboys.

                         (1.1.204a/b/c/205)

'Has your Worship / So short a head?' exploits the rhetorical form of curtailed or shortened name that already came with a bodily or sexual significance, like the 'Apocope' or verbal shortening identified in Alain de Lille with the 'cutting' or unmanning of castration (Ziolkowski 1985: 18). The curtailed, cut or shortened 'Ambo' here simultaneously evokes 'boys' and the 'both sides' of 'ambo' itself, exploiting the same pun on 'bois' (also spelled 'boyes') and 'boys' that appears in *As You Like It*, where a plot involving a 'Ganymede' and 'De Boyes' similarly evokes the 'hyena' which could turn sexually in 'both' directions (DiGangi 1997: 55, 57).

'Ambo' and 'ambodexter' thus came with associations that connected writing with 'both hands' (or in reversible directions) with its sexual counterparts.[27] Florio's *Worlde of Wordes* (1598) defines Italian 'Ambo' as 'both' and 'Ambodestro' as having 'the use of both hands alike', an ambidexterity that simultaneously designated 'both ways' in the sexual sense. The 'ambidextrous' (defined by Minsheu as 'ready to play on both sides') connected ambiguity of all kinds with the 'shifting' evoked in Peele's 'Such shifting knaves as I am the ambodexter must play' (Peele 1952–70: III, 44).[28] Anti-theatricalist Phillip Stubbes links 'doble dealing ambodexters' with 'masking Players' and the Hebrew Pharisees ('beware therefore you masking Players, you painted sepulchres, you doble dealing ambodexters').[29] Within the work of Chapman himself, the other 'D'Ambois' (of *The Revenge of Bussy D'Ambois*) is linked with the 'ambo' or 'both' ('How strangely thou art lov'd of both the sexes'), though he values 'friendship chaste, and masculine' (5.1.188) over 'loue of women' (5.1.156).[30] In *Bussy D'Ambois* – where the 'Ambo' of the name is most directly exploited – the situation in which Chapman's Senecan original is caught between (stoically leaning to 'neither side') is charged with the more ambiguous sense of being caught 'between', in which 'Ill plays on both sides'.

The 'ambo' associated with 'both sides' (front and back, behind and before) as well as the reversible directions of 'left' and 'right' connects the double-meaning 'Amboys' with the sexual ambiguity of the 'ambo' and with an ambidextrous (or reversible) writing, including the threat of a 'sinisterly' written 'Hebrew' imprinted on the body from 'behind'. Spelling backwards thus combined the backward spelling of Hebrew with the inverse of 'right writing' in its sexual as well as other senses. But it also – in its multiple overdetermined senses in the period – extended to the larger cultural stakes of reading the Hebrew scriptures themselves in the 'right' direction, from left to right, Old Testament to New, rather than 'preposterating' them in what was described as an 'arseward' direction. For a Protestant polemicist such as John Bale, 'Roma' was 'Amor spelled backwards' not only because of the 'sodometryes' of its popes or priests, but because it turned

Gospel truth itself back to idolatry and the Judaising of law or works. In Bale's play *Three Lawes*, which claims that 'At Rome for prelates are stewes, / Of both kyndes', sodomy and idolatry are conjured by the Latin 'ambo', in a scene where the Hebrew 'Tetragrammaton' is directly invoked and sodomy's 'Ambo is a name full clean' suggests precisely the reverse.[31] In the works of Bale as a whole, the palindrome '*Roma/Amor*' figures the danger not just of the individual's turning 'back' to this 'unclean' pair but of England's own reverse conversion or turning, in polemical writings that repeatedly condemn Rome's 'praeposterous' abuses, as well as its turning backward to 'Hebrew' ceremonies as the 'Synagogue of Satan'.

***

These roguish Arsmetrique gibbets or flesh-
hookes, and cyphers or round oos.
                                   Nashe, *Saffron Walden*

I am very comptible, even to the least sinister usage [. . .]
What should that alphabetical position portend?
                                   Shakespeare, *Twelfth Night*

The association with the 'sinister' that conflates Hebrew with 'prepos-terous amor' may not appear to the same extent in relation to Arabic or other languages read or written from right to left, though it is hinted at in the lines of Jonson's *Sejanus* on 'Egyptian' as well as 'Hebrew' sexual 'prints'. But it does appear in relation to the 'backwards' or 'sinister' writing of Arabic numerals, part of the growth of both usury and mercantile capitalism in Europe or what Thomas More called the 'Arithmetricke meete for marchauntes'. For us, Hindu-Arabic numbers have been naturalised for so long into the telelogy of reading from left to right that it may come as a surprise that in early modern instruction they were written 'backwards' or *sinistrorum*.[32]

   This system of counting (with its so-called infidel 'O')–which was increasingly replacing both Roman numerals and calculation by 'compters' – brought with it the zero, cipher or 'O' (from Arabic 'as-sifr' and Hebrew *Saphar*) that crucially depended on its place-ment or place. It is this feature which is exploited in *Bussy D'Ambois*, for example, when the Monsieur comments that 'there is no sec-ond place in numerous State / That holds more than a cipher' (1.1.34–35), an 'O' that registers both as hierarchical place and in relation to this play's explicit images of 'back-part upwards' and 'right open-arses' (5.1.155–7; 3.2.237–9), as well as its reversal of 'left' and 'right', 'behind' and 'before'. The 'zero' or 'cipher' was not only 'the infidel symbol', but an example of the 'curved' rather than the erect or straight. This infidel 'O', from a system of numbers written 'backwards', *sinistrorum* or towards the 'left hand' was associated by opponents of this 'saracen' form (also identified with Jewish merchants and usurers) with conjuring, witchcraft and other kinds of backwards spelling. It was identified not only with the 'infidel' system of 'backward' numbering but with the 'O' that was the distinguishing sign of Jewish identity, as well as the multiplying 'O's' of usorious increase, characterised by metaphors of barrenness and sterility, including the 'sterility' of the 'preposterous sin' of Sodom, associated (as in Drayton) with the Jews.

The 'O' that we may be used to identifying with the misogyny of *Hamlet*'s reference to the 'nothing' that lies between 'maid's legs' (or the hetero-semantics of the 'nothing' or 'nought' of *Much Ado about Nothing*) was thus available for both sexual orifices, 'before' and 'behind'. Even the early English spelling of the Arabic 'arithmetic' (as 'arsemetric') led to associations with the 'backwards' and bodily 'arsy-versy'. The Arab roots of 'algebra' and the 'algorism' (as well as 'arithmetic') – signalled in texts such as Jonson's *The Alchemist* (1.1.607), which couples 'alchemy' and 'algebra' as 'sciences' traceable to 'Arab' or 'infidel' arts – are repeatedly commented on in early modern writing, while the common English spelling of 'arsmetrik' (or of the astrolabe as the 'ars-table') linked the sinister or 'backwards' form of 'Saracen' numbering with the bodily 'preposterous' or arsy-versy. Even before the early modern period, Chaucer – whose treatise on the astrolabe, together with other aspects of his writing, make clear his familiarity with 'Saracen' learning – alludes in the *Knight's Tale* to 'geometry or arsmetrike' and strikingly exploits 'ars-metrike' in its bodily arsy-versy sense at the end of *The Summoner's Tale* where (in a satire directed against fraternal orders long associated wih sodomy), a 'fart' is divided according to the principles of 'ars-metric', associated with Arabic learning and its backward writing.[33]

'Arsemetry' remained a common early modern spelling, continuing to be used by Robert Greene and others.[34] Nashe's reference to 'rogish arsmetrique gibbets' and 'cyphers or round oos' in the epigraph to this section is from a passage in which Piers Pennilesse disdains to write such 'figures' in the 'margent' of his 'Booke' lest it be 'bescratcht' with them 'like a Merchants booke'. The mercantile 'arsemetrique' here, in Nashe's scatalogical text (with its anal 'rope-rhetorics' and 'envois' associated with bodily 'excrements') comes with an already bodily and potentially sodomitical resonance as well as connections with the arsy-versy in its other early modern senses. [35]

Nashe's reference to 'Arithmetique' in a later passage of this text is associated with heterosexual 'multiplication' or increase (Nashe 1958: III, 120).[36] But its appearance as 'Arsemetrique', in a passage where reference to 'Pages vnfigured' and 'disfigure(d)' joins the punning on 'pages' and 'Pages' elsewhere in Nashe, simultaneously evokes the 'arsy versy' bodily sense of 'cyphers or round oos', or 'O's', in a text filled with allusions to an 'Ambodexter' (Nashe 1958: III, 104) as well as 'Ganimede' (92) and other 'beloued Boy(s)' (108). Nashe's text is famously directed against Gabriel Harvey, upstart 'sonne of a Rope-maker' (1958: III, 56–7), described as seeking 'to raise his estate and inuent new petegrees' (56), satirically linked by Nashe with the assbackwards (including 'such men as ride with their face to-wards the horse taile', 60). At his birth, it is claimed, a 'calfe' was born with 'his feete turned backward, like certaine people of the Tartars, that neuertheles are reasonable swift' (Nashe 1958: III, 63). Immediately after the text's explicit evocation of (a leftwards or sinister) spelling backwards – in a passage on 'retrograde' heavenly signs' and 'Hebrue Rabbines' who would 'enforce vpon vs' the 'inuersed denomination' (or backward spelling) of certain words – it goes on to treat of the '*Dick* that set *Aristotle*, with his heels vpward, on the Schoole gates at Cambridge, and asses eares on hys head' ('This is that *Dick* of whom *Kit Marloe* was want to say that he was an asse', Nashe 1958: III, 85). His opponent (along with his 'printer' Wolfe) is described by Nashe's persona in another passage as 'saracenly sentencing it against mee' (1958: III, 90).

Teachers of the system of 'Arabic' notation repeatedly emphasised that it was to be written in a 'backward' or 'sinister' direction. Sacrobosco's *De Arte Numerandi* connects the writing backwards (or *sinistrorum*) of this 'arsemetrike' with Arabic itself, written not from left to right but the reverse ('We writene in this art to the lift side-warde, as arabiene writene, that weren fynders of this science').[37] A fourteenth-century 'Treatise on the Numeration of Algorism' advises its readers to begin at the 'rithe syde and to rekene backwarde', to produce '1000' not as we do by writing the '1' first and proceeding to the right with each successive 'O' but in the reverse, proceeding from right to left or 'O' to '1'. Robert Recorde's *Grounde of Artes* – dedicated to the 'Arithmetic' that 'some cal [. . .] Arsemetrike' – similarly teaches students to 'recken your order of places backeward, I meane from the right side towardes the left', reversing the familiar spelling of the ABC from left to right.[38] The confused student complains that he has to learn to put 'first' what he would otherwise put at the end or

44	*Patricia Parker*

'last' and confuses the Arabic numbers '6' and '9', cited by More in relation to the danger of 'Mysse-pryntynge those fygures of Algorisme, because the figure of .9. and the figure of .6. be all in maner one, if thei be contrary turned' (More 1533: 496) – a confusion and a 'contrary turning' associated with 'Arabic' numbers that takes us back to the association of these particular 'Arabic' numerals with sodomy in Middleton's *Game at Chess*.

Like 'alphabetical position', which (though the ABC was to be read in the 'right' direction, from left to right) could be turned or 'spelled backwards' in all senses, this system of 'backwards' or 'sinister' counting associated with 'saracens', 'arsemetrike', and infidel 'Oos' is important for the reading of early modern texts. Shakespeare's repeated references to the 'O' or 'cipher' – including in *Henry V* and *The Winter's Tale* – makes clear that he understands that it was written backwards, that what counted was the 'place' where the 'O' was located, and that it could be used to suggest mathematical and sexual 'O's' at once. In *Much Ado about Nothing* – whose title famously puns on 'noting' as a form of 'notation' as well as on things that are 'nought' – this 'O' has been assumed to be (as in *Hamlet*) the 'nothing' that 'lies between maid's legs', or what Benedick terms a woman's 'invisible baldrick' (1.2.34). But since the 'nought' or 'O' of the new system of numbering depends entirely on its placement, it may simultaneously suggest another (posterior) bodily orifice.[39] The desire of Beatrice (both female character and transvestite boy actor) for 'an H' (in the exchange that evokes the figure of 'turning Turk') comes in a passage that is ambiguous about how precisely to read this alphabetical letter, suggesting the 'deformation' in which this 'H' (which in one reading stands for 'husband') could simultaneously figure (as desire for a 'nache') the bodily 'preposterous' or posterior. Benedick's complaint, similarly, against the 'base (though bitter) disposition of Beatrice' (2.1.207–8) depends on the sense of 'disposition' as placing, and hence of Beatrice's putting Benedick 'in a false position'.[40]

Given the Shakespearian playing on '*a, b*, spell'd backward' in relation to the bodily and other reversals of *Love's Labour's Lost*, Nashe's reference to 'posterior cornugraphers' and the bodily figures of letters, numbers and other forms of notation in early modern writing, the 'backwards' and 'sinister' sense of the new system of counting (along with its rival 'compters') may even be behind some notoriously puzzling lines in Shakespeare's *Twelfth Night*, a play in which the order of letters (or 'alphabetical position') is famously altered by placement in different 'positions' in the 'letter' that Malvolio attempts to read.

Viola swears to Olivia 'I would be loath to cast away my speech; for besides that it is excellently well *penn'd*, I have taken great pains to *con* it. Good beauties, let me sustain no scorn; I am very comptible, even to the least sinister usage' (1.5.176). Editors (less focused on 'sinister') have been baffled by Viola's 'comptible', to the point of suggesting that the text itself is corrupt and should be altered. But the enigmatic line may be suggesting the various senses of what it meant to count backwards in a 'sinister' direction, especially since the 'Viola' who speaks of being 'comptible' (the term that evokes 'compters' as well as 'counting') as well as the possibility of a 'sinister usage' is herself a transvestite boy, who plays the part of a 'eunuch' and is by the end of the play coupled with Orsino, in a plot that features 'backtricks' of all kinds.[41]

Twelfth Night is filled with preposterous (or arsy-versy) exchanges of place as well as of alphabetical letters. The bank of 'violets' (1.1.6) at its opening suggests 'viol' as well as 'Viola', the Italian *for* 'violet' and emblem of the gender and other violations that ensue. Olivia, Viola and Malvolio are linked not only as characters but by the reversals or exchanges of the same letters within the names themselves. The wordplay on 'hart' and 'heart' in the opening scene turns (like the later 'C, U, T' that may figure a bodily cut or 'cu[n]t') on an added or a missing letter, just as Malvolio (in the 'letter' scene) has to construe what 'follows' from the order of particular letters of the alphabet. The preposterous or 'backward' is explicitly introduced not only in Sir Andrew's boast of his skill at the 'backtrick' (1.3.115), with its suggestion of sexual entry as well as of dancing, but in the carnival reversal of 'early' and 'late' (2.3.5–7), 'elder' and 'younger' (2.4.29–36), the wordplay on 'except before excepted' in the scene that begins with Maria's attempt to bring Sir Toby 'within the modest limits of order' (1.3.7–8), and the reversible 'chevril glove' that traditionally figured reversals of gender (3.1.1–25).

The obsession in *Twelfth Night* with letters, bodies and alphabetical place or 'position' links the reference to Olivia's 'very c's, her u's, and her t's' as well as 'her great P's' with the incontinent female body, as Gail Kern Paster has argued (Paster 1993: 33–4). But in a play in which 'Viola' announces that she will play the part of a 'eunuch', this 'C-U-T' suggests the unmanned or castrated body of the 'eunuch' as well, just as Viola's 'A little thing would make me tell them how much I lack of man' (3.4.302–3) may be read not only as designating the traditionally imperfect 'female' but also (with the emphasis on 'little') the 'boy' who plays this prominent female part, whose want of a 'beard' (and desire for a man with a 'beard') is emphasised elsewhere within it. 'P' itself anciently figured 'a visual image of the male genitals', as in the pun exploited in Ausonius's Epigram 87.[42] Olivia (the other transvestite boy player who falls for Viola, the doubly transvestite boy who embodies the 'viol' of her/his own name) in fact possesses the 'little part' of 'man' that this 'Cesario' ('eunuch' or 'cut') professes to lack. Even the letter whose 'alphabetical position' Malvolio attempts to read aright ends with an 'O' and 'I' capable of being read in both directions:

Mal.: [. . .] A should follow, but O does.
Fab.: And O shall end, I hope.
Sir T.: Ay, or I'll cudgel him, and make him cry O!
Mal.: And then I comes behind.
Fab.: Ay, and you had any eye behind you, you might see more detraction at your heels than fortunes before you [. . .]

(2.5.130–8)

The exploitation of 'alphabetical position' here is even clearer in the Folio text: the letters of the letter Malvolio attempts to construe – attempting to read what 'alphabetical position portend[s]' – ends with an 'I' or (as in Chaucer, nether 'eye') that 'comes behind'

Fa.: And O shall end, I hope.
To.: I, or Ile cudgell him, and make him cry O.
Mal.: And then I comes behind.
Fa.: I, and you had any eye behinde you, you might see more detraction at your heeles, then Fortunes before you.[43]

These lines in which an 'I' and 'O' associated with a female 'cut' are transposed from 'before' to 'behind', just as in the lines on the 'halting' or limping Sir Toby, 'he would have tickled you othergates than he did' (5.1.192–4), suggests the 'postern' or 'other gate' opposite to sexual right writing. Inversions of all kinds might be expected in a play of '*Twelfth Night*' carnival (or arsy-versy) overturning. *Twelfth Night* itself ends with multiple puns on 'write' and 'right'. But it famously troubles the teleology of 'right writing' or orthography by pairing 'Viola' (while still a transvestite 'boy') with the older male figure of the Duke, the 'beard' this 'Cesario' has desired throughout. The play that features a 'eunuch' page and this final vision of an unrighted pederastic coupling takes place, moreover, in Illyria – a place which may appear to modern readers to be merely the invented name for a placeless 'de lyria' of carnival overturning but which in fact locates its entire plot within a territory on the Adriatic closely linked with Constantinople and the empire of the Turk, associated with the preposterous *amor* that was ascribed in contemporary English writing to Italian and eastern courts. Critics of *Twelfth Night* have been puzzled by Viola's plan to become a 'eunuch' in Illyria, frequently assuming that it must be a textual mistake or slip. But given that the place in which she assumes the identity of 'Cesario' (from *caesus* or 'cut') was routinely associated with the Turk and the cutting, circumcising or culturally assumed castration or 'unmanning' that was part of contemporary representations of converting or turning Turk, and that Malvolio himself is termed a 'renegado' after his crucial transformation in this scene, its scene of letters and 'alphabetical position' – with its 'C-U-T' and its 'I' and '0' capable of both 'forward' and 'backward' reference' – may suggest (like 'comptible' and 'sinister') the overdetermined cultural contexts of the various 'backtricks' it performs.

Notes

1 On Eve as the first witch and this Ave/Eva palindrome from Robert Southwell's 'The Virgins Salutation', see Clark (1997: 113).

2 Jonson's marginal notes cite Pliny's description of the 'Priests of Cybele' (from the *Natural History* XXVIII, Chapter 2). The chief among them is Attis, whose transformation from 'he' to 'she' is featured in Catullus 63.

3 See Jonson (1925–52: VII, 290), for Jonson's marginal note citing Lucan, Book 6 on the hyena and the 'sinister'; and DiGangi (1997: 57), on the hyena in *As You Like It*.

4 See Masten (1997: 75–107), especially pp. 79 and 101, n.15, citing Alexander Hume's dedication to his *Of the Orthographie of the British Tongue* (1865: 2).

5 See *Nashes Lenten Stuffe* (1599) in Nashe (1958: III, 141–226), Ziolkowski (1985, *passim* and 14–15) on the unmanning 'witchcraft' of Venus; Leupin (1989: 60–4 and 76), on the 'limping' left hand (from Latin *claudus*) and 'orthography' and 'falsigraphy' in Alain de Lille.

6 'Turn'd orthography' suggests among other things a turning toward the 'straight' (*orthos*) and upright, the basis of the English translation of 'orthography' as 'right writing'. On this passage, see Masten (1997: 80).

7 For text and commentary here, see Ziolkowski (1985). Ziolkowski's English translations are from de Lille 1980.

8 See *OED* 'retrograde' 4b, for spelling backwards in the (more modern) sense of reversing the letters of the alphabet. See also Heywood and Brome (1979: 145), for 'retrograde' in the astrological sense.

9 See *OED* on 'crab', which cites 'the signe of Cancer which is cleped the Crabbe' from Lydgate, *Pylgremage of the Sowle*, V.xiii. (1483: 104). 'Cancer, a sygne retrogradant' appears in George Cavendish, *Poems* (1825: II, 3). Under 'retrograde' 6 ('In a backward or reverse direction') *OED* quotes

for 1634 Sir Thomas Herbert, *Some Yeares Travels into divers parts of Asia and Afrique*: '[The priest] crab-like goes retrograde from the Idoll' (1638: 188). See also under 'retrograde' for 1564 Chaloner in J. A. Froude, *History of England*: '[I am] now further from wealth [. . .] than I was eighteen years agone. Methinks I became a retrograde crab' (1881: 8.45).

10 See, respectively, Philipp Ludwig Elich, *Daemonomagia; siue libellus erotematikos, de daemonis cacurgia, cacomagorum et lamiarum energia* (1607: 132, 135), cited by Clark (1997: 14); and Brathwait (1620: 139), which compares a shrew to 'a very Crab, if shee affect any pleasures, they must be backward'. The *OED* on 'crab' makes clear its link with the 'arsy versy' or 'backward' as well as the 'contrary' and 'perverse'.

11 See also Florio (1598): 'Retrorso, backward, akeward'; 'Retrosita, frowardnes, waywardnes, peevishnes, skittishnes'; 'Retroso, froward, wayward, peevish, akeward, backward, wittish'.

12 See Farnaby (1647: 107) on Martial's Epigram 2.86.

13 See Richard Sanders, *Physiognomie and Chiromancie, Metoposcopie the symmetrical proportions and signal moles of the body*, (1653: 37).

14 See Hawkes (1985: 310–32), and *OED*, which cites under 'arseward' 2 ('Backward, contrary, perverse') for *c.*1500, *Almanak* for 1386: 'A crab es an arsword best' (1812: 12) or in modernised spelling 'arse-ward beast'.

15 For the Roma/Amor palindrome, see Bale (1551: Viv, Aiiv). For the preposteration of the testaments, and other 'arseward procedynges' associated in Bale with the Roman Church, see Bale (1550: Oir).

16 Richard Huloet's *Abecedarium Anglico-Latinum* (1970) comments that 'backedore or posterne, and which by circumlocution, signifieth the arse, or all thynges that is behynde us, as Antica be all thynges before us'. For references for the examples of the 'preposterous Italian way' cited here, see Williams (1994: II, 721).

17 See Jonathan Swift, *Micellanies in Prose and Verse* (1733: 95) 'On Poetry': 'To Statesman wou'd you give a Wipe, You print it in *Italick* Type. When Letters are in vulgar Shapes, 'Tis ten to one the Wit escapes'), cited in *OED* under 'italic' 3.

18 See Justinus (1564: 18): 'They [the Egyptians] write their letters aukelie [i.e. from right to left, backwards or in reverse]'.

19 On the association of hyena and Jew, see Hassig (1995: 145–55).

20 On Hebrew, Jews and witchcraft, see Newall (1973: 95–124).

21 On Jonson's Sejanus, see DiGangi (1997: 121).

22 See the Geneva Bible (1560) glosses on the 'governance of the Lawe' as 'an ABC' to be spelled in the right direction (Galatians 4) and Galatians 2:14 ('they went not the right way to the trueth of the Gospel', where 'right way' is glossed in the margin as 'Word for word, with a right foot, which he setteth against halting & dissembling, which is backeward'). In relation to Hebrew, the Tetragrammaton, and witchcraft's 'backward' spells, see also Wills (1995: 67) on 'Jehovah's name / Forward and backward anagramatis'd' from Marlowe's *Doctor Faustus* (A1.3.813). See also Mellinkoff (1991: 1.107 and 1.59–94) on Jewish hats and headgear.

23 DiGangi (1997: 12), who also cites Palmer (1988: 112, Emblem 107).

24 This gloss is taken from the Revels Plays edition of *Bussy D'Ambois*, ed. Nicholas Brooke (Chapman 1964: 9).

25 On the 'O' and horned hat (as well as jewels in the ear) as signs of the 'Jew', see Hughes (1986).

26 Maurice Evans, editor of the New Mermaid edition of *Bussy D'Ambois*, comments that 'Judas in tapestries was popularly represented as having red hair, and stage Jews, such as Shylock, traditionally wore red wigs' (Chapman 1965: 90).

27 Medieval writers already identified the 'ambidextrous' with the sexually 'hermaphrodite' in contexts that echoed Romans 1:267 on turning back to idolatry and unnatural sexual use (as in the 'men of duble astate' identified as 'hermofodrita or ambidexter' by Wycliffite writers who condemned both clerical sodomy and 'nigromancie' or spelling backwards). See 'Twelve Conclusions of the Lollards', in Hudson (1997: 24–9).

28 See the entry in Florio (1598), under 'Ambodestro, that hath the use of both hands alike'; and Minsheu (1617), under 'Ambidexter or Ambodexter'.

29 For Stubbes, see Drew-Bear (1994: 32).

30 See these lines involving Clermont d'Ambois at 5.1.154–64 of *The Revenge of Bussy D'Ambois*, in Chapman (1987: 498–9).

31 See Bale (1548: Civ-Cijr), cited in Stewart (1997: 53).

32 See More (1528: v.B). On Hindu-Arabic numbers, see Eugene Ostashevsky (2004: 205–28). On the 'O' as the 'infidel symbol' and the connections between the 'Hindu' or Indian system of numbering (transmitted through the Arabic) and the beginnings of mercantile capitalism in Europe, see Rotman (1987: 8 ff).

33 For the Arabic roots of 'algebra' itself, as 'ars-table', and the variant spellings of 'arsmetryke', see *OED* on each of these words. See Chaucer's *The Knight's Tale* for 'ars-metrike' (l. 1898) and *The Summoner's Tale* (l. 2221) where the afflatus of this 'fart' is simultaneously a parody of Pentecost, in F. N. Robinson's edition of *The Canterbury Tales* (Chaucer 1957: 41, 119).

34 OED cites, inter alia, Greene, *A Looking-Glass for London and England* ([1594] 1861: 132): 'Have I taught you arsmetry'.

35 See Thomas Nashe, *Have with you to Saffron-walden* (1596) in Nashe (1958: III, 44). In a passage filled with references to 'so foule a jakes for my groaning stoole as hys mouth' and to 'two or three mouth fulls of my Oo yes yet behinde', Nashe speaks of Harvey's 'tynie titmouse Lenvoy' and 'a third Lenvoy, like a fart after a good stoole' (1958: III, 132–3).

36 The 'Rhetoricall figure of amplification' is compared here to the 'multi-plication' and other operations of 'Arithmetique', in a passage that clearly links it to generation ('So hee is to Multiplication too, hee having, since I parted with him last, got him a Gentlewoman').

37 See Sacrobosco ('John of Holywood') in Steele (1992: 34–5). For 'sinistro-rum', see Sacrobosco in Halliwell (1841: 5), with Ostashevsky (2004: 225). Karl Menninger traces the rise of Arabic (or 'Indian') numbers, including the rivalry with 'compters' (or 'counters') and the abacus, and comments on the 'backwards' numbering system: 'the Arabs certainly counted from low to high as we do now [. . .] but wrote the numerals from right to left according to their alphabet' (1969: 415).

38 See Steele (1992: 70) and Recorde (1969: Biv).

39 Recorde comments on the importance of placement, in a system where the 'ciphre' or 'O' can multiply value simply by occupying a particular

'place' (1969: Bv). See also *The Winter's Tale*, 1.2.6–7, on the 'cipher' standing in 'rich place'.
40 See *OED* on 'nache' and the gloss on 'disposition' in F. H. Mares (ed.) *Much Ado About Nothing* (Shakespeare 2003: 284).
41 For 'backtrick', see Sir Andrew's 'I think I have the back-trick simply as strong as any man in Illyria,' (1.3.123–4).
42 See Williams (1994, vol. III), under 'queue'.
43 The 1623 Folio text is quoted here from TLN 1139–43 of the Norton Facsimile of *The First Folio of Shakespeare* (Shakespeare 1968: 282).

3 Caught *in medias res*

Female intercession, 'regulation' and 'exchange'

Rachel Heard

Images of suppliant women abound in English drama of the early modern period. The affective power of such figures clearly captured the imagination of Henry Peacham, inspiring him to sketch a scene from *Titus Andronicus* in which Tamora is shown, flanked by male characters in a curious mix of Roman and Elizabethan dress, 'pleading for her sons going to execution'.[1] Outside the wooden walls of the theatre, no such direct methods of appeal were available to women. Some sought redress in the same way as men. Indeed, according to Tim Stretton's estimates, not hundreds but thousands of women went to law in this period and participated 'in civil litigation in a variety of courts' (Stretton 1998: 42). Pleading by women, however, was not permitted in any legal setting. Women could be litigants but they could not be judges, jurors or lawyers. Along with heretics, excommunicants and criminals, no woman could plead on behalf of someone else before a judge (Stretton 1998: 67).

How, then, were such proscriptions reflected in literary forms which had, traditionally, been less inclined than the drama to provide a platform from which women could argue their own cases? This chapter will focus on the representation of female pleaders in the so-called 'Tradition of Women Worthies', a specialised genre that influenced and contributed to the body of medieval and early modern writings known as the 'controversy over women' or *querelle des femmes*.[2] These texts theorised on the nature of woman and reflected on her place in the world. Shaped by their heavy reliance on panegyric and denunciation, they defended or attacked women through appeals to classical and biblical authority and supported their arguments with examples from history and myth. Unsurprisingly, the ideological imperatives that deemed certain kinds of female speech unacceptable meant that women famed for their oratorical prowess were subjected to special scrutiny. The aim of this chapter is to uncover the recognised potency of their petitions while exploring, simultaneously, the rhetorical strategies used by male writers to deal with such unwanted articulation. And 'unwanted' it often proves to be, even in texts whose titles might at first suggest otherwise. A self-styled reporter on 'The Excellency of Good Women', Barnaby Rich clearly believed that the laws forbidding women from pleading before a judge did not always deter them from approaching some other male authority in order to do just that. To illustrate this, Rich tells a story involving four principal characters: the ruler Epaminundus, his captain Polipodius, a nameless woman, 'openly knowne to be a common Curtizan', and a third man, imprisoned for his loose manner of living and described only as a 'base fellow' (Rich 1613: 18). Although it has caused him considerable trouble, this anonymous man's alleged wantonness has not robbed him of supporters. His first champion is the philanthropic Polipodius, whose argument for the 'inlargement' of the accused makes no inroad whatsoever in the ruler's original verdict. The base fellow's 'suite' is quickly taken up by the courtesan, who, 'comming to Epaminundus [. . .] obtained his liberty, and had the prisoner presently delivered unto her' (Rich 1613: 18). Learning of the Curtizan's success, Polipodius confronts the ruler with the 'unkindnes' of this strange decision and is instructed to accept the following explanation for it: 'Content thy selfe Polipodius', Epaminundus counsels, 'for if thou couldest advisedly consider of the matter, thou wouldest not let to confesse that the suite was fitter to be granted to a *Curtizan* than to a Captaine' (Rich 1613: 18).

Whether Polipodius is made easy by this sententious reasoning is not a question that occupies Rich. Instead, he drops the story, but not before passing an unmistakably moral judgement upon the heretofore-undisclosed practices of the courtesan-pleader. The example, Rich admits, forces him to 'note the impudency of these common creatures',

> that dare insinuate themselves into any presence, be they never so great nor never so good and dare adventure to undertake any suite be it never so base or never so shamefull, and by this againe I doe further gather, that this kind of cattle shall prevaile, when those that be honest shall have a deniall.

> (Rich 1613: 18)

In these desperate tones Rich completes his anecdote, declaring himself 'afraid' that 'there be too many of these women suiters in these dayes if all were knowne' (1613: 18). The final verdict of an exasperated moralist, Rich's words bear witness to his automatic correlation of female 'impudency' and sexual incontinence. Only a sexually shameless woman would 'dare' to undertake such a suit; in this instance, in fact, the anonymous woman's roles as 'common Curtizan' and female pleader seem to be inevitably predicated one on the other. In the words of the early Dutch humanist, Henricus Cornelius Agrippa, there 'exists nowhere an orator more persuasive than the least of prostitutes' (Rabil 1996: 84). Similarly, when Rich admits, regretfully, that 'there be too many of these women suiters in these dayes', it is unclear whether he is objecting to female pleaders per se, or simply calling for a reform of the work done by female inhabitants of the stews. The point of this narrative is to elide the differences between the two occupations.

A keen commentator on this woeful state of affairs, Rich also reassures his readers, implicitly, that times have been better. The touch of nostalgia apparent in his reference to 'women suiters in these dayes' gestures backwards to the beginning of his text, sharply delineating the antics of these 'cattle' from the pleading strategies of women who existed in a now lost golden age. This group of women, famed for their skill in public speaking, have been presented rather as shining examples of their sex than as objects of castigation. Far from being instructed to avoid them (as one might be told to shun the company of 'common Curtizans'), Rich's reader is actively encouraged to investigate these women's histories. 'If we should look into a virtuous life', he muses, 'who more famed than *Aemelia, Claudia, Tusia, Nicaulia*? [. . .] for rethorike *Hilernia*; for oratory *Cornelia*, for eloquence *Hortensia*?' (Rich 1613: 3). Yet even the most obedient reader is obliged at this point to extend his search beyond the boundaries of this volume. For details of what these unusual women actually did or said he must 'look' elsewhere, for Rich has effectively finished with them. *The Excellency of Good Women* merely provides a list of proper names: here, Hilernia, Cornelia and Hortensia function more as suggestions for further reading than as principal speakers in Rich's discourse. And since they are never heard to practise 'rethorike', 'oratory' or 'eloquence', the difference between the persuasive techniques used by these women and those used by the similarly silent Courtesan pleader, is left for the reader to decipher, as best he or she may.

As his narrative proceeds, then, Rich decisively undermines his earlier praise of female eloquence, eventually seeming to confirm the commonplace 'long association in which a "public woman"', and especially one who spoke in public, could only be called a whore' (Parker 1987: 104). Contempt for female pleaders was often expressed indirectly, though; frequently, female speech is evoked in order to 'praise' qualities that the knowing reader is invited and expected to condemn. Richard Brathwait, for instance, suggests that the tendency of 'Feminine Disputants' 'to *flow* in words, but *droppe* in matter' makes them incapable of choosing compelling arguments from a stock of commonplaces (Brathwait 1640: 70). His next assertion, that women shall be found 'copiously [. . .] worded, but for matter penuriously stored', plays revealingly on women's reputation for garrulity, but it also presses the 'feminine disputant' back into specifically domestic territory, a conceptual space in which her speech is linked to her management of household affairs. Unlike the good housewife, 'that's so discreet knows when to spare, / When to expresse herselfe in bounty' (Brathwait 1618: B2v), the inept helpmeet will allow the substance of her 'store' to 'flow' inefficiently away.

The tenor of such complaints is responsible for lending a 'distinctly early modern flavour' to works that consist primarily of 'misogynist claims dating back to antiquity'. As Barbara McManus and Katherine Usher Henderson have shown, early modern contributions to the *querelle des femmes* appeal to their bourgeois audience by placing alongside 'the age-old picture of women as dangerous sexual temptress [. . .] the portraits of the scolding, domineering shrew and the vain spendthrift ruinously draining her husband's finances' (Henderson and McManus 1985: 24–5). Other methods of dealing with unwanted female articulation apparently owe less to historical circumstances. Focusing on the appearance of female speakers, whose 'very presence [. . .] accompanies their discourse with an applausive grace' (Henderson and McManus 1985: 70), allows Brathwait to imply, as Rich had, that to 'look into a virtuous life' will be far more edifying than to listen to it. Indeed, the rhetorical figure *philophrenesis* (literally *kind treatment* in Greek) or 'the attempt to mitigate anger by gentle speech and humble submission' is closely associated with the 'countenance' of its user in Brathwait's scheme.[3] 'Gentleness of speech', he explains,

> is an affable treaty or conference one with another, or a winning kinde of Rhetorick, which of all others, purchaseth most friends with least cost. An excellent grace it gives to Hospitality: especially, where a cheerefull countenance is delivered with the mouth: and an entertaining eye becomes ready to usher in that speech.
> (Brathwait 1640: 102)

An account so dominated by talk of 'friends', 'hospitality', 'welcome' and 'entertaining' makes one suspect that Brathwait is envisaging his perfect hostess, whose attractive features will recommend her to her husband's guests. Again, the suggestion that gentle speech gives an 'excellent grace' to 'Hospitality' seems to confine its usefulness to a conventionally feminine domain. What is more surprising in the context of this discussion is that Brathwait does not distinguish between the 'winning kinde of Rhetorike' used in the 'affable treaty' of civil conversation and the kind used when matters of public interest are at stake. '*Gentle speech* graced with a *pleasing presence*', he goes on to claim, have also 'produced [excellent fruits] both in affaires of peace and warre' (1640: 104). And in order to demonstrate the efficacy of female speech in matters of state-craft, Brathwait introduces 'that princely *Sophonisba*, whose attractive Majesty and unaffected Eloquence' proves 'that a sweet and debonair speech works wondrous effects' (1640: 105). But like the women famed for their achievements in oratory who were paraded silently before Barnaby Rich's reader, the attractive Sophonisba never utters a word.

Not, at least, on this occasion. Like many others of its kind, however, Brathwait's text is arranged around a list of qualities or virtues, and Sophonisba reappears several chapters later as the embodiment of 'Prudence'. As if inadequate to the task of describing the '*wisdom* that excellent *Sophonisba* manifested to the world' (Brathwait 1640: 174), Brathwait allows Sophonisba a rare opportunity to take the stage herself. Startling the reader with its material incongruity, the next page of text is dominated by a left-hand column of quotation marks that instruct the reader to hear in what follows the authentic voice of this paragon. The anecdote he chooses describes Sophonisba's characteristic reaction to any 'Counsellor or Conscript Father' who 'seemed troubled' or 'shewed the least irresolution'. Discovering such behaviour, says Brathwait, 'she would usually interpose herself and chide their weakness in this manner': 'Is it fit, grave Fathers, that your advice should be to seeke, when the state is ready to sinke? Will dejected spirits cure our distempers? Must Fathers turne Children, and put finger in th' eye when imminency of perill menaceth the States ruine?' (1640: 175)

With its aggressive stacking of rhetorical questions, its emphasis on conduct that is 'fit', Sophonisba's speech savours more of Lady Macbeth's incitement of her husband to murderous deeds than it does of the 'sweet and debonair speech' in which she was allegedly so expert. In a contemporary dramatic representation, John Marston painted an idealised portrait of Sophonisba as a model of stoic virtue: 'women's right wonder, and just shame of men', according to the obsequies spoken at her funeral (Marston 1986: 5.1.59). In Shakespeare, the kind of 'shaming' practised by Brathwait's Sophonisba is the speciality of such female unworthies as Lady Macbeth, Goneril and Dionyza, all of whom use similar tropes to 'chide their [husbands'] weakness' by subjecting their voluntary regression from manliness to derision. Far from producing 'wondrous effects', these rhetorical strategies are designed to encourage the severance of filial and social bonds – urging Macbeth to commit regicide, Albany to disregard his duty to Lear and Cleon to relish his complicity in the planned slaughter of Marina. In this instance, Brathwait does not suggest that female intervention in government will have such violent and treacherous repercussions. But by allowing Sophonisba an encore, he does undermine his earlier approval of her talents by suggesting that she only qualifies as an exemplary user of *philophronesis* for as long as she stays silent. His lofty pillar of quotation marks provides material evidence of Sophonisba's 'real' compulsion to chide; the practitioner of 'unaffected eloquence' is presented ultimately as a fine example of the 'scolding, domineering shrew'.

That the sincerity of Brathwait's praise would leave much to be desired might have been predicted from the title of his text. The plaintive cry of a wakeful wife, *Ar't Asleepe Husband?* clearly cannot be included among the most serious contributions to the Tradition of Women Worthies. It is better described, in Elizabeth Harvey's terms, as a 'ventriloquization': 'an appropriation of the female voice' that 're-flects and contributes to a larger cultural silencing of women' (Harvey 1992: 12). In this text, Brathwait chooses not to adopt the blatantly masculine speaking voice apparent in texts such as John Taylor's *Juniper Lecture* (1639), or Thomas Heywood's *Curtaine Lecture* (1637), both of which are quite clearly written by *and for* men.[4] Here, the process of incrimination is more subtle. Like Chaucer's *Wife of Bath's Prologue and Tale*, Brathwait's narrative is supposed to be 'spoken' by a woman, and its subtitle, *A Boulster Lecture*, acts to steel the reader for a deeply prejudicial account. That this unrelenting torturer, a ready cache of examples to her credit, seems intent on selecting ones that undermine her own argument for early modern 'maistrie' is, of course, part of the joke. This discourse on female excellence is served up as a case of special pleading at best; at worst, it is easy to read as an exercise in nocturnal nagging, and an extremely prolonged one at that. *Ar't Asleepe Husband?* consists of hundreds of pages of harping on daughters, the very form of which seems designed to demonstrate, by example, the utter folly of allowing women to argue their own cases.

In the words of the 'Satyrist' cited in Daniel Tuvil's *Asylum Veneris*: 'Brawles, chidings, jarres, attend the marriage bed; / And where a Wife lies, seldome sleepes the Head' (Tuvil 1616: 76).

Raised in protest against female speech, the voices of like-minded 'Satyrists' are audible even in texts that claim to defend their subjects from male disapproval. More earnest panegyrists did exist, however, and the rhetorical strategies they used to valorise female speech deserve closer attention. Writers committed to this cause were confronted by a paradox that shapes the representation of virtuous female pleaders in quite specific ways. In order to liberate female speech from its association with prostitution or shrewishness, these writers had to challenge the stereotypes imbedded in mock-encomiums such as those just mentioned. One of the most common of these gives rise to the title of John Taylor's *Juniper Lecture*, so-called because the tongue of its female speaker resembles the leaves of a plant renowned for being 'bytinge', 'sharpe', and 'hote' (Turner 1562: 25).

Even without any prefatory clues from its author, Taylor's reader would have been prepared to hear from an anathematised female whose ambition was to dominate her husband – one of the stereotypical wives 'whose aggressiveness ranges from shrill scolding to physical violence' (Woodbridge 1984: 193). 'Women's tongues are very often, in early modern literature, said to be sharp', argues Linda Woodbridge, 'and the submerged metaphor suggests a weapon' (1984: 208). The 'heat' of the female tongue was also legendary, however, even though the notion threatens to undermine the tenets of Galenic medicine which placed a cultural value on the innate goodness of bodily heat and which therefore worked 'in collusion with patriarchal ideology to give a physiological "explanation" to the asserted inferiority of women', whose temperaments were supposed to be colder, and whose bodies wetter, than men's (Schoenfeldt 1999: 36). Perhaps because it troubles what Gail Kern Paster identifies as the 'conventional early modern association of women and water used [. . .] to insinuate womanly unreliability' (1993: 25), excessive heat in women is often linked to an equally objectionable inability to control their own passions.[5] And indeed, this idea seems to provide the inspiration for the means of self-defence used by the husband in *Johan Johan, the Husbande, Tyb, His Wife, and Syr Johan, the Preest*, who fights fire with fire by shielding himself from his violent and scolding wife with a shovel full of hot coals.

Such stereotypes clearly damaged the case for female eloquence and were therefore best avoided. But the effort to defend their female subjects from charges of heated aggression also obliges male panegyrists to deny them access to what the most influential authorities of the period clearly identify as a cornerstone of eloquence: namely, the requirement that for the orator to move others, he must first be moved himself. Horace, Quintilian and Cicero were all exponents of the 'contagion theory', in which, as Wayne A. Rebhorn puts it, 'the orator's emotion [. . .] directly affect[s] the feelings of the listener, spreading from one to the other like a contagious disease or like a fire encountering kindling' (Rebhorn 1995: 49). On this matter, Quintilian states his position unequivocally: 'All emotional appeals will inevitably fall flat', he warns, 'unless they are given the fire, that voice, look, and the whole comportment of the body can give them' (Quintilian 1921: IV, 11.3.3).[6] This imperative is captured in early modern rhetorics in a series of metaphors that imagine the successful orator 'burning', 'glowing' or 'on fire', but such images are seldom evoked in positive accounts of female pleaders. It is not hard to see why. To claim that women possessed the 'fire' required by Quintilian was to emphasise the heat associated with the undesirably aggressive character and discourse of the scalding scold.

Consequently, far from endorsing Quintilian's insistence that a pleader bring to his appeals all 'the fire, that voice, look, and the whole comportment can give them', sympathetic commentaries on eminent female pleaders focus instead on their special ability to *moderate* their own emotions and, in turn, the emotions of those around them. Evidence of this particular aptitude appears in Abraham Darcie's *The Honour of Ladies*, where the widowed Queen Alexandra is reported to have spoken so persuasively that she 'mittigated the fury and anger' of the countrymen left in bondage by her husband, a population previously vengeful and 'inflammed with fury and rage to exterminate her two Sonnes' (Darcie 1622: 35). Analogous effects are achieved by Volumnia, who succeeds where numerous other pleaders have failed to 'abate the heate of [her son's] choler' (Darcie 1622: 28), so that 'all his desire of revenge was quenched, and sodainely his army departed' (1622: 31). Volumnia proves to be a popular example, with earnest panegyrists such as Anthony Gibson also attributing the survival of Rome to her happy application of 'so manie great maximes of and for the state' (Gibson 1599: 6).

It is unusual for a male author to admit so ungrudgingly that a woman could speak persuasively and effectively on matters usually reserved for men – using 'great maximes', for example, instead of 'dropp[ing] in matter' as Brathwait claimed. But what might, on one hand, be enjoyed as rare praise for Volumnia's rhetorical prowess also has the less positive effect of making her virtuoso performance seem rather dry, a little cold, vaguely academic. No commentator familiar with the Coriolanus story could have been ignorant of the indisputably 'emotional' nature of Volumnia's appeal to her son. Yet Gibson deliberately ignores this aspect of her plea, sweeping it aside along with the 'fire' Quintilian considered so essential a part of such petitions.

As panegyrists such as Darcie and Gibson continue to defend female participation in civic affairs, their concern with very specific qualities becomes ever more apparent. Neither man ignores the more horrific details of his heroines' histories. Indeed, Gibson dwells with gruesome interest on Rhea's ability to 'temper the prodigious crueltie and tyranny of *Saturne*, who not onely would disinherit her sonnes, but devoure them' (1599: 6v). This sensational tale of savagery follows that of the Romans who, when 'surprized by the Sabines', 'were warrented from death and utter destruction of their Cittie, by the meanes of women, who knew how to quenche the anger justly enflamed in their fathers against their husbands' (Gibson 1599: 5v). But what links Alexandra and Volumnia, Rhea and the Sabine women more strongly than their fearlessness in the face of peril is the fact that their rhetorical activities are without exception propitiatory. Bearing in mind the strengths of these women helps explain why, some fifteen pages later, Gibson rebukes himself for 'forget[ting] Oratours', and adduces 'Nature' as his proof that 'women are or may be the most eloquent', 'considering the organes and instruments of theyr voyce is more mylde and gentle, than those in men, whose pronounciation is very rough, sharpe and coorsely shapte, by reason of the abundance of choller, which (with their words) drives foorth so much vehemencie of spirit.' (1599: 20r–v).

Reluctant to rest his case on examples, Gibson offers a more compelling reason for why readers should accept his defence of female eloquence. Grounding his theory in physiological necessity, Gibson lends 'scientific' weight to the ideological imperative that disapproved of feisty women. Implicated in this project is the idea that women are not so much disinclined to 'vehemencie' as they are physically incapable of achieving it. Thus, the appeals made by these women are never fiery; they are discreet, temperate and softly spoken. Their oratorical successes are born out of their ability to 'temper' and 'quenche' the boiling blood of their listeners, not to 'enflame' an already disaffected audience. Finding herself in the midst of such disputes, the virtuous female pleader is clearly required to imagine herself as extinguisher, not kindling. And what is more, these eloquent women of antiquity are presented in this way consistently, their rhetorical fervency dampened and their pleas made more consistent with appropriate female behaviour, even if to do so demands a judicious and largely silent correction of source material by their sympathetic early modern male biographers. One such canny handling of a source occurs in John Shirley's *Illustrious History of Women*. Shirley plunges boldly into a chapter entitled 'Of Learning' by asserting how 'In Oratory women have been found skilful Proficients, as appears in many Examples' (Shirley 1686: 76). From this supposed embarrassment of riches Shirley produces two gems: Amasia and Hortensia. Amasia appears first, with Shirley acknowledging the classical master of reportage, Valerius Maximus, in his marginalia. Of this Roman woman Valerius Maximus had written:

> Amasia Sentia, being guilty, before a great concourse of people, pleaded her own cause. [*Lucius*] *Titus*, the Praetor then sitting in Court; and observing all the parts and elegancies of a true Defense, not onely diligently but stoutly was quitted in her first Action by the Sentences of all. And because that under the shape of a woman she carried a manly resolution, they call her *Androgyne*.
>
> (Maximus 1684: 8.3.1)

With such raw materials at his disposal, the author of the *Illustrious History* painted his portrait of '*Amasia*, a virtuous Roman Lady', who,

> being accused of a Crime, and ready to undergo the Sentence of the Praetor, she in the midst of a great confluence of people, step'd up and pleaded her own cause so effectually, and with such Eloquence, that by the publique suffrage, she was Acquited of the Aspersion Layd to her charge, and in that great Affair, used such Decency and Modesty, that she got her self thereby the Sir-name *Androgyne*.
>
> (Shirley 1686: 76)

Shirley's deviation from the models available to him is certainly revealing. The description of the praetor and the swelling crowd are common to both accounts; their difference lies in the apparent gulf between the ancient and early modern understanding of the kind of behaviour constitutive of 'androgyny'. As Valerius Maximus has it, Amasia is called *Androgyne* because she carries 'under the shape of a woman' a 'manly resolution'. From the Greek for *man* plus *woman*, *androgyne* is not a word, presumably, whose etymological origins would have left Shirley baffled. And yet he seems peculiarly anxious to protect his Amasia from the threatening encroachments of masculinity: here she is a 'virtuous Roman *Lady*', whose androgyny is inexplicably related to her ability to behave with 'Decency and Modesty'.

Contemporary evidence shows that this particular reading of Amasia's 'androgyny' hinges on an unusually charitable interpretation of the term. The circulation of texts such as the infamous *Hic Mulier; or, the Man-Woman* made the 'androgyne' an instantly recognisable figure in the early modern period and one more likely to receive censure than praise. As Phyllis Rackin observes, 'in life as on the stage, masculine women were regarded as whores' (Rackin 1993: 43). One of the most notorious contributions to the controversy over women, the anonymous *Hic Mulier* offers itself as an antidote to the 'disease of the Staggers in the Masculine-Feminines of our time' (Henderson and McManus 1985: 271). The ensuing declamation instructs women to shield themselves 'with modest and comely garments such as are warm and wholesome', thus distinguishing themselves from the 'masculine women' who have exchanged 'for Needles, Swords [. . .] for modest gestures, giantlike behaviours; and for women's modesty, all mimic and apish incivility' (Henderson and McManus 1985: 268).[7] This latter group of women are accused of having 'cast off the ornaments of [their] sexes to put on the garments of Shame' and of discarding 'the bashfulness of [their] natures to gather the impudence of Harlots' (Henderson and McManus 1985: 266). Drawing on the commonplace that associated women's use of cosmetics with their moral depravity, Thomas Tuke described the 'painted woman' as 'both a substantive and an adjective, and yet not of the neuter gender: but a feminine as well consorting with a masculine' (Tuke 1616: 57). In both texts, as well as in dramatic works such as Ben Jonson's *Epicoene*, androgyny is envisaged as the antithesis of all that is 'decent' and 'modest', a fact that clearly posed serious difficulties for writers such as Shirley, whose self-imposed task it was to prove meritorious the conduct of such mannish women.

Finding sufficient material in Valerius Maximus to portray Amasia in a positive light must have tested Shirley's powers of *inventio* to the limit. One of his most formidable challenges is to disguise this classical authority's barely concealed disapproval of his subject. 'Nor must we omit those Women', the Roman historian had written, by way of introducing Amasia, 'whom the condition of their Sex, and the Garments of Modesty could not hinder from appearing and speaking in publike Courts of Judicature' (Maximus 1684: 8.3). The implication here is that the actions of such women prove them so unencumbered by the

Garment of Modesty that they are quite literally indecent. In this case, Shirley's representation of Amasia's oxymoronic 'modest' androgyny involves a wilful misreading of his literary precursors. Where writers such as Darcie and Gibson tend to 'temper' the potency of female speech, Shirley's adaptation of earlier sources manages the ambiguous figure of the female pleader by seeming to 'domesticate' her. With his careful editorial manoeuvres, Shirley affects Amasia's transformation from infamous classical pleader to desirable early modern woman. Here, the qualities of 'Modesty' and 'Decency' shown by Amasia are privileged (or invented if they seem not to exist) in the interests of presenting a worthy figure fit for female emulation. These are the qualities, of course, that pervade seventeenth-century discourses dedicated to promoting proper feminine conduct: 'Modesty', declared Samuel Torshell in 1620, 'is as proper [. . .] to the womans Sexe, as flying to a bird, swimming to a fish, beautie to a flower' (Torshell 1620: 111). With a sharp eye on such requirements, Shirley constructs from earlier, more antipathetic, accounts a figure of the suppliant woman who has more in common with the behaviour expected of all gentlewomen.

The main advantage of this technique is obvious: it allows Shirley to champion the virtues of female pleaders while suggesting that what makes them virtuous is their difference from men. But by focusing on modesty as the traditional marker of female virtue, Shirley does more than he might have realised, or even intended, to associate these women with a form of eloquence that the best male orators strove to perfect. To claim that 'Modesty' was a quality appropriate in female petitioners only, in fact, is to distort the evidence, for theorists and practitioners from antiquity through early modernity privileged a pleader's ability to deliver a 'decent' oration. Indeed, as Valerius Maximus pointed out, the renowned orator Quintus Hortensius, 'thinking there was very much to be ascribed to a decent and com[e]ly motion of the Body, spent more time in practising that than in studying for Eloquence' (cited in Glenn 1997: 191 n.50). Similarly, the subtitle of John Bulwer's *Chironomia; Or, the Art of Manuall Rhetorique* (1644) tellingly identifies the 'Naturall Gestures of the HAND' as the '*Regulated* Accessories or faire-spoken Adjuncts of Rhetoricall Utterance'. Punning relentlessly throughout the 'Praeludium', Bulwer argues that a proper understanding of the principles of decorum can guard against shameful failures of erudition. '*Decencie* is properly spoken of *Gesture*', he writes,

> and is so looked for at the Hand of an Orator, that the defects of extemporarie and jejune Orations, have been covered by

the Elegancies of this Artifice; and those that have come off unhandsomely with their expressions, for want of these comely and palliating graces of Elocution, were ever laughed at, and justly derided.

(Bulwer 1644: The Praeludium)

Introduced so early, Bulwer's thoughts on the threat of oratorical humiliation add an uncomfortable frisson to his account, but the means of avoiding it, by the judicious use of 'regulated', decent and comely gestures, is advice given as standard. Even Shakespeare's Henry V, the perpetrator of outrageously indecorous youthful acts, is alert to the propriety of following such conventions. Unless one counts his advances to Katherine, of course, there is no point in this play at which Henry assumes the role of a suppliant petitioner. Nevertheless, on the eve of the battle of Agincourt he is still responsible for persuading a reluctant body of men to undertake a course of action unlikely to be particularly advantageous to themselves. Treating his soldiers to a little touch of Harry in the night does not involve subjecting them to a fiery or impassioned oration. On the contrary, as he mingles with the crowd, the King's solicitations bear more resemblance to the 'winning Rhetorick' delivered with a 'cheerefull countenance' by Brathwait's gentle speaker. Indeed, the Chorus speaks fondly of how Henry bids the soldiers

good morrow with a modest smile,
And calls them brothers, friends and countrymen.
[. . .] Nor doth he dedicate one jot of colour
Unto the weary and all-watched night;
But freshly looks, and overbears attaint
With cheerful semblance and sweet majesty.
(Shakespeare 1974: 4.33–40)

Shakespeare's description of a male sovereign who is seldom accused of effeminacy or sexual emasculation is replete with the same language of modesty and cheerfulness as pervades prescriptive texts such as Shirley's. In similar terms did James I instruct his own son, another Henry, to exercise the virtues of modesty and moderation in all his dealings. 'In your language be plaine, honest, naturall, comely, cleane, short, and sententious', advised the King. '[E]schew [. . .] both the extremities', and 'let the greatest part of your eloquence consist in a naturall, cleane, and sensible forme of the deliverie of your minde', '*temper[ed]* [. . .] with gravitie, quicknesse, or merrinesse, according to the subject, and occasion of the time' (James VI and I 1971: 183–4).[7] Reading both Shakespeare's and James's descriptions of masculine exemplarity against those of the ideal woman should therefore alert us to something important. One effect of this comparison is to complicate the received view of a culture that endorsed 'a different morality for women' and ensured their subjection to 'a different array of moral restraints, obligations and virtues' (Lloyd 1996: 151). Recognising that many of the qualities considered essential in pleading were not necessarily 'masculine' virtues raises an intriguing possibility. If eliminating the 'fire' from female discourse disqualified women from setting their audience alight, accounts that emphasise their comeliness and modesty, their ability to 'temper' or mitigate anger by gentle speech, all suggest that virtuous women already possessed the qualities prized in 'mild' oratory, the very qualities that will make them successful pleaders.

These were qualities, moreover, which the aspiring male orator failed to cultivate, and then to display, at his peril. Some measure of their importance in pleading can be taken from discussions in the most prestigious and popular textbooks of the period. In Book II of *De Oratore*, Cicero, the universally acknowledged classical master of rhetoric, uses his own experienced orator and pedagogue, Antonius, to confirm that 'vigorous language is not always wanted' to achieve success, 'but often such as is calm, gentle, mild: this is the kind that commends the parties' to an arbiter (Cicero 1996: 2.183). This lesson forms part of Antonius' larger claim that 'nothing in oratory [. . .] is more important than to win for the orator the favour of his hearer, and to have the latter so affected as to be swayed by something resembling a mental impulse or emotion, rather than by judgement or deliberation' (2.178). To this end he postpones dealing with the arrangement and distribution of 'proofs' in order to underline the importance of securing goodwill and to outline the qualities required by the orator to win that favour:

> Attributes useful in an advocate are a mild tone, a countenance expressive of modesty, gentle language, and the faculty of seeming to be dealing reluctantly and under compulsion with something you are really anxious to prove. It is very helpful to display the tokens of good-nature, kindness, calmness, loyalty and a disposition that is pleasing.
>
> (2.182)

Antonius' description of 'mild' oratory is later compared to the 'impetuous and violent' style (2.200) in which the 'assailing speaker is [. . .] aglow with passion' (2.190). Sulpicius is praised for his efforts in this area, but the implication remains that any petition that ignores the importance of mildness, gentleness and modesty will distance an audience so irrevocably that no amount of 'rhetorical fireworks' (2.205), however accomplished, will regain their confidence in a cause.

An awareness that virtuous women are innately equipped to triumph over male opponents in 'publike courts of judicature' is clearly evident in positive accounts of female pleaders. Similarly, and more crucially, an analogous recognition of women's potential may be responsible, in part, for the persistent and determined efforts made in male-authored narratives to contain it. These efforts range from explicit criticisms of female petitioners (Rich) to more subtle erosions of the efficacy and integrity of the pleas they make (Brathwait). Some scholars have suggested that the fear and suspicion behind such satirical outbursts are a direct response to the burgeoning number of women participating in central court actions during this period (Stretton 1998: 60–1). This theory sounds entirely plausible and may be developed still further. Even though women were forbidden from speaking before a judge on their own behalf, the increased presence of women in legal contexts may also account for the special animosity reserved for women who pleaded their own causes: the marked tendency, even in positive accounts, to deny women agency in their own pleas.

Not that there is anything uniquely 'early modern' about this particular containment of female potential. It is rooted, as many social historians have shown, in classical proscriptions against female participation in civic affairs. In her now classic account, Sarah Pomeroy, for instance, compares the political manoeuvrings of Fulvia, Mark Antony's ambitious first wife, with those of Octavia, his second: 'While Fulvia's policy had been to steer Antony against Octavian, Octavia's was to mediate between the two men, and for her efforts she won the approbation of her brother and later historians' (Pomeroy 1994: 186). Acting as an intercessor between men, Pomeroy insists, 'was the only traditionally commendable, active political role for women in Rome' (1994: 186). Mary Lefkowitz describes the same restrictions in no uncertain terms. Women of antiquity 'take political action only under closely defined conditions', she argues, and 'unless they do so at least ostensibly on behalf of a male relative, they and others around them come to a bad end' (Lefkowitz 1983: 49).

Ancient antagonism to women who argued their own cases survives in many early modern texts, as is shown by the gleeful alacrity with which Thomas Heywood rehearses Juvenal's detraction of Manilia, 'a bold fac'd Roman Matron, who being full of controversie, and through her wrangling having many suits in agitation, blusht not in open Court to bee her owne Advocate, and plead her owne causes in publike assemblies' (Heywood 1637: 10–11). As common as they are, such contemptuous dismissals of female pleaders are less revealing, in some respects, than the more subtle ways in which male writers attempted to curtail their potential. Several of the rhetorical strategies examined so far are combined in a quite different example from Heywood, an example that seems deliberately contrived to deny a successful female pleader agency in her own petition. In this scenerio, a winning plea, delivered by a woman on her own behalf, is not considered on the basis of its rhetorical merits, as a model for persuasive speech, but is presented instead as an exemplary narrative designed to 'encourage all maidens how to behave themselves that they may be better married' (Heywood 1637: 48). The story itself concerns a chance encounter between Galbrata Bertha, a girl of 'extraordinarie beautie and vertue' and daughter to a private Florentine, and one Emperor Otho, visiting the city at that time on urgent business.

Participating one day in a tour of the city, Otho notices the beautiful Galbrata whom he singles out from a crowd of well-wishers. Back at the Duke's palace, he proceeds to describe her to the company assembled there for dinner, one of whom happens to be the girl's father, Bellincionus. Heywood does not elaborate on the motives behind Bellincionus' next move, which is to summon his daughter with all speed to the palace. Galbrata obeys this command without question, being an innocent girl and little expecting to be prostituted by her own father. With Galbrata safely arrived, Bellincionus suggests that a more remote chamber will be required for what is about to transpire and presents to the Prince 'the Virgin by him so much praised ready to prostrate herself to your Majesty' (Heywood 1637: 54). Otho is evidently far from repulsed by this prospect; Galbrata, on the other hand, is horrified and begins a defence of her right to preserve her chastity.

Unlike the defence mounted by Shakespeare's Isabella, a virgin in similarly awkward circumstances, Galbrata's plea is an object lesson in female deference and subservience. Her first action is to deny 'the Emperour her right hand, and with her left modestly put him back' (Heywood 1637: 55). Then, apologising to the Prince's 'high and sacred Majesty', she informs him of the vow made between herself and her Saviour never to lend her hand to any man but her husband. Galbrata's petition continues in this vein and ultimately proves so persuasive that the amorous Otho withdraws his advances and, in a dramatic renewal of purpose, determines to find her that husband instead. Conscious that to refuse would signify a 'great rudeness & indiscretion' (Heywood 1637: 58), Galbrata accepts his offer. Stripped of its local colour, Heywood's story is simple: a man prostitutes his daughter, who makes an eloquent plea that succeeds in persuading a second, more powerful, man to alter his intended course of action. The woman is then offered in marriage to a third man, himself under the patronage of the second. The story has a conventionally comic ending, but several of its features deserve attention. Although Heywood initially makes much of Bellincionus' 'base Pandarisme', all censure for his conduct in the affair is, as the narrative progresses, effectively overshadowed by Otho's magnanimity in bestowing Galbrata on a gentleman 'whom hee much favoured' (Heywood 1637: 59). As soon as the Prince assumes control, in fact, the Florentine pimp drops out of the narrative altogether. Coinciding with a change in the structure of authority in the story, this shift may be read in almost graphic terms. The story begins with a situation in which Bellincionus played the bawd, going between Otho and Galbrata; it ends with Otho rejecting decisively the role of beneficiary and assuming that of benefactor. The lucky recipient of Otho's generosity is told how the Prince has at length 'found out a gift to reward him, and to remunerate his long and faithfull service; such a one as might become the giver, and (withall) prove worthy his acceptance: and in the closure of these words presented unto him the Virgin Galbrata Bertha' (Heywood 1637: 59–60).

The ideological implications of Heywood's story will be all too familiar to anthropologists and cultural historians interested in the ties that bind. Theories originally posited by Marcel Mauss, in his seminal *Essay on the Gift* (1969), have subsequently been developed by Claude Lévi-Strauss (1969), Gayle Rubin (1975) and Luce Irigaray (1991: 118–32). It was Mauss who first noticed the 'significance of one of the most striking features of primitive societies: the extent to which giving, receiving, and reciprocating gifts dominates social intercourse' (Rubin 1975: 171). Adapting Mauss's idea of primitive reciprocity, Lévi-Strauss argued that marriages are the most basic form of gift exchange, in which women become the most precious of gifts. Precious, perhaps, but as Gayle Rubin has adroitly observed,

> if it is women who are being transacted, then it is the men who give and take them who are linked, the woman being a conduit of a relationship rather than a partner to it [. . .] And it is

the partners, not the presents, upon whom reciprocal exchange
confers its quasi-mystical power of social linkage.

(1975: 174)

The centrality of this schema to kinship systems is indisputable, but
Heywood's story suggests that it provides a paradigm for other social
practices as well. The question remains, though, as to why Heywood
found it necessary to manage the outcome of Galbrata's petition in
the way he did. Galbrata's cause is a good one and her plea itself
obeys prescriptions about female modesty harped on by writers such
as Shirley: the whole petition, Heywood tells us, is characterised by
its 'bashfull shame, and well becoming modesty' (1637: 56). In spite
of possessing these ubiquitous features, this plea provokes enough
anxiety in its male hearer to ensure that the woman who makes it is
manoeuvred, swiftly and conspicuously, into a position 'between men'.
    The phrase 'between men' originates with Eve Kosofsky Sedgwick,
who uses it, in her own gloss on Lévi-Strauss, to describe the conceptual
space occupied in patriarchal cultures by a less powerful third party,
usually a woman, whose presence allows for the strengthening of
bonds between male partners in any social transaction (Sedgwick
1985). At the end of Heywood's story, as in the famous Peacham
drawing, a female pleader is captured *in medias res*. Rather than
admitting that Galbrata has prevailed in a rhetorical exchange – that
she has spoken and her male opponent has been persuaded by her
words – Heywood transforms her plea into the vehicle for affirming
a quite different relationship between men and confirms her status
as object rather than agent in *this* exchange in spatial terms. In this
respect, Heywood's narrative reflects the tendency shown by the most
sympathetic of writers on this subject to valorise the efforts of female
intercessors – another group of pleaders whose rhetorical activities
are confined to the resolution of disputes between men. The decision
taken by Darcie and Gibson to champion the virtues of Alexandra,
Volumnia, Rhea and the Sabine women is not haphazard, of course.
Both men imply that the female pleader's ability to moderate the
emotions of others makes her particularly suited to the *action* of
moderation. What lingers even in these accounts is a very real sense
that these women are only allowed to practise oratory because to
do so is also to confirm their status as wives, mothers or daughters.
Following similar principles, Heywood may have intended to put
Galbrata in her place, quite literally, by undermining her status as
a female pleader and presenting her as a wife. Like many others
examined in this chapter, however, this strategy does not really

succeed in negating the potency of female rhetoric. On the contrary, such anxious reinforcements of patriarchal structures prove that the woman whose speech could move a man was considered genuinely powerful enough to place them under threat.

Notes

1 On the importance of this drawing as an 'imaginative reconstruction', see Orgel (1994: 43–5).
2 On the 'Tradition of Women Worthies' see Davis (1976). More general discussions of the controversy over women can be found in Woodbridge (1984) and Hull (1982).
3 Definition in Lanham (1991: 115).
4 In his 'Epistle to the Reader', for example, Heywood extends his sympathy to the husband who has 'been often terrified with his *Curtaine clamours*' (1637: A3v).
5 On the cultural implications of early modern humoral theory, with its tendency to describe fluidity as the defining characteristic of female corporeality, see Paster (1993).
6 On the importance of this tenet see Graf (1991: 40). See also Vickers (1989: 75–6).
7 A facsimile of the 1616 edition. On 'moderation' (which was closely related in this period to the notion of the Aristotelian 'mean') as a guide to ethical conduct, see Scodel (2002).

4 Speaking women

Rhetoric and the construction of female talk

Danielle Clarke

This chapter sets out the case for considering the relationship between women and rhetoric as central to early modern understandings of articulacy, self and society. In the course of making this argument, I will aim to suggest some ways in which the question of the female voice, frequently inscribed by men, or through masculinist frameworks, might be approached. The attempt to trace and isolate authentic, unmediated voices that are unequivocally female has been central to the development of critical approaches to gender and discourse in the early modern period. Yet this approach, I argue, is ultimately flawed; we need to find more nuanced and historically alert ways of reading both canonically central representations of female speech and of contextualising the material traces left by women themselves. In this chapter this will be undertaken through reading early modern versions of the myth of Echo, from translations of Ovid through to Milton's representation of Eve in *Paradise Lost*, as well as looking briefly at versions by Shakespeare and Lady Mary Wroth.

Even where Echo is not specifically evoked either thematically or acoustically, her doubling duplicity haunts early modern descriptions of female speech. Echo as exemplarity produces contradictory effects in relation to women as users of language – paradoxes that seem to me to structure the ways in which images of female speech are produced in the early modern period. On the one hand, echoing is often presented as the ideal image of the relationship between husband and wife. In John Davies' *Epithalamion*, written for the marriage of Lady Elizabeth Vere to the Earl of Derby, the figure of Echo is adapted to represent the marital bond:

> That as the voice and Echo doe agree,
> So maye you both, both doe, and saye the same,

And as your eyes beinge two, but one thinge see,
So maye ye to one end your actions frame.
So shall your Lyves be a sweete harmonye,
And with your dayes your Joyes shall multiplie
(Davies 1975: 204.37–42)

Voice and echo are imagined as an ideal harmony, with neither loss nor augmentation, giving way to the power of echo to generate and reproduce, 'your Joyes shall multiplie'; interestingly, Davies does not specify who is the 'voice' and who the 'Echo'.

Women learning to write are also encouraged to cultivate an echographic relationship to the texts they copy; virtuous women are to imitate models of piety from the Bible.[1] Their role is to engage in the reproduction of ideology and culture. On the other hand, Echo can be seen as a model of doubleness, duplicity, desire and lack of control in speech. For Brathwait, for example, echoing turns up in his character of a shrew, where it threatens a terrible homology: 'her mothers sole note (being the voyce of her vocation) eccoed, New wainflete Oysters' (1620: 134). Shirley writes 'Wherefore should men love women? / Such aery mockeries, nothing but meer Eccho's, / That owe their being to our opinion', suggesting the idea of secondariness that haunts both early modern ideas of physiology and notions of female speech (Cotgrave 1655: 306).[2] Yet echoing and imitation also permit the formation of perfect speech, as in the much-cited example of Cornelia and the Gracchi in addition to providing a powerfully feminised figure for linguistic instability. In *The Duchess of Malfi*, for example, the device of echo is used to create illusion and to prefigure Antonio's fate; it thus subverts his words and places them into a new semantic context, where the advice he gives to Delio more properly should be applied to himself: 'you'll find it impossible to fly your fate' Antonio advises; the echo rebounds '*O fly your fate*' (Webster 1975: 5.3.33–5). As Delio remarks, 'the dead stones seem to have pity on you / And give you good counsel' via a voice which is feminised in terms of function, but also, implicitly in relation to point of origin, as it comes '*from the DUCHESS' grave*' (5.3.sd). Voice and origin are effectively fused. Echo therefore bequeaths a contradictory legacy, open to interpretation. That Echo remains such a contested figure suggests that this story signified something important about language, its origins, speakers and effects. In the end, Echo represents the ways in which women's language is framed and contained by models expressed for quite different reasons and to distinct ends. The point here is not so much that women are excluded from rhetorical culture – evidence increasingly suggests that modern critics have fallen victim to early modern prescriptivism on this point – but that they are central to its sense of itself as a culture, what it includes and excludes, and the terms in which it expresses abjection, specifically linguistic abjection. As rhetorical power was increasingly represented through the eloquent use of the vernacular, its restriction to men must have started to look potentially precarious, if not arbitrary. There was, logically, no reason why a woman could not equip herself with any one of the plethora of handbooks on rhetoric (and some did), nor why her reading and writing should not extend to the mastery of the stylistic code represented by tropes and schemes.[3] There were, of course, several ways in which women's language was positioned as trivial or marginal, but, equally, fissures and contradictions that enabled representations of female speech as power, agency, comfort, piety or necessity. The figure of Echo and its afterlife gives us an example of the female pretext to early modern rhetorical power, the ways in which the contrary legacy of Echo gives rise to a powerful paradox and a model of female speech that may be reductive but nevertheless remains central to early modern notions of language, sexuality and desire.

One of the most persistent *topoi* in critical and historical accounts of the early modern period is that rhetoric is the exclusive preserve of masculinity; that textual intervention in the period is defined by *homo rhetoricus*.[4] In this manifestation of the classical heritage, rhetoric can be seen as an exclusionary model, which is primarily utilitarian in the cultural and ideological work that it does.[5] The acquisition and dissemination of rhetorical skills is grounded in masculine institutions (schools, universities, inns of court), which are defined by their capacity to generate and cement homosocial bonds, and which rhetorical skill comes in turn to symbolise and consolidate. The means of instruction is largely dictated by the perceived end – that of service in the public sphere – from which women are systemically excluded.[6] Rhetorical skill is an ideological and cultural badge of personhood, indicative of a social identity that marks an individual as belonging to various institutional networks. As such, it is implicitly gendered, as well as marked by class and status, as Portia's shocking transgression of these norms in *The Merchant of Venice* demonstrates. But as the status of the vernacular changes, the meanings of literacy mutate, and linguistic boundaries are redrawn to preserve social structures, even if these, overall, become more fluid. Latinity enables a certain degree of social mobility, yet this very fact renders the marginal relationship of women to it arbitrary at best.[7] This is illustrated in Erasmus's

Colloquy of the Abbot and the Learned Woman, where Antonius (a monk) instructs Magdalia (a nun) on the correct relationship of women to Latin:

An.: I can endure books, but I cannot endure Latin books.
Ma.: Wherefore?
An.: Because that language is not fit for women.
Ma.: I would know the reason.
An.: Because it little avails to maintain their chastity.

(Aughterson 1995: 172)

The point here rests on the question of *suitability*, not *ability*, compounded by the fact that this text was largely circulated in Latin. My argument here is that the shift to the vernacular opens up the potential of female competency in discourses that mark male superiority; this possibility requires a series of cultural adjustments to ideas surrounding female speech in order to contain women's capacity for eloquence and to preserve homosocial structures. Echo seems to me to be one classical *topos* that brings together these contrary impulses, as she both imitates and repeats, but subverts and generates; on the one hand, she represents the possibility of copious female discourse, but on the other, the impossibility of its realisation. Equally, echo and echoing are central to early modern ideas about copiousness and imitation: on the one hand, a fear of pointless repetition; on the other, an anxiety about the infinite capacity of language to generate meaning, to the point of meaninglessness.

One of the central debates in Reformation thought concerns access to scripture and thus the politics of literacy and, specifically, the role of women in disseminating the word in a domestic and familial setting; the 'permission' to read is closely allied to maternity, and, through this, to the reinforcement of existing norms and the dissemination of socially conservative moral principles: for the reformers, women should be learned enough to instruct young children, but also contained or managed in this role. The early modern position on education for women remains remarkably stable in the period between the initial interventions of humanist educators and the more radical arguments advanced after the Civil War, and it is predicated entirely on a philosophy of education based upon function, namely that whilst (exceptional) women are capable of intellectual endeavour, such efforts are largely fruitless because women can have no sphere in which such skills can be exercised, and, thus, a systematic rhetorical education is pointless in relation to women.[8] This is clearly a circular argument, and the rest of this essay seeks to explore some of the ideological and cultural means by which its key tenets are held, shakily, in place, but also to suggest some circumscribed areas where mutation, via the myth of Echo, might permit some form of intervention; echoing is inherently rhetorical, as the intense interest in its formal aspects in early modern poetry suggests.

Feminist readings of the early modern period have been preoccupied with notions of voice and articulation, a telling reprise of early modern anxieties about female speech. The former have tended to concentrate upon articulacy as a key vector of subjectivity and individuality, but I argue that early modern culture viewed female speech and eloquence through the categories bequeathed by rhetoric, and by rhetorically inflected readings and imitations of both classical and Christian texts. In other words, ancient texts provided an ontology for female speech, which functioned in effect as teleology, as classical and biblical models served as either restrictive or exceptional *exemplae* for early modern women. Early modern conceptions of the relationship between women and eloquence bear all the marks of the contradictions inherent in positioning widely different ancient texts (even within the Bible itself[9]) on a single plane, that of a textual authority to be mined for contemporary models of conduct. Models for female articulation are thus contained within and by those very cultural systems that structure early modern discourse. I will concentrate specifically upon Echo because she is a resonant site for the issues I am concerned with. It is important to recognise that the *topoi* that represent female talk in the early modern period are indicative of an accretion of traditions, variously inflected by context, of which the state of English in the age of Shakespeare is but one. We may wish to call these commonplaces by different names – cliché, adage, misogynist tag – but the point is that such terms and terminologies structured not only how women's language was viewed, but also how women viewed language and its potential for individuation, subjectivity and political intervention. Ovid is a particularly interesting example, because of his own profound interest in the question of a female voice (or, less kindly, the poetic potential of *prosopopoeia*). For many writers, Ovidian inscriptions of the female voice were some of the most powerful and primary that they encountered.[10]

Women's speech in the early modern period is a matter of inscription. Its transmission is enmeshed in provisionality, temporality and the frameworks bequeathed by early modern ways of interpolating female eloquence into a hierarchised system provisionally marked as masculine. There are many possible explanations for this, but two central and related contexts concern us here: first, the culturally and historically specific form of misogyny found in classical and early Christian (especially Pauline) texts and, second, the complex ideological disruptions posed to a male-coded system of rhetorical authority by the shift to the vernacular, changes in rhetorical function, and the sidelining/transition of key institutions that had embodied (though not necessarily practised) oratorical power. I want to suggest that the persistence of masculine rhetorical models for female speech, including Ovidian ones, was one way of ensuring that women remained largely outside of those forms of eloquence that constituted social status and advancement for men in early modern Britain.[11] That the textual bodies of Ovid's heroines, and the established tropological models for female speech, continued to be almost exclusively passed between men at a point where they were theoretically available to many women would lend support to this notion. In short, the movement to the vernacular (troped from Cicero onwards as feminine) required a complex realignment of linguistic and stylistic hierarchies and of institutional and rhetorical markers (Cicero 1996: 3.44-6). In the early modern period, this process consists of re-establishing and recirculating a series of negative models for female speech, alongside highly restrictive models of virtuous speech and language. Just as it is Echo who is 'the initiative of speech', transforming sounds into words, it is the feminine that is simultaneously the abjection, precondition and agent of early modern eloquence (Berger 1996: 630).

We have become so accustomed to the conventional frames for women's speech in the early modern period that critics have developed their own slightly inaccurate cliché(s), which, like those of the sixteenth and seventeenth centuries, have begun to arrogate their own authority. Suzanne Hull's 'chaste, silent and obedient' has been repeatedly recycled as a historically grounded description of the status of early modern women, a kind of metonymic shorthand for the plurality of representations, not to mention historical realities (see Hull 1982). The phrase has no early modern authority, other than approximating the vows taken by the religious of both sexes in the Roman Catholic faith, and yet it has formed one of the foundational *topoi* for discussing the relationship of women to early modern discourse, effectively becoming a kind of source for the oppositional model, where women are systematically excluded from early modern verbal economies. This process is both more complex and more ambiguous than recent criticism in the area allows. To take just one specific example, the injunction to silence for women is not in any sense a given. It is found repeatedly in strongly Protestant conduct books and in reworkings of classical texts. However, it is rarely unqualified, and the degree to which the passage in 1 Corinthians – and other key scriptural passages – is the subject of exegesis and debate, suggests that the question of women's speech/silence is a key locus for other kinds of cultural and ideological battles.[12] For example, the degree to which a model of virtuous and eloquent speech becomes a powerful convention in the representation of exemplary women, notably in funeral sermons, is striking, particularly in the seventeenth century. The validation of women's speech in such contexts is heavily indebted to a model of rhetorical utility, albeit largely in a devotional, domestic context rather than a public or political one. Boreman's funeral sermon on Alice, Duchess Dudley, for example, repeatedly returns to a model of exemplary literacy, as his subject is praised because she 'spent as much time (or more) in reading of God's word, and other godly books the extracts of it, as others do in their Glasse' (Boreman 1669: 6). In relation to speech, Dudley is praised not for silence, but for the useful and judicious employment of speech, with the explicit end of instruction: 'she had a great command over her Tongue, and Passions[. . .] she therefore seldom spake but to the benefit of the Hearer[. . .] [h]er mouth had a watch set upon it, which then opened when she was to give rules of Instruction' (Boreman 1669: 8–9).

The positive value afforded to useful speech is a repeated trope of exemplarity in early modern sermons on women. Edmund Barker's sermon on the wife of Lord Capel states that anyone who 'had but happily heard, and listned to her discourse, must needs have learned excellent gravity from thence' (Barker 1660: 32).[13]

Women's linguistic engagement with the complex symbolic orders of early modern English is frequently indebted to inaccurately recycled historical commonplaces. One clear early modern example of this kind of recycling of commonplaces as if they described contemporary realities can be found in the woman debate, or *querelle des femmes*. It is now well understood that these texts (and their looser generic offspring in the shape of stage plays, jests and poems) are structured by rhetorical imperatives that have little to do with observed reality, which primarily intrudes as a form of exemplification (see Purkiss 1992 and Clarke 2001: Chapter 2). Whilst much conventional misogyny focuses on the specific issue of women's speech (as evinced by the number of proverbs devoted to precisely this topic), the form in which it is expressed more usually involves allusions closely related to early modern notions of literary value, namely a tendency to frame women's speech as the negative image of culturally valued norms for eloquence (see, for example, Breton 1916: A4v–A7r, Ray 1670, Tilley

1950). In other words, women's speech and what is said about it are two of those perennial topics to which early modern writers return over and over again – the minor writers engaging in tedious reiteration, the major ones in powerful acts of imitative transformation. The issue here relates less to the ways in which such classical and early Christian assumptions are circulated than to their significance in a contemporary context. It is not purely and simply high literary culture that is relevant either; these ideas float free of their original moorings and circulate as popular truths in themselves. These unmarked 'truths' are all the more powerful for being de-historicised and de-contextualised, less like echoes of distant cultures than accurate descriptions of reality, with the status of unchallenged, universal truths. Returning to the discontinuities that structure perceptions of women's language, I wish to consider the extent to which conventions regarding the desirability of female silence, fears of uncontrollable speech and garrulity and vexed issues around prestige languages are counterbalanced by a sense of the power and agency of female speech, albeit in specific situations and contexts, often through the exploitation of the power of echo/Echo to subvert the point of origin and her capacity to bridge antithetical ideas about language and speech.[14]

As the work of Jonathan Bate and others has demonstrated, Ovid was central to early modern notions of the self (see Bate 1994, Enterline 2000 and Lyne 2001). Bate acknowledges that the self that Ovid articulates, and that the early moderns imitated, is implicitly coded as masculine. Yet Ovid might also be seen to be unique amongst the poets revered and imitated by the early moderns for his sustained interest in the self-negating, self-cancelling power of female speech. By this I mean the way in which Ovid undoes any kind of causal relationship between the temporal, biological female body and the inflection of the female voice. This uncoupling has proved difficult for feminist readers, uncomfortable with male-authored inscriptions of the female voice that often sound more 'authentic' than those scripted by women themselves. What does Echo figure? She is the nymph punished by Juno for her protection of Jove through talk – for detaining Juno in chat. Thus Echo symbolises plural, empty speech, which nevertheless carries huge power: the power of deception, the betrayal of female solidarity and flagrant disregard for social hierarchy. Her speech is both sexualised and a means of exercising sexual control. She is described by Ovid as

> resounding Echo, one whose speech was strange;
> for when she heard the words of others, she

could not keep silent, yet she could not be
the first to speak. Then she still had a body –
she was not just a voice. Though talkative,
she used her voice as she still uses it:
of many words her ears have caught, she just
repeats the final part of what she has heard.
(Ovid 1993: 91)

This is an epitome of the way in which early modern texts represent
female speech – unstoppable, yet unable to initiate, able only to copy
(or parrot, to take one of the most common parallels) (see Baxter
1673: 433). Yet, as many critics have suspected, a troubling agency lurks
beneath the surface here. Echo hears many words, but repeats few; the
implication is that those few are at least selected, if not chosen: 'she
cannot begin / to speak: her nature has forbidden this; / and so she
waits for what her state permits: /to catch the sounds that she can then
give back / with her own voice' (Ovid 1993: 92). It is clear from her
responses that echoing the words of others enables her to articulate
her desires, as language slips away from the control of Narcissus and
confounds his intentions. Even so in Ovid's version of the story Echo
is relegated to the role of marginal recorder of Narcissus' drama of
self-destruction, a witness to her own secondariness, as her name is
over-written by her function. Anne-Emmanuelle Berger asks the key
question: 'Why would an echo, in the fantasy that anthropomorphizes
it, be feminine rather than masculine?' (Berger 1996: 628). It may be
due to 'inherent' secondariness, yet, as Berger makes clear, the very
operation of echo undoes any kind of straightforward relationship
between utterance and repetition. For the early modern period,
Echo's secondariness coalesces a real fear of pointless repetition and
diminution, particularly in relation to the unstable prestige of the
vernacular, one which is powerfully symbolised by Echo's female
status – a status, incidentally, that depends, in the first instance, on
an understanding of the inflections of the Latin language. This
anxiety about replication lies at the heart of early modern imitation
and copiousness, as the work of Terence Cave has demonstrated.
Echoing may be transformative imitation; equally, it might function
as a synecdoche for 'the dry repetition of hackneyed topoi and stories
raided from the classics' (Kilgour 2005: 321; see also Cave 1979).
Early modern versions of Echo as a character and a rhetorical figure
follow through both aspects of echo; on the one hand as exemplarity,
on the other as a specific formal and structural quality, a duality
that finds its apotheosis in Milton's appropriation of Ovid's myth

to situate the creation and self-awakening of Eve. These two aspects are often conflated in imitations and versions. Arthur Golding, for example, adds a moralising cast to his characterisation of Echo, using early modern keywords strongly associated with the negative aspects of female speech: 'A babbling nymph that Echo hight (who, hearing others talk, / By no means can restrain her tongue but that it must needs walk, / Nor of herself hath power to gin to speak to any wight' (Ovid 2002: 3.443–5). Howell's 'caulyng nimph' (1560: Aiiv) 'nether ever lettes / To taulke to those that speke, nor yet hath power of speeche', she is 'the dobbeler of skreeche' and 'wyth dobling sound the wordes she heareth, and sendeth againe with screch'. Thus Echo is a figure simultaneously of augmentation and diminution, of creative imitation and slavish copying; as such she is at the symbolic centre of early modern cultural and linguistic fears. For Sandys in 1626, she is 'the vocall Nymph', whose fate is to copy forever, excluded from the selfhood that autonomous articulation might proffer: 'of words she wanted choyce; / But onely could reiterate the close / Of every speech' (Sandys 1626: 54). In the commentary he added to the 1632 edition, she turns up again as 'the babling Nymph Eccho' who pines away to 'an unsubstantiall voice' (Sandys 1632: 156). In a sense, it is Echo who is punished for Narcissus' self-obsession: 'who rejected, converts into a sound; that is, into nothing' (Sandys 1632: 156). Sandys tries to be more scientific than earlier writers, but presents Echo, like Narcissus, as an operation in self-consumption, 'the repercussion of the voice[. . .]returning directly from whence it came' (1632: 156). Echo thus becomes the mediating term by which the male self engages in self-contemplation – a dynamic that is also at work in Milton's use of the myth of Echo to structure the relationship between Adam and Eve in *Paradise Lost*. In Sandys' translation, the term used is '[s]hee yet ingeminates / The last of sounds, and what she heares relates' (1626: 55). The verb 'ingeminate' (a transliteration of Ovid's *ingeminare*) means, according to the *Oxford English Dictionary*, 'to utter a sound twice or more often; to repeat, reiterate[. . .]use for emphasis or to make an impression; to double; to couple'. This sounds suspiciously like a description of the male-coded rhetorical culture of reproduction of which Sandys himself is, at this precise moment of lexical choice, a central part, depending heavily upon the precursor text that the act of translation at least purports to displace or disrupt. At one level, Echo's involuntary repetition of sound privileges the reader/translator, who processes strings of sounds into contextualised meanings; when Echo's words appear to give Narcissus the come-on, it is because the reader has turned sounds into language. The lack of clarity as to whether Echo really knows what she is saying means that it is the male reader who smiles knowingly to himself at her expense – part of a series of conventions by which women's speech is positioned as not meaning what it says (the no-means-yes situation), or their words are interpolated into a register to which they have no access (the spectacle of women using *double entendres* of which they remain unaware).

The wresting of this power to echo from Echo and its reassignment in turn to reader and imitator indicates the way that linguistic and semantic anxiety about potential meaninglessness and verbal chaos is figured through the feminine and hints at why Echo is such a resonant figure in the early modern period.

One of the most resonant and complex examples of the deployment of the myth of Echo occurs in Milton's *Paradise Lost*, where it both figures and embodies the systematic exclusion of women from rhetorical culture, yet simultaneously admits the potential for their inclusion through the inversion of order that Milton undertakes as he inverts and dilates the account of the creation of Adam and Eve as found in Genesis. Milton's account of Eve's narrative in Book 4 is one example of what Schwartz claims is a Miltonic obsession with origins, the extent to which they can be identified, and how far language can convey such origins: this is particularly problematic in relation to prelapsarian language and its temporal dimension (or lack of it), and echoic allusion is one way in which Milton attempts to grapple with this issue (Schwartz 1988). It is fascinating, but problematic, that Milton uses such an incongruous figure as Narcissus to represent the moment when Eve awakens as a conscious human being. Although Milton is heavily indebted to Ovid throughout *Paradise Lost*, this passage in Book 4 is perhaps the most directly Ovidian in both theme and method. Whilst there are numerous examples of self-obsession in the poem, the powerful precedent set by Narcissus is specifically reserved by Milton for the representation of Eve's sense of self. This seems, at first, to be doubly inappropriate. Not only is Narcissus male, although beloved of both sexes, he is also a by-word for self-absorption, as Tiresias' prophecy that Narcissus would see old age 'if he never knows himself' suggests (Ovid 1993: 91). Where Adam argues from divine authority, Eve's moment of revelation is predicated on a non-Christian text, and on a figure that was a virtual synonym for the vice of vanity. As Sandys' translation recounts (a version that Milton knew well), Narcissus 'unconsiderately himselfe desir'd' leading to his confusion of his self as subject with self as object, 'Ah, He is I! Now, now I plainly see; / Now is't my shadow that bewitcheth mee' (1626: 57). The error of mistaking subject for object is one that requires specific 'correction' by external authority. The consequences of misreading and misinterpreting in *Paradise Lost* are literally fatal: it is clear in Book 9's account of the fall that Eve has understood only the surface meaning of the prohibition, not the larger rational context so painstakingly outlined by Raphael to Adam. In this sense, Eve's 'natural' response to her creation requires interpolation via a divine authority into the patriarchal order that she is to serve; thus, her ability must, in the end, be subordinated to what is considered suitable. Her rhetorical potential is quickly rendered secondary, derivative. Eve's tendency to prefer the outside, the physical, the sensual above the inner, the abstract and the rational is precisely what makes Satan exclaim so joyfully, 'behold alone / The woman, opportune to all attempts' (Milton 1971: 9.480–1). On the other hand, it is Eve's arguments and perceptions that shape Adam's decision to eat the apple; her rhetoric may be applied to the wrong end, but it is effective nonetheless. Milton's construction of Eve suggests that her rhetorical potential cannot ultimately be contained, although it can elicit punishment, just as the nymph Echo does.

Adam, whose account of his creation underscores his greater proximity to God, recalls that '[s]traight toward heaven my wondering eyes I fed' (8.257). By contrast, Eve requires guidance and intervention to select the 'correct' objects of worship and love. That Eve first forms an attachment to her own image is telling enough; it prefigures her inability to 'read' objects correctly, and her tendency to elevate image above substance, body above spirit, the senses above reason and appearance above all. The terms in which Milton frames this (self-)encounter deliberately recall Ovid's account of Echo and Narcissus and the tradition of moralising commentary on *Metamorphoses*. While Adam awakes on 'flowery herb' (8.254), Eve finds herself '*[u]nder* a shade of flowers' (4.451), a significant preposition in a poem that so frequently spatialises moral states. The setting metamorphoses Ovid's account of Echo, as well as earlier and subsequent traditions relating to the dilemma of how to locate Echo: 'Not distant far from thence a murmuring sound / Of waters issued from a cave and spread / Into a liquid plain' (4.453–55).[15] The setting is not simply a lyrical extension of the *locus amoenus* that Milton creates earlier in Book 4, but is significant in its broader allusive context, recalling a Homeric image often interpreted as a symbol of the descent of the soul (*Iliad* 5.872). The allusion is clearly ironic when read in the more proximate context of Ovid. The river from the cave becomes a pool, to which Eve finds herself drawn by 'unexperienced thought' (4.457), a phrase that epitomises lack of self-knowledge, yet retrospectively and proleptically recalls Tiresias' prophecy that Narcissus would see old age 'Except himselfe to know'. Adam immediately proceeds to order and name the animal kingdom, his awareness that he can speak coming from a process of self-discovery: 'who I was, or where, or from what cause, / Knew not; to speak I tried, and forthwith spake, / My tongue obeyed and readily could name / What e'er I saw' (8.270-3). Adam shapes a verbal economy whilst Eve attempts to intervene in one that has already been created. Eve cannot initially make differentiations and cannot perceive boundaries; the pool 'to me *seemed* another sky' (4.459, emphasis added), and the Narcissus myth is used to articulate the fact that she cannot distinguish between her self and her image:

> As I bent down to look, just opposite,
> A shape within the watery gleam appeared
> Bending to look on me, I started back,
> It started back, but pleased I soon returned,
> Pleased it returned as soon with answering looks
> Of sympathy and love; there had I fixed
> Mine eyes till now, and pined with vain desire,
> Had not a voice thus warned me.
>   (4.460–7)

Her relationship to her self is posited as echoic, yet this moment of self-consumption explicitly resists the central idea of cultural and sexual reproduction to which Eve must be led. The parallel is powerful and suggestive and enfolds within it some key aspects of Echo (repetition, the disembodied voice); the extended allusion is transformative and ironic, as Eve's later actions reveal that she seeks an end for herself (the possession of knowledge, goddess-like status, equality/superiority to Adam) and thus demonstrates the negative potential of female rhetorical power within a masculine hierarchy based upon the separation of gender roles grounded in obedience to male authority. Here though, as yet unfallen but with the potential to fall, her desire must be directed away from the shadow that is the image of her self towards Adam, who is substance. Like Narcissus, here she 'thinks the shadow that he sees to be a lively body' (Ovid 2002: 3.417). Despite Eve's awakening in 'shade' (a significant phrase given Milton's use of light and dark as moral indices, and a direct echo of Sandys' Ovid, 'fleeing shade', 'flying shade'), God's voice guides Eve towards Adam: 'follow me, / And I will bring thee where no shadow stays / Thy coming' (4.469–71). Significantly, Eve requires the concrete evidence of the senses to fulfil God's plan, as later she requires instruction in the proper governance of the senses by reason. At first she sees Adam, but cannot comprehend him in terms other than self-reference, is unable to view him as an object separate from herself: 'methought less fair, / Less winning soft, less amiably mild, / Than that smooth watery image; back I turned' (4.478–80). However, Eve makes the transition to viewing Adam as object of desire instead of her self: the 'image' and the subject 'I' are separated, at least at the level of articulation, if not yet desire. Here the dynamic of Ovid's myth is replicated in terms of the position occupied by each sex: Eve seeks Adam like Echo seeks Narcissus; by the same token, the myth is inverted, as it is Eve who rejects Adam in favour of the satisfactions provided by being both desiring subject and object of desire. In this moral and structural scenario, it is Adam who (temporarily) plays Echo. Like Ovid's Echo he follows Eve, but he echoes himself and the Old Testament, *not* the composite Narcissus/Eve:

> Return fair Eve,
> Whom fly'st thou? Whom thou fly'st, of him thou art,
> His flesh, his bone; to give thee being I lent
> Out of my side to thee, nearest my heart
> Substantial life, to have thee by my side
> Henceforth an individual solace dear;
> Part of my soul I seek thee, and thee claim
> My other half.
>
> (4.481–8)

He seeks, she flees; and as she does, Adam echoes Echo (in Golding's version 'why fly'st?', Ovid 2002: 3.478) as well as Genesis 2:23 ('This is now bone of my bones, and flesh of my flesh') and the other account of the creation of Eve in Book 8, 'like of his like, his image multiplied' (8.424), 'Bone of my bone, flesh of my flesh, my self / Before me' (8.495–6) or 'Best image of my self and dearer half' (5.95). The fact that Eve herself gives her own account of her creation prior to Adam's more text-bound version in Book 8 suggests her capacity to function metaphorically as a foundational element of early modern ideas of poetic value, as she productively transforms both the Ovidian source and provides a point of departure for Adam's act of imitation. As Maggie Kilgour notes, 'while Eve is made in Adam's image, her story, told before his, becomes the model to which we compare his later version' (Kilgour 2005: 331). Moreover, like Echo, she is repeatedly associated with abundance, with *copia*, with all of its attendant dangers.

Much like Ovid, so Milton makes a transition in this short but allusively dense passage from visual mirroring – with its additional implications of vanity and resonances of specific injunctions to early modern women to substitute the mirror of the Bible/soul for the mirrors of vanity/glass – to sound mirrors or echoes. Elements of the Narcissus/Echo story are dispersed through the text of *Paradise Lost* in order to create a network of symbolic allusions: these are not always, or necessarily, simply thematic or allegorical. John Hollander's wonderfully suggestive book, *The Figure of Echo*, attempts to classify the bewildering array of types of echo into categories, arguing that 'potentially it can augment and trope the utterance it echoes, as well as reduce and ridicule[. . .] the scheme of echoing covers a wide array of sorts of controlled repetition of word or phrase' (Hollander 1981: 31). This transformative capacity is inherently generative and thus closely related to the key idea of *copia*, in short, the capacity of language to work infinite variation and transformation on a given source. It should be noted that despite Milton's efforts to contain Eve's rhetorical potential, she does voice many of the key arguments in *Paradise Lost*; it is, paradoxically, the figure of woman who teases out the discontinuities at the heart of seventeenth-century ideologies of gender. In Eve's final and vain attempt at resisting the wiles of Satan in Book 9, the notion of echo is placed in a scriptural and theological context. Eve explains, punning as she goes, that their visit to the tree of knowledge is 'fruitless to me, though fruit be here to excess' (9.648). Once again, Eve is rhetorically central, in signalling to the reader how s/he should interpret. Eve repeats God's injunction, as she has overheard it relayed to Adam by Raphael, and then repeated to her, 'Adam relating, she sole auditress[. . .] from his lip / Not words alone pleased her' (8.51, 56–7):

> But of this tree we may not taste or touch;
> God so commanded, and left that command
> Sole daughter of his voice; the rest, we live
> Law to our selves, our reason is our law.
>   (9.651–4)

Yet this passage also draws attention to Eve's position as repeating without authority and implies the ironic diminution and alteration of meaning that echo produces and that was so beloved of early modern poets. The phrase 'sole daughter of his voice' not only re-engages stylistically with the very relationship that Eve has recklessly abandoned to go her own way (Adam's 'Sole part and sole partner' in Book 4, 'Sole Eve, associate sole' in 9.227, and Eve's 'O sole' address to Adam in 5.28), but also deploys what Fowler argues is a deliberate Hebraism, 'daughter of the divine voice', for the biblical formula 'voice sent from heaven' (Milton 1971: 476). This phrase reproduces Bat Kol, or Hebrew 'echo', or as Hollander glosses, 'a secondary, or derivative, voice of the holy spirit often uttering a scriptural text, such a voice, as it were an echo of heaven, [which] seem[s] to have had at best a contingent authority' (Hollander 1981: 16). Eve's deployment of it would seem to confirm this through mutually reinforcing cross-reference. Its use here illustrates the way in which Milton enfolds one sense of echo within another to create powerfully allusive, but ambiguous cruxes within the text as well as combining numerous different echoes. Equally, this dense layering of allusion suggests the need to re-enfold Eve into a cultural history of misogyny, where female speech carries little or no authority. Her statement about reason being their law is telling, partly because here Eve appropriates Adam's authority to herself, but also because she seriously mistakes and misapplies the text from Romans to which Milton has her refer: 'When the Gentiles, which have not the law, do by nature the things contained in the law, these, having not the law, are a law unto themselves' (Romans 2:14). The biblical text argues that even if the law is followed without conscious knowledge, these acts do not constitute the law; Eve's rather grandiose interpretation, once again, does not view God as an authority, but elevates human reason to the level of divine law.

Milton's axis of potential and containment is perhaps the prevalent interpretation of the relationship between the myth of Echo and female speakers in the early modern period; however, other writers utilise the transformative possibilities in the myth to create more resonant images of female subjectivity. Interestingly, the idea of echo is frequently invoked in the context of female loss and abandonment, where it becomes a trope for the loss of self and, thus, a key element in the articulation of desire and loss. Whilst Echo tracks the disconnection between the female self and the masculine world to which she remains ancillary, paradoxically she also links the female speaker to a larger rhetorical economy. When Adonis breaks free from Venus's embrace in Shakespeare's *Venus and Adonis*, Venus's response connects her not only to the natural world that images her sorrow, but to verbal augmentation:

> And now she beats her heart, whereat it groans,
> That all the neighbor caves, as seeming troubled,
> Make verbal repetition of her moans;

Passion on passion deeply is redoubled:
'Ay me!' she cries, and twenty times, 'Woe, woe!'
And twenty echoes twenty times cry so.
(Shakespeare 1974: 829–34)

This suggests that doubling maps interiority, and thus echoing does not imply Venus's diminution but rather her full participation in a dense layering of literary echoes that places her at the heart of rhetorical invention and variation. In *A Lover's Complaint*, the idea of echo is framed in such a way as to provide a model for female authorship, and the transmission of the maiden's tale:

From off a hill whose concave womb reworded
A plaintful story from a sist'ring vale,
My spirits t'attend this double voice accorded,
And down I laid to list the sad-tuned tale,
(Shakespeare 1974: 1–4)

One might argue that the model of mediated speech is the central one structuring the inscription of female voices in the early modern period; yet this particular form of mediation also hints at the connectedness of these voices to the inherently rhetorical character of literary production in the period and the ways in which the feminised figure of Echo coalesces a series of anxieties about literary dependency and language's precariousness.[16]

I would like to conclude by looking briefly at an example where the deployment of the myth and trope of Echo seems to offer a model, albeit a circumscribed one, for female authorship. As I have suggested, imitation and copying are central to early modern rhetoric and poetics; echo is frequently generically deployed in relation to elegy, complaint and lament, all forms which were culturally available to women, precisely because at one level they reinforce the female speaker's dependence on the (lost) male term (see Sacks 1985 and Clarke 2000b). The potential for female authorship that Echo offers is, first, that echoing ties the speaker firmly into a male rhetorical economy to which her relationship is – at first glance – marginal, secondary and derivative. In the second instance, the echoing voice is, by definition, a disembodied voice, hence freeing the speaker from a troubling corporeal femininity (see Wall 1993 and Maus 1993). Mary Wroth's sonnet, 'Unseene, unknowne' exemplifies both of these elements, yet also complicates them. The poem occurs at the very beginning of *The Countesse of Mountgomeries Urania*; the speaker, Urania, of course is herself a marginal character plucked from Sidney's *Arcadia*, but the character herself is an example of echoing as augmentation rather than diminution, as well as a subversion of the point of origin, as she is moved from the margins of a male-centred text, to the centre of one that concentrates on female subjectivity (see Quilligan 1990). The poem is a remarkable intervention in the tradition of Echo and echoing poems, precisely because Urania does not mourn the loss of a male lover (as Echo does) but the loss of her *self*. Rather than repeating what others say, the echo here augments what Urania says:

> Unseene, unknowne, I here alone complaine
> To Rocks, to Hills, to Meadowes, and to Springs,
> Which can no helpe returne to ease my paine,
> But back my sorrowes the sad Eccho brings.
> Thus still encreasing are my woes to me,
> Doubly resounded by that monefull voice
> Which seemes to second me in miserie,
> And answere gives like friend of mine owne choice.
> (Wroth 1983: U1, 1–8)

Here Urania herself is the point of origin for the utterance, and rather than having to subvert it to articulate her self, the echo and the voice are joined together to create a complex interchange between self and other. This is not a form of containment, but a model for intervention and authorship, based upon the ambiguous legacy of the myth of Echo.

Acknowledgement

I would like to acknowledge the Irish Research Council for the Humanities and Social Sciences for the award of a fellowship during which the research for this essay was carried out.

Notes

1 For example, see Baxter (1682).
2 See Laqueur (1990) on the one-sex model and accounts of early modern ideas of physiology in Maclean (1980) and Aughterson (1995).
3 Puttenham, for example, repeatedly envisages a female as well as a male readership: 'our chiefe purpose herein is for the learning of Ladies and young Gentlewomen[...] desirous[...] for their private recreation to make now & then ditties of pleasure' (1936: 158).
4 This term is used by Lanham (1976). Whilst Lanham does not explicitly address the gendered basis of rhetorical education, his book supplies extensive evidence of this.

5 See Halpern (1991); the theoretical model invoked here derives from Guillory (1993), and it is applied in a way germane to my argument in Goldberg (1990).

6 See Vickers (1989) and Aughterson (1995), 'One of the eventual consequences of the humanist educational revolution was to intensify the developing split between men's public function and place and women's private function and place' (Aughterson 1995: 165).

7 See Lanham (1976), Fleming (1993), Stevenson (2005). Wall (1993) addresses some of these questions from the specific point of view of literary production, print in particular.

8 See Astell (1696), Makin (1673), Drake (1696). On women's education, see Gardiner (1929), O'Day (1982), Fletcher (1995), Mendelson and Crawford (1998) and Ferguson (2003).

9 See Proverbs 31:26 'She openeth her mouth in wisdom; and in her tongue is the law of kindness'; this is the text on which Aylmer (1559) bases his argument for female regiment. Contrast this with Becon's rehearsal of the example of Mary to encourage female silence, citing Luke 2:19 'this noble virtue may the virgins learn of that most holy, pure and glorious virgin Mary, which when she either heard or saw any worthy or notable thing, blabbed it not out straightways to her gossips, as the manner of women is at this present day, but being silent she kept all those sayings secret and pondered them in her heart, saith blessed Luke', Becon, *Catechism* (1564) quoted in Aughterson (1995: 27).

10 See Martindale (1988), Bate (1994), Lyne (2001), Hardie (2002). Most of these readings of Ovid deal with the *Metamorphoses*.

11 For a version of this argument in a different context, see Fleming (1993).

12 For useful background see Luckyj (2002).

13 For some other examples, see Fuller (1628: 26), on Francis Clifton, '[j]udicious in all discourse beyond degree of her sex'; Horneck (1699), Hoby (1998), Provoste (1698). Rainbowe (1677) cites Donne's comment '[t]hat she knew well how to discourse of all things, from Predestination, to Slea-Silk' (1677: 38), Wolcomb (1606), Rainbowe (1647).

14 See Kilgour (2005: 320, n.41), 'Echo's status is ambiguous: she is both a character separate from Narcissus and simply his own voice copied and thrown back to him[. . .] she exists on the boundary between self and other. Through her power, Narcissus's words are transformed into dialogue'.

15 See note in Milton (1971: 221) for relevant contexts.

16 For a discussion of these issues in relation to Spenser's 'Doleful Lay', see Clarke (2000b).

5 Letter-writing Lucrece
Shakespeare in the 1590s

Huw Griffiths

Shakespeare's *Lucrece* has usually been thought of as a version of the Lucretia narrative that, unlike many of its sources and predecessors, steers away from an overtly political rendering of the story (Burrow 2002: 53). In place of a founding myth for the Roman republic, Shakespeare deals instead with the psychological and familial aspects of this story of rape, suicide and revenge. However, this essay will argue that the poem purposely thematises that avoidance and, in doing so, explores the possibilities for effective communication of grievances in the stifling political atmosphere of the 1590s.

The last decade of Elizabeth's reign has long been seen as particularly turbulent, marked by an intensification of court factionalism, a series of economic crises and a deterioration in the systems of client and patron through which not only the business of government, but also the related activities of writing and print publishing were facilitated.[1] There have been analyses of the literature from this period which have taken into account the oppositional positions that some writers took up as a result of these changes; this has especially been the case with Edmund Spenser who has, in recent years, emerged not so much as Elizabeth's panegyrist but as one of her biggest critics (Hadfield 1994, 1997, Norbrook 2002). However, little attention has been paid to Shakespeare's contribution to this aspect of 1590s printed literature, even though his two works – *Venus and Adonis* (1593) and *Lucrece* (1594) – are both dedicated to Henry Wriothesely, a significant figure in the Essex circle who eventually took part in Essex's failed *coup d'état* of 1601. This is because where we might expect the most political content from these two works – in *Lucrece* – we seem to get an exercise in complex rhetorical forms and a studied avoidance of the story's political implications in favour of its potential for developing a psychological portrait alongside moral debate. However, this poem's excavation of the possibilities for female speech within a society where communication has broken down can be seen as a reaction to the political circumstances of the 1590s. Rather than pursue a masculinist line against the potentially effeminising tyrannies of monarchy, as might be expected of more obviously oppositional literature, *Lucrece* develops an ironic response in which the possibilities for speech are always shown to be compromised and where nobody is ever listened to. In place of a political territory that is marked out on gender lines, with Elizabeth's male courtiers expressing dissatisfaction with their ageing female monarch, Shakespeare's poem goes in search of a smothered female voice, tracing the possibilities for that voice as well as its frustrations. This emerges as a poetic intervention in the circumstances of the 1590s that may be just as attuned to the problems of that decade as Spenserian epic, albeit in a very different register.

This is accomplished through the figure of Lucrece herself and specifically through the way that she is written into the poem with reference to Ovidian predecessors from the *Heroides*. Ovid's sequence of poems, an important source for the early modern genre of complaint poetry in general and, I will argue, explicitly referenced in *Lucrece*, comprises mostly a sequence of fictional letters composed by women who demand a response from men who they feel have abandoned them, or from whom they require some assistance. At the same time, the reader is, through prior knowledge of the myths from which Ovid's letter-writers are taken, ironically aware that no response will ever come. Shakespeare's *Lucrece*, whilst fitting into the republican narrative in which the protagonist's private grief is listened to and translated into action, nevertheless betrays many of the same ironies of miscommunication as the *Heroides* and also features a writer and speaker who remains unread and unheard.

Despite a pervasive masculinism within republican theory and practice, the representations of women, and particularly of dead women, are of fundamental importance to the tradition. Melinda Matthes argues that republicans, in retelling the story of Lucretia, participate in a wider republican project of defining the public sphere as masculine against a feminine private sphere. The dead body of Lucretia reminds her male survivors of the tyranny of their previous oppressors and, in doing so, inaugurates a political system that is dependent upon public spectacle, upon the privileging of the public over the private and, concomitantly, of the masculine over the feminine. A paradoxical situation then emerges in which a political system identified with the masculine is heavily reliant on the stories of women for its founding myths. 'At its genesis,' Matthes writes, 'what must later be absent and silent – what is most destabilizing to, and vulnerable about, the incipient republic – is most exposed' (Matthes 2000: 3). However, as republicanism needs continually to restate its own origins in order to reproduce the political conditions in which it operates, this exposure is unlimited. That is, as much as republicanism is a political doctrine that excludes the feminine and celebrates the masculine, it constantly reveals its dependence on narratives that bring this binary division into question.

However, Matthes's account of what she calls the 'deeply gendered' nature of republican political theory needs to be modified if we are to think at all about Shakespeare's *Lucrece* as a participant in the ongoing restatement of republicanism through the repetition of one of its founding myths. In the examples that Matthes uses – Livy, Machiavelli and Rousseau – she is dealing with figures who are writing within political circumstances and philosophical traditions that were potentially conducive to the elaboration of a republican politics; however much these writers may have felt at odds with the regimes under which they existed, their writings are able to participate in the constitutive act of producing a forum for republican debate through the retelling of its founding myths. This is not the case with Shakespeare in 1594. Rather, the particular circumstances in which he is writing – under a political regime headed by a woman who is being seen by some as increasingly capricious and tyrannical and whose gender is sometimes seen as linked to that tyranny – result in a significantly different representation of gender relations.[2] In place of a story in which the mute body of a dead woman produces the possibility for a public forum of debate between men, Shakespeare places much greater emphasis on the experience of the silenced woman. This is not done to highlight the positive aspects of a world after Lucretia in which men are no longer prevented from addressing the tyrannies of their ruler; rather Shakespeare, as writer, identifies his own voice with that of the silenced Lucrece, thus stalling any movement towards a public resolution of Lucrece's 'private woes'. This feminine 'muteness' then becomes, in Shakespeare's poem, not an opportunity for the restatement of a masculinist 'public sphere' but rather an ironic commentary on the lack of just such a sphere in Elizabeth's 'second reign' (Guy 1995b).[3] Just as Lucrece's 'muteness' is investigated in the poem, so Shakespeare's text is, itself, deflected away from communicating the celebratory potential that the Lucretia narrative might ordinarily contain, in terms of bearing witness to the inauguration of the Roman republic. *Lucrece*, then, reveals the difficulties attendant on articulating a republican politics, or even on setting up a public forum for debate, in the stifling circumstances of the 1590s.

There has, in the past few years, been a concerted attempt on the part of some literary critics and historians to locate the emergence of something like a Habermasian 'public sphere' in periods other than the latter part of the seventeenth century that Jürgen Habermas himself identifies as the decisive point of origin for his model of a bourgeois public sphere (Habermas 1989). David Zaret has insisted on the importance of print culture in the sixteenth and seventeenth centuries as a 'prototype for democratic models of the public sphere' (Zaret 2000: 133) whilst acknowledging the necessary political limits to this development given what he calls the 'restrictive norms of secrecy and privilege in pre-Revolutionary England' (2000: 131). Whilst Zaret's primary focus is the development of an audience for polemical texts, Michelle O'Callaghan and Andrew McRae both identify the early years of Stuart rule as a period in which audiences for particular forms of poetry ('Spenserian' poetry and verse satire respectively) also seem to anticipate, with qualifications, the later formation of a less restricted public sphere (O'Callaghan 2000; McRae 2004). Again, I think *Lucrece* and the 1590s offer us something slightly different. McRae's suggestive comments that in earlier periods we might rather think about writers trying 'to think towards something that we might choose to call a public sphere, but which for them was unclear and untested' and that 'forms of unreason' might be more identifiable than a strictly Habermasian form of rationality are still more appropriate for the 1590s than they are for the early years of James's reign (McRae 2004: 14). In this period, it is not so much that poetry works as a forerunner for a later development of clear public forums for debate, but that it offers a rather more veiled outlet for oppositional arguments. Shakespeare's *Lucrece* is both part of this search and, in foregrounding breakdowns in communication within the poem, a commentary on it. What Andrew Hadfield has said about *The Faerie Queene* – that it is 'a dark political work, searching for a space to articulate a critical voice' – is true of *Lucrece*, but the latter also reveals a deep scepticism about the possibility for that voice, even if it is found, of ever receiving an audience (Hadfield 1994: 200). This scepticism about the communicative function of language in *Lucrece* extends as far as the choice of rhetorical tropes and figures that Shakespeare has made in composing the poem. One of these is *adynaton*, the figure of inexpressibility.

Shakespeare and the practice of *adynaton* in the 1590s

Shakespeare's use of *adynaton* is central to an understanding of *Lucrece*. On the one hand, this text explores a need for communication that functions on the basis that language is adequate to move private griefs into public action; on the other hand, it comments ironically on the impossibility of that ever being achieved. *Adynaton* is a rhetorical figure that bears particular witness to what it is possible to say in any given context and can, therefore, be linked to the poem's avoidance of the political message that the Lucretia narrative might ordinarily carry. A clear example of the figure in *Lucrece* would be Lucrece's response to her maid's enquiry that, 'She would request to know your heaviness' (Shakespeare 1974: l. 1283). Lucrece replies that, 'more it is than I can well express' (l. 1286). That is, words are inadequate to the feelings that she would have to convey if she were able fully to respond to her maid's question. *Adynaton* specifically uses the failure of expression as a means to express extreme emotion. One of the genres of writing from this period that makes habitual use of this figure is lyric verse, and Petrarchan poetry in particular. An example would be Sidney's lyric from the third book of *The Old Arcadia* which begins, 'What tongue can her perfections tell / In whose each part all pens may dwell?' (Sidney 1985: 207) and then proceeds to a 140-line blazon of the woman's beauty in which her every part is lovingly traced by the poet's pen before ending, 'As I began, so must I end: / No tongue can her perfections tell, / In whose each part all pens may dwell' (1985: 211). Here, as elsewhere, the function of *adynaton* seems as though it might be something like a straightforward expression of overwhelming emotion. However, in a move typical of Sidney's adaptation of Petrarchan conventions, it also comments ironically on the inadequacies of language and the impoverishment of the Petrarchan tradition. The crude pun on pen/penis in conjunction with a reference to the woman's 'each part' does not so much evoke a sense of the woman's ability to transcend all that is written about her as it does reduce her to a common pool of tired and tawdry tropes and figures. *Adynaton*, then, is not only particularly attuned to what can, or rather cannot, be said in any given context, but can also offer the careful reader a critique of the very language being used and expose the limitations of that language. It reveals its user as sceptical about the rhetorical strategies that they are employing. As such, its use in *Lucrece* is part of the wider scepticism the poem has about the possibilities of finding a 'critical voice', about such voices finding an audience and about the establishment of a public forum for debate.

Adynaton is, perhaps, one of those 'forms of unreason' that McRae has identified as characteristic of a period where there is a struggle for debate in hostile circumstances.

In Shakespeare's dramatic writing, the figure of *adynaton* is twice used by women who are seeking to assert their presence at court. At the start of *King Lear*, when Lear asks his daughters, 'Which of you shall we say doth love us most?' (Shakespeare 1974: 1.1.51), Goneril answers, 'I love you more than [words] can wield the matter' (1.1.55). That is, her feelings for her father are so strong that it would be impossible to find words adequate for the occasion. Of course, Goneril does go on to speak. If she had not, she, like her younger sister Cordelia, might have lost her inheritance. One of the things that is particularly striking about Goneril's use of *adynaton* is that she is using the language of love poetry within a public arena. ('Dearer than eyesight, space and liberty, / Beyond what can be valued, rich or rare' (1.1.56–7).) This kind of language was being used with great skill in the increasingly self-reflexive poetry of the late Elizabethan period, as seen in the Sidney lyric cited above. In addition, something of that lyric's sense of the emptiness of the language is also present in Goneril's use of *adynaton*. Her father is devalued as much as he is praised in his daughter's mechanical repetition of over-familiar lines. His acceptance of Goneril's hackneyed description as properly flattering shows the king willing to sell himself short and shows his court as a place where emotions are sold cheap. There is, then, an implication in Goneril's statement other than the obvious one, that she loves her father so much that words could never be adequate; there is also the sense, for us, that in the oppressive atmosphere of Lear's court, open communication is not possible.

The other notable Shakespearian woman who deploys *adynaton* is Queen Margaret in *Henry VI, Part 3*. In the powerful denouement of this play – the onstage murder of her son and potential heir to the throne – Margaret responds with customary forthrightness.

> What's worse than murtherer, that I may name it?
> No, no, my heart will burst and if I speak,
> And I will speak, that so my heart may burst.
> Butchers and villains! Bloody cannibals!
>   (Shakespeare 1974: 5.5.58–61)

Typically for Margaret, who is a dominating presence throughout this play, her use of *adynaton* ('my heart will burst and if I speak') does not last long and she insists instead on naming her enemies for what they are: 'Butchers and villains! Bloody cannibals!'. What is particularly effective about this example, though, is that it comes in a scene which, for all its bloody spectacle, is concerned in minute detail with who is allowed to speak at court. It opens with King Edward refusing to hear Oxford and Somerset speak, which is then immediately followed by his insistence that the young prince does speak out and give his reasons for bearing arms against the king. The prince then claims to be speaking with the voice of his father, whom he considers still to be the rightful king. He is called 'malapert' (5.5.32) and his mother Margaret a 'captive scold' (5.5.29), both of them condemned for speaking out of turn. Margaret's *adynaton* is more than a tired falling back onto clichéd tropes and figures. Rather, it forms part of a larger pattern in this scene where it is evident that some things are not allowed to be said, or heard, within the court.

That both of these examples from Shakespeare's plays are women speakers is not an accident. *Adynaton* operates on the border between private feeling and public action. In *Lear* and *Henry VI, Part Three*, it is the compromised position of women in the otherwise masculine world of the court that lends itself particularly to this form of speech. Although not immediately condemned for speaking out of place, Goneril's forthrightness is being compared to Cordelia's more reticent use of a similar verbal strategy – 'Unhappy that I am, I cannot heave / My heart into my mouth' (1.1.91–2) – and it is Goneril's monstrous femininity that becomes an increasing focus in the play. Margaret is explicitly condemned as a scold in her scene, revealing the gendered lines along which the ability to speak out is being policed. *Adynaton* can, then, be a figure which merely reinforces the standard equation of femininity with the private sphere and masculinity with the public. However, as these examples show, even when compromised by the disreputable intentions of Goneril, it may also be a figure that reveals the difficulties of negotiating a position within court in potentially prejudicial circumstances. This is what makes it a rhetorical figure which is peculiarly apposite to understanding *Lucrece*, not just in terms of specific instances where it is used, but also in relation to the structure of the narrative as a whole. The borderline between a private feminine sphere and a public masculine sphere is precisely what structures the Lucretia narrative as her private woes are translated into public revenge. In *Lucrece*, though, as in these instances of *adynaton*, it is the problems attendant on this translation that are brought to the fore.

Complicating further this gendering of the figure is an example of 'real-life' *adynaton* that may lead us closer to the motivations behind

Shakespeare's identification of his authorial voice with a feminine voice, structured through *adynaton*, in *Lucrece*. In the first appearance of Robert Devereux, the Earl of Essex, at Elizabeth's Accession Day Tilts, on 17 November 1586, he arrived dressed in black. He was advertising the fact that he was in mourning for Philip Sidney. His motto for this occasion was '*Per nulla figura dolori*' ('Nothing can represent [my] grief') (Hammer 1999: 55–6). Despite this protest that he is unable to express himself, this performance must have made his position in relation to the Sidney circle, and to the vexed question of their militaristic foreign policy, obvious to his audience of fellow courtiers. This use of *adynaton* in the public arena of the Accession Day celebrations obliquely asks questions about the extent to which public displays of grief for Sidney may have been considered acceptable by Elizabeth at all, in so far as such expressions may have been uncomfortable for a monarch opposed to the actions and policies of her dead, but popular, subject. As well as proclaiming his political and familial affiliations, Essex's appearance comments on the stifling of debate at Elizabeth's court, revealing the inadequacies of the court for expressing clear opposition even as it takes part in the game. Although in 1586 Essex's stepfather, the Earl of Leicester, had yet to die and create the power vacuum that helped inaugurate the factionalised politics of Elizabeth's later years, Essex was seeking to position himself within court and was searching for a means to speak out on the part of his extended family and their connections, especially given Leicester's marginalisation within court after his marriage to Lettice Knollys.

Lucrece is related to these issues in two ways. As well as concerning itself with the subject matter of how personal grief might be turned into political action, the poem also marks Shakespeare's own entry into a public world of political affiliation and patronage systems. The dedication to Henry Wriothesley, Earl of Southampton, and the 'Argument' of the poem, taken from Livy, seem to announce a contribution to the kind of displaced republicanism that has been identified in this period by literary critics such as David Norbrook and Andrew Hadfield, as well as historians such as Markku Peltonen.[4] Southampton was associated with Essex both before and after his disgrace at court and imprisoned by Elizabeth at the time of the Essex rebellion in 1601, and so would have been potentially receptive to this kind of political reading of the Lucretia narrative. However, the main body of the poem resists an overtly political reading, even as it is invited. The difficulties of the poem's uses of rhetoric – its deployment of *adynaton* and of other forms of communicative breakdown – offer an oblique commentary on a language that is seen as inadequate to the occasion. Rather than articulate deliberate resistance to the stultifying atmosphere of the 1590s – something that is at least potentially available to him with the story of Lucretia – Shakespeare develops a rhetoric that embodies rhetorical failure. This works both through a conspicuous avoidance of the political import of the narrative and through the various breakdowns in rhetoric that occur within the poem.

Adynaton in *Lucrece*

For a poem that is famously verbose, *Lucrece* actually centres on moments where verbal and written communications break down and where there are difficulties in finding the right form of words to match the occasion, or problems in interpreting the intentions of another person. Each turning point in the poem is marked by a failure in rhetoric. The first such moment comes when Lucrece's husband, Collatine, is accused by Tarquin of having a 'shallow tongue' when it comes to praising his wife.

> The niggard prodigal that prais'd her so,
> In that high task hath done her beauty wrong,
> Which far exceeds his barren skill to show.
> Therefore that praise which Collatine doth owe
>   Enchanted Tarquin answers with surmise,
>   In silent wonder of still-gazing eyes.
> (ll. 79–84)

Collatine fails fully to take possession of Lucrece with his description of her and allows Tarquin room to see in her what *he* wants. The oxymoron, 'niggard prodigal' (miserly wastrel) highlights the risk that Collatine has taken. In not fitting the words to the occasion, he has squandered those words he has used and, with them, Lucrece's reputation. Tarquin's answering silence creates, for Tarquin, the ability to interpret without himself being interpreted.

Lucrece's own lack of skill in interpretation leaves her vulnerable. On her first meeting Tarquin, her interpretation of a stranger's looks and behaviour is given a specifically textual gloss.

> But she that never cop'd with stranger eyes
> Could pick no meaning from their parling looks,
> Nor read the subtle shining secrecies
> Writ in the glassy margents of such books.

> She touch'd no unknown baits; nor fear'd no hooks,
> Nor could she moralize his wanton sight
> More than his eyes were open'd to the light.
>   (ll. 99–105)

And when Tarquin begins to consider the morality of his proposed rape of Lucrece, he imagines it in terms of a rhetorical exercise, but one that he cannot do. He imagines himself, as if he were a student of rhetoric, composing a courtroom defence.

> 'O, what excuse can my invention make
> When thou shalt charge me with so black a deed?
> Will not my tongue be mute, my frail joints shake?
> Mine eyes forgo their light, my false heart bleed?
> The guilt being great, the fear doth still exceed;
>   And extreme fear can neither fight nor fly,
>   But coward-like with trembling terror die.'
>   (ll. 225–31)

In Collatine's inadequate, but also inappropriate, description of his wife's beauty and virtue, in Lucrece's lack of skill in reading the book that is Tarquin, and in Tarquin's failure to justify his actions in the imagined public arena of a courtroom, Shakespeare shows us a public world that is in the process of collapse, and one whose participants do not share a language in which they can participate as equals. Lucrece, of course, is most in need of finding the appropriate words.

> Her pity-pleading eyes are sadly fixed
> In the remorseless wrinkles of his face;
> Her modest eloquence with sighs is mixed,
> Which to her oratory adds more grace.
> She puts the period often from his place,
>   And midst the sentence so her accent breaks,
>   That twice she doth begin ere once she speaks.
>   (ll. 561–7)

Lucrece's voice and her grammar both break down under the stress she is feeling as Tarquin himself breaches decorum in a much more serious manner, by making sexual advances on his hostess and crossing the carefully demarcated boundaries of the Roman household as well as those of male friendship.

However, when it comes to her speech pleading with Tarquin, Lucrece proves herself a remarkable rhetorician, appealing to logic, ethics and emotion. She is, of course, not listened to. In the situation that she finds herself in, Lucrece is unable to establish any *ethos*, a speaking position within a rhetorical situation from which one's words are listened to, believed and trusted. *Adynaton* itself, particularly in its close proximity to *litotes*, the figure of modesty, is potentially an attempt to establish *ethos*. What we witness in the ongoing story of Lucrece's failure to find the right words is, however, a struggle to gain that position from which she may be listened to and believed. Following the rape, there are some of the poem's most innovative moments in terms of the way that Shakespeare chooses to tell the story. The long section between the rape and the arrival of the male members of her family witnesses Lucrece's lengthy disputation with herself. This is Shakespeare's addition to the story, but it is almost as if this is a type of extended *adynaton*. The more that she speaks, the more impossible it becomes for her words to 'wield the matter'. It is after this that she is still unable to say what has happened when questioned by her maid and comes out with the clear use of *adynaton* referred to earlier.

> 'But, lady, if your maid may be so bold,
> She would request to know your heaviness.'
> 'O peace,' quoth Lucrece. 'if it should be told,
> The repetition cannot make it less;
> For more it is than I can well express,
>   And that deep torture may be call'd a hell,
>   When more is felt than one hath power to tell.'
>   (ll. 1282–8)

The long monologue, with the apostrophes to night, opportunity and time and even the famous identification of Tarquin with the treacherous Sinon on a tapestry of the fall of Troy have all been inadequate to what she wants to express. From this moment on in the poem, despite her extended rehearsal, Lucrece fails to communicate in a number of different ways. It is notable, for example, that as she dies, there is even some doubt as to whether she names Tarquin as her attacker or not.

> Here with a sigh as if her heart would break
> She throws forth Tarquin's name: 'He, he,' she says,
> But more than 'he' her poor tongue could not speak,
> Till after many accents and delays,
> Untimely breathings, sick and short assays,

She utters this: 'He, he, fair lords, 'tis he,
That guides this hand to give this wound to me.'

(ll. 1716–22)

The narrative first says that 'she throws forth Tarquin's name' and then we get Lucrece's repeated, almost pre-verbal utterances, 'He, he' and the narrative changes its mind – 'more than "he" her poor tongue could not speak'. Of course, she must have communicated the name or the subsequent story of revenge could not have occurred. Nevertheless, at the most politically important moment in the story, when she passes on the baton of revenge to her male relatives and her grievances into the public realm of politics, so initiating the move towards the Roman republic and the overthrow of the kings, Shakespeare offers us a moment of broken communication. And then she kills herself. Even at the moment when her personal woes are being translated into the public arena of political revenge, Shakespeare has his heroine seeming to fail in her language or, at least, goes out of his way to cast doubt on the status of her final words and what her male relatives may have heard and been able to respond to. Although the poem does move on, however briefly, to the political story of revenge and the foundation of the Roman republic, Lucrece's dying words seem to resist entry into this more public realm even as they attempt to do just that. If, as Lynn Enterline argues, Shakespeare's great success in this poem is to give the voiceless Lucretia from the *Fasti* a voice constructed from various speakers in the *Metamorphoses* (notably Hecuba and Philomela), he also reveals a profound scepticism about the reception of this voice. I will argue that this scepticism reveals itself most fully through the poem's other Ovidian source, the *Heroides* (Enterline 2000).

The moment when Lucrece tries, but initially fails, to write to her husband is, perhaps, the most suggestive of a long sequence of rhetorical breakdowns in the poem. Having been raped by Tarquin, her husband's friend and fellow soldier, she disputes with herself what the consequences of this event will be for her and her family. She calls for a pen in order to write a letter to her husband asking him to return home. She is initially confident that, given the urgency of the task ('The cause craves haste'), there will be no problem with getting the words down on paper ('and it will soon be writ').

'Go get me hither paper, ink, and pen,
Yet save that labor, for I have them here. –
What should I say? – One of my husband's men

Bid thou be ready, by and by, to bear
A letter to my lord, my love, my dear.
  Bid him with speed prepare to carry it,
  The cause craves haste, and it will soon be writ.'
Her maid is gone, and she prepares to write,
First hovering o'er the paper with her quill.
Conceit and grief an eager combat fight,
What wit sets down is blotted straight with will;
This is too curious-good, this blunt and ill:
  Much like a press of people at a door,
  Throng her inventions, which shall go before.
                              (ll. 1289–1302)

The terms within which Shakespeare asks his readers to make sense
of Lucrece's uncertainty when it comes to writing the letter are taken
directly from formal instruction in rhetoric. A governing concept
in classical and early modern rhetoric is *decorum*; rhetorical systems
demand that there should always be a correct form of words for any
occasion, measured according to the event and to the audience. It is
precisely the question of *decorum* that Lucrece struggles with when she
starts to write to her husband. In rhetorical terminology, the discovery
of the subject matter for a composition is called *inventio* ('inventions'
in the poem) and its arrangement is called *dispositio*. Lucrece is having
problems with the latter; she cannot arrange her material in any kind
of decorous order, 'which shall go before'. Whatever she writes does
not match the situation: 'This is too curious good, this blunt and ill.'
The phrase, 'curious good', is an oxymoron in this context. It relates
to sixteenth-century assumptions about the necessity of good writing
style being highly elaborate, in a Ciceronian style, and in this context
'curious' means sophisticated and highly decorative. However, like
the word 'subtle', its near synonym in early modern English, 'curious'
can also carry slightly negative moral overtones. Lucrece is either
writing too elaborately, and so not accurately representing the awful
nature of what has happened to her and the urgency of her current
situation, or her writing is too coarse and so, presumably, not suitable
for a Roman matron addressing her husband. If her writing were too
good, perhaps she would not be believed. Her very stylishness could
call into question the veracity of the content. If it were ignoble in
any way, then it might reveal something else about her nature. Again,
what Lucrece is attempting to establish is her *ethos*, a position from
which her word is to be trusted. Her struggles indicate an awareness
that this attempt is in danger of failing.

It is evident that Lucrece's writer's block is described using key ideas from formal rhetoric, but there is a specific branch of rhetoric to which this event refers: the art of letter-writing. Lucrece does eventually write the letter but remains unable to find the words to say what has happened to her. She asks her husband to return to Rome and again ends the short letter with an *adynaton*: 'My woes are tedious, though my words are brief' (l. 1309). This is then echoed in the narration: 'Here folds she up the tenure of her woe, / Her certain sorrow writ uncertainly' (ll. 1310–11). The whole letter, even when it is completed, is an extended exercise in *adynaton*: her words are uncertain and brief, inadequate to express the certainty and the interminable nature of her pain and sorrow. That Shakespeare focuses on letter-writing as a specific area of rhetoric in which Lucrece encounters difficulties is key to understanding the poem's relation to the politics of the 1590s, in that the letter, as a particular genre of writing, was one of the most vital ways in which the related dealings of patronage and government were conducted in early modern England. The importance of the letter was underlined by the popularity of letter-writing manuals throughout the period, one of the most influential of which was Erasmus' *De conscribiendis epistolis*. In this book, Erasmus outlines a programme of education through which tutors are encouraged to instruct their students in a style of letter-writing that promotes an easy equality between writer and recipient. Shakespeare, however, was writing in a culture that had not taken Erasmus' lessons completely to heart. As Lynne Magnusson has shown, in English letter-writing manuals, such as Angel Day's *The English Secretary*, this potentially radical idea of how the world of politics might be constituted through reciprocity and equality was reorientated to take account of the hierarchical relationships of patronage and client, master and servant that structured Tudor political culture (Magnusson 1999). English letters had to be a lot more circumspect in their expectations of response, performing elaborate verbal displays of self-abasement and flattery in order that any hierarchical relationship be sustained rather than threatened by the potentially risky event of the letter.

It is in this letter-writing context that Shakespeare turns to Ovid's epistolary fictions, the *Heroides*, when writing *Lucrece*. The *Heroides* also feature in Erasmus' *De conscribiendis epistolis*. By establishing Shakespeare's turn to Ovid at this stage of the poem, and by comparing his treatment of the *Heroides* to the negative and masculinist reception that those poems receive in Erasmus' humanist tract, it is possible to gain a further understanding both of *Lucrece*'s commentary on the political atmosphere of the 1590s and of the gendered nature of that critical intervention.

Lucrece **and Ovid's** *Heroides*

As Lucrece initially starts to write her letter, Shakespeare's description follows the actions of many of the women writing letters in the *Heroides*. As Lucrece writes and the 'wit' of her letter is blotted by her 'will', this echoes the more material blots that are mentioned in Ovid's poems at moments that allude directly to the status of his poems as epistolary fiction. In the third letter of the series, the slave girl Briseis writes to Achilles asking why he has not called for her to be returned to him from Agamemnon who has abducted her. The letter elaborates on a relatively short but important interlude from the *Iliad*, significant in that it is at the heart of Achilles' anger at the start of the poem. In Ovid's version we witness events from the point of view of a character who has hitherto only been a bit-player in the military epic, on the margins of her own story. Ovid's Briseis opens her 'letter' as follows.

> *Quam legis, a rapta Briseide littera venit,*
> *vix bene barbarica Graeca notata manu.*
> *quascumque adspicies, lacrimae fecer lituras;*
> *sed tamen et lacrimae pondera vocis habent.*
> (From stolen Briseis is the writing you read, scarce charactered
> in Greek by her barbarian hand. Whatever blots you shall see,
> her tears have made; but tears, too, have none the less the weight
> of words.)

(Ovid 1977: 32–3)

The opening lines of this poem can be understood as a kind of material embodiment of *adynaton*. They articulate similar ideas around expressing the inexpressible, but in writing rather than speech. Briseis writes that she cannot write, but the material signs of her inability to write, her tears, are just as, if not more, expressive ('weighty') than her words. The letter from later in the series which Canace writes to her brother and lover, Machareus, has a similar opening. This letter is a suicide note to her brother. She is being forced into killing herself by their domineering and violent father Aeolus who, having found out that she has had a child with her brother, has killed the baby and sent her a knife with which, she understands, she is to kill herself.

Siqua tamen caecis errabunt scripta lituris,
  oblitus a domnae caede libellus erit.
dextra tenet calamum, strictum tenet altera ferrum,
  et iacet in gremio charta solute meo.
haec est Aeolidos fratri scrbentis imago;
  sic videor duro posse placere patri.
(If aught of what I write is yet blotted deep and escapes your eye,
'twill be because the little roll has been stained by its mistress'
blood. My right hand holds the pen, a drawn blade the other
holds, and the paper lies unrolled in my lap. This is the picture
of Aeolus' daughter writing to her brother; in this guise, it seems,
I may please my hard-hearted sire.)

(Ovid 1977: 132–3)

Here it is blood rather than tears that blurs the lines of Canace's
letter. But again, these splashes of blood, potentially obliterating the
words that she writes are just as, if not more, expressive than the letter
itself.

The blurred lines of Lucrece's letter are not as material as those
in the Ovid poems – 'What wit sets down is blotted straight with will'
(l. 1299). If the moments taken from the *Heroides* allude directly
to the act of letter-writing by referring to the paper and the ink
with which the epistolary poems have supposedly been produced,
Lucrece's letter-writing is still more self-conscious than this.[5] It is not
her tears, nor the blood from the knife with which she is planning to
kill herself that are blotting her writing, but a kind of writer's block.
Shakespeare uses this blotting motif from Ovid's *Heroides* to indicate
a breakdown in the transparent communication in which the letter is
traditionally supposed to engage.

This effect, in *Lucrece*, is aided further by the odd position that these
particular epistolary poems occupied within the literature of letter-
writing proper. In *De conscribiendis epistolis*, Erasmus mentions the
Heroides in his attempt to define what the genre – the letter – might,
or might not, consist of.

> Some critics may exclude certain letters from the general category,
> for example, letters composed for practice or to show off one's
> virtuosity, like those of Phalaris, attributed by scholars to Luciana,
> and the amatory letters of Philostratus, which are indeed very
> elegant (if only they were as chaste!); to these may be added
> the *Heroides* of Ovid, and others of that sort, – I should have no
> objection to calling them short declamations as some prefer.

(Erasmus 1985: 20)

The *Heroides*, alongside other fictional epistles, do not fit easily into the kind of writing that Erasmus wants to discuss. He is, I think, right to be circumspect, especially given his understanding of the definition of the letter as it appears shortly after in the book.

Even if the name 'letter' be restricted to interchanges between friends on private matters, it would still not be possible to settle on any fixed form. Nevertheless, if there is something that can be said to be characteristic of this genre, I think that I cannot define it more concisely than by saying that the wording of a letter should resemble a conversation between friends. For a letter, as the comic poet Turpilius skilfully put it, is a mutual conversation between absent friends, which should be neither unpolished, rough, or artificial, nor confined to a single topic, nor tediously long. Thus the epistolary form favours simplicity, frankness, humour and wit.

(Erasmus 1985: 20)[6]

The reason why Erasmus excludes the *Heroides* is not their status as fiction, as might be expected, but that they might be more properly understood as 'declamations'. In calling them 'declamations', Erasmus is differentiating between letter-writing proper, which moves out of the classroom, and letter-writing as nothing more than a schoolroom exercise. He sees Ovid's poems as 'declamations', presumably inasmuch as they seem deliberately to take sides in an imagined debate in the classroom tradition of *in utramque partem* (taking both sides).[7] What Erasmus misses, in this reading of the poems, is the deliberate way in which Ovid places the experience of these women at the centre of narratives to which they are otherwise marginal. They do not participate in a debate of equals, *in utramque partem*, in that the women who write the letters are not responded to and so cannot really be 'declamations' in the sense that Erasmus intends. This elision, on Erasmus' part, is further compounded in *De conscribiendis epistolis* by the rewritings of the *Heroides* and of the Lucretia story which he encourages his schoolboys to engage in. When Erasmus comes to the *Heroides* slightly further on in the letter-writing manual, it is in the context of searching for suitable topics that tutors might give their students to write letters on.

One should seek them out in the stories of the poets or the historians, [. . .] – for instance, a suitor seeking a girl in marriage with cajoling letters, or Helen restraining Paris from an illicit love. Penelope's letter to Ulysses is perfectly chaste, as is that of

Acontius to Cydippe. Similarly one may compose a letter from a wife to her husband who is tarrying abroad, telling him to hasten home; or a letter from the aged and eloquent Nestor urging Achilles to bear nobly Agamemnon's seizure of Briseis, showing that even a wicked king must be obeyed, that the common good must take precedence over private grief, and finally that it is utterly unbecoming of Achilles' high birth, noble spirit, and brilliant career that he should forget his valour for the love of a foreign slave girl. This topic gives a splendid opportunity to attack disreputable pleasure, and also to dwell on the immortal glory to be won by exceptional heroism.

(Erasmus 1985: 24)

Whilst he approves of the letters of Penelope and Acontius, one written by the chaste wife of Ulysses and also of one of the later epistles, written by a man, demanding that Cydippe keep an oath to marry him that she had been tricked into, other letters from the *Heroides* he sees as needing to be rewritten from an alternative perspective, to be given proper responses that refuse to allow Ovid the radical ironies of a letter that has no real recipient. His pupils are not, then, to imitate Briseis complaining about being abandoned, but rather to write to Achilles in the person of Nestor, advising him to abandon Briseis and, presumably, to ignore her letter asking him to call for her. Erasmus and, within the fictional letter, Nestor, understand this as calling Achilles back to his properly Greek duty; Briseis' foreignness and her status as a slave and a woman should be superseded by the demands of the Greek king, Agamemnon. Whilst this is being advertised as an exercise in rhetorical training in which students may be encouraged to state both sides of an argument, it should be considered alongside the example from further on in his list of historical and literary topics for use in the schoolroom practice of letter-writing: 'a letter dissuading the violated Lucretia from taking her life'. In Shakespeare's poem, of course, it is Brutus who most forcefully makes this particular point at the end of the poem. Erasmus, under the cover of a rhetorical training in deliberately taking sides, ignores the implications of the particular positions that he does adopt. When looked at more closely, a pattern is revealed in which women read men's letters but not the other way round. In the claustrophobic political atmosphere of the 1590s, the *Heroides*, which depict women in fictional acts of written supplication, may seem more helpful than Erasmus would have his students believe, in that acknowledging the possibility of not getting a response may be a key strategy in the writing of letters to a superior. They may also be available as a critique of this particular form of political culture. Time and again, Ovid's women write without response, and the familiar stories that they are placed within starkly reveal the ill effects of this one-sided form of correspondence.

As Lucrece sets to writing her letter, she is unable to judge the terms of the conversation into which she might be entering and thus reveals herself as uncertain of the response she will be met with: she is either too 'unpolished or rough' or too 'artificial', not simple and certainly not frank enough to conform to the letter-writing model set up in Erasmian humanism. But the *Heroides* also could never match up to the model of communication taking place in a way that is transparent, and between two equal parties, as was demanded in the formula of a 'mutual conversation'. They, for the most part, rely on an awareness of their lack of effect for their irony. We know that the letters of the *Heroides* are never listened to, or even that the person to whom the letter writer addresses herself is already dead, or that the letter is actually a suicide note and that the writer will be dead before it is read. Whilst this is true of the first sixteen poems written by women, it is not true of the last six written by men. Their replies are, importantly, included. Men expect and receive a response in the fictional letter-writing community of the *Heroides*. Women do not.

In making particular use of the *Heroides* as one of his sources for *Lucrece*, Shakespeare is making a very different point about their position in rhetorical culture than that which can be inferred from their presence in Erasmus' book. Shakespeare seems more attuned to the potential that these poems offer for an ironic critique of the possibilities for transparent and equitable communication. If the letter as 'mutual conversation' is an ideal, then it is not one that is available either to Lucrece or her antecedents in the *Heroides*. Similarly, clear communication is not available to Shakespeare in the 1590s as he presents his retelling of the Lucretia narrative, not as a celebration of the virtues of the ensuing republic, but as an ironic foreshadowing of that republic's failure.

The 'everlasting' ends of *Lucrece*

In the penultimate stanza of the poem, Lucrece's surviving relatives make a vow to avenge her rape and suicide. The final stanza then continues as follows:

> When they had sworn to this advised doom,
> They did conclude to bear dead Lucrece thence,

> To show her bleeding body thorough Rome,
> And so to publish Tarquin's foul offense;
> Which being done with speedy diligence,
>   The Romans plausibly did give consent
>   To Tarquin's everlasting banishment.
>   (ll. 1849–55)

Between the fourth and fifth lines of this stanza something monumental takes place, something 'everlasting' even – the change of an entire political regime and the birth of the Roman republic. This is 'speedy diligence' indeed. The chronologies of this final stanza, though, bear further examination. The first four lines of the stanza, despite being in the past tense, actually announce events to happen in the future – you might suppose beyond the end of the poem. Once they have sworn their vengeance, Lucrece's male relatives discuss further how to act, deciding to carry Lucrece's dead body through the streets of Rome. By the next line, this has already been done ('Which being done') and the remaining two lines of the poem give a brief narration of the positive reaction of the Roman people. What might be played centre stage in Shakespeare's Roman plays – a public interaction between conflicted political leaders and the gathered populace – here slips silently by in the spaces between a few lines. And then the reader is told that they are living in the time of the poem even as they read it – the banishment of the Roman kings, the Tarquins, is, after all, 'everlasting'. And yet, is that reader also supposed to be aware of the irony that the Roman republic was not 'everlasting' and that even the Roman Empire which succeeded it now lay in ruins? The chronologies of this final stanza are highly complex in the way that they implicate the reader in the promise of an everlasting republic that has already failed to last forever.

There is a sense in which the poem as a whole is oriented towards future events, but it is a future that has already been compromised. The story of rape, suicide and revenge that inaugurates the Roman republic was well known to Shakespeare's readers and yet the promised ending – promised not only in the prior reading of those readers in Ovid and Livy, but in this poem's prefatory argument taken from those Roman sources – is endlessly deferred by the poem itself. The deliberate frustration of this deferral, which I have identified as a type of structural *adynaton*, allows time and space for Shakespeare's great achievement in *Lucrece*: to produce a voice for the mute body of Lucretia, whose usual role in her own story is precisely to remain mute, to kill herself and to be borne through the streets, her corpse the site on which is played out the major historical and political event of the birth of the republic. And yet that achievement takes place in a poem which consistently illustrates voices not being heard or responded to. In previous versions of the Lucretia myth, she had been marginal to her own story. Ovid-like, Shakespeare places her back at centre stage and we witness events from her perspective. But, as in the *Heroides*, this is a perspective that proves difficult to communicate. Alongside this irony – that Ovid's female letter writers are never read – Shakespeare also gives us an irony of a political future which is endless, but which we know has already ended: the promise of a republic that can never be achieved. That Shakespeare has elected to produce for himself an authorial voice which is structured through the figure of *adynaton*, a mode of speech which in his work acquires a specifically feminine inflection, is a product of the difficulties that those interested in the potential of republican narratives faced in the claustrophobic 1590s. A particular strength of Shakespeare's poem is in refusing merely to adopt a masculinist stance against the ageing queen, but instead to excavate the possibilities for a feminine speech even within the structures of communicative impossibility that *adynaton* represents.

Notes

1 For a collection of essays relating to a wide range of developments in the 1590s see Guy (1995a).
2 For a detailed discussion of an earlier poet's resistance to the effeminising tyrannies of monarchy, see Worden (1996). David Norbrook has pointed out similar ideas in *The Faerie Queene*, noting a sense that Britomart's 'womanly qualities may become dangerous without strong male guidance' (Norbrook 2002: 123) and also that Fulke Greville's 'critical scrutiny of the cult of the female ruler was sharpened by a streak of misogyny' (2002: 149).
3 Alastair Fox (1995) has produced a detailed analysis of the distinct decline in expectations for literary patronage throughout Elizabeth's reign and during the 1590s particularly, deducing that by the 1590s, 'very few [writers] were getting the rewards from patronage that they thought they deserved, and once would have had a right to expect' (1995: 240).
4 All these writers (Peltonen 1995, Hadfield 1998, Norbrook 1999) identify a form of classically inspired republicanism that predates J. G. A. Pocock's original identification of the 1640s as the proper date of arrival in England for classical republicanism (Pocock 1975).
5 This apparent self-consciousness about the processes of writing is also supported by an apparent reference to Philip Sidney in the uses of the words 'wit' and 'will'. It echoes the famous passage from *A Defence of Poesy*, 'our erected wit maketh us know what perfection is, and yet our infected will keepeth us from reaching unto it' (Sidney 1989: 217). Sidney's understanding of the word 'will' in the *Defence* seems to be something like

our natural sinfulness and that must be at least part of what is meant in *Lucrece*. She also feels that her 'will' is 'infected' by the rape.

6 Turpilius was a Roman comic writer, active in the second century BC.

7 See Rhodes (2004), especially Chapter 3: 'Both Sides Now', for a discussion of how Shakespeare's drama emerges out of the grammar school exercise of declamation, the process of arguing opposing points of view.

6 'Presbyterian sibyl'

Truth-telling and gender in Andrew Marvell's *The Third Advice to a Painter*

Martin Dzelzainis

One of Andrew Marvell's most distinctive practices as a poet is that of speaking through the voice of someone who is evidently not himself. These voices can be more abstract than human, as in 'A Dialogue between the Soul and Body' where the speakers articulate the views of the two halves of a divided self. At other times the speakers, although human, are still pastoral types, such as the Mower who only acquires a name (the entirely conventional 'Damon') in one of the four mower poems. Frequently, however, Marvell appropriates the voices of actual persons, especially writers. In *Tom May's Death*, he conjures up the ghost of the poet and dramatist Ben Jonson – one of the royalists' favourite authors – to deliver a denunciation of the recently deceased republican historian and translator of Lucan, Thomas May. And in *The Loyal Scot* we hear the ghost of another royalist, the satirist John Cleveland, retracting the anti-Scottish views formerly expressed in his poem *The Rebel Scot*.

This leaves an even more distinctive group: his female speakers. Admittedly, Marvell was far from original in simulating a woman's voice since there were classical precedents for this kind of verbal cross-dressing by a male poet. Ovid, for example, impersonated some of the most famous women of antiquity in his *Heroides*. Early-modern practitioners of transvestite ventriloquism included Shakespeare and John Donne as well as contemporaries such as the Earl of Rochester (see Harvey 1992 and Greer 2000: 45–53). The most famous such Marvellian figure is, of course, the nymph complaining for the death of her fawn, whose naivety is in sharp contrast to the deviousness of the 'subtle' nun in *Upon Appleton House*, who entices the heiress Isabel Thwaites into entering the nunnery (Marvell 2003a: 219, l. 94; see Goldberg 1986: 14–32). More loquacious than either, if much less well known, is Anne, Duchess of Albemarle (1619–70), the 'Presbyterian sibyl' of my title, who delivers a speech of no fewer than 234 lines in *The Third Advice to a Painter*, an opposition satire which appeared at the height of the second Anglo-Dutch war of 1665 to 1667. Reputedly opinionated and coarse in life, the Duchess exhibits none of the pathos of the nymph or the finesse of the nun and poses an interpretative challenge of an entirely different kind. Not only is the sheer length of her utterance suggestive of the garrulousness routinely attributed to women in the early modern period, but she herself is enigmatically figured as 'Half witch, half prophet' (Marvell 2003a: 348, l. 199).[1] Her status as a truth-teller is, in consequence, in doubt and indeed raises in an acute form the problem of the relationship between truth and female speech. My aim in this essay is, accordingly, to try to explain why, at a time when rhetoric was often 'depicted as an enticing, wanton woman – in short a harlot or prostitute', Marvell should have handed over the body of his poem to a female speaker and to this female speaker in particular (Rebhorn 1995: 140).[2]

   The Second Advice to a Painter and *The Third Advice to a Painter* began to circulate in manuscript in April and October 1666. What makes these poems – now widely agreed to be the work of Marvell – so important is that they effectively inaugurated the tradition of state satire (see Love 1998: 238–42).[3] For it is a striking fact that, while several radical prose pamphlets appeared in the early years of the Restoration, there were apparently very few verse satires criticising the Cavalier regime. What triggered a change in this situation was the appearance in print of two panegyrics by Edmund Waller on the Duke of York, the King's brother and Lord High Admiral. Modelled on a translation of an Italian poem by Giovanni Francesco Busenello in which a poet instructs a painter commemorating a Venetian triumph at sea over the Turks, Waller's *Instructions to a Painter for the Drawing of a Picture of the State and Posture of the English Forces at Sea, under the Command of his Royal Highness in the Conclusion of the Year 1664* was registered in March 1665. This sixty-line broadside dealt only with the skirmishes with the Dutch that took place in 1664 prior to the declaration of war and was later expanded into a 336-line celebration of the Duke's victory at the Battle of Lowestoft in June 1665 – the high point of the war, as it turned out, for the English. Waller's *Instructions to a Painter for the Drawing of the Posture & Progress of His Maties Forces at Sea, under the Command of His Highness Royal. Together with the Battel & Victory Obtained over the Dutch, June 3 1665* was licensed on 1 March 1666. Within weeks, Marvell's manuscript reply, *The Second Advice*, viciously parodying Waller's poem and sharply questioning the victory at Lowestoft, was in circulation. And when the Four Days'

Battle of June 1666 – with the Navy now under the joint command of George Monck, Duke of Albemarle and Prince Rupert – was likewise trumpeted as a victory by the government, Marvell at once set about exposing it as all but a disaster in *The Third Advice.*

Marvell's intention in writing *The Third Advice* was to nail a government lie. Assuming prophetic powers (in a passage written, of course, after the events it predicts), the poet eagerly looks forward to the punishment in store for the powers that be.

> Now joyful fires, and the exalted bell,
> And court-gazettes our empty triumph tell.
> Alas: the time draws near when, overturned
> The lying bells shall through the tongue be burned;
> Paper shall want to print that lie of state,
> And our false fires true fires shall expiate.
>   (Marvell 2003a: 347, ll. 163–8)

The Great Fire of London (September 1666), he 'foretells', will erase the triumph falsely proclaimed by bells, bonfires and newspapers earlier in the year. But besides exposing a lie, Marvell was also undertaking to tell the King the truth when those who might be expected to do so – his ministers and courtiers – had failed. As lines 439–40 in the envoy to the King put it, 'What servants will conceal, and couns'llors spare / To tell, the painter and the poet dare' (Marvell 2003a: 353). However, the problem for the poet, as for many other would-be truth-tellers in the early modern period, is that telling the truth, which ought to be straightforward, turns out to be fraught with difficulties. At the heart of this essentially rhetorical problem is *parrhesia*, that is, the practice, as distinct from the right, of free speech. So when, for example, Shakespeare's Henry V tells the French ambassadors to speak 'with frank and with uncurbed plainness' (Shakespeare 1974: 1.2.244), or when Milton assures Parliament and the Westminster Assembly in the preface to the 1644 edition of *The Doctrine and Discipline of Divorce* that he is speaking with 'a fearlesse and communicative candor', they are both referring to *parrhesia* – the act of speaking freely (Milton 1953–82: II, 226).

For an illuminating analysis of *parrhesia*, we can turn to Michel Foucault's *Fearless Speech*, the recently-published transcript of a series of six lectures he gave at Berkeley, California in 1983 devoted to the topic. *Parrhesia*, he points out, is merely one of several ancient Greek terms relating to freedom of speech, first appearing in Euripides' *Hippolytus* and *Ion*, where it refers to a salient feature of Athenian democracy:

the right of the citizen to speak freely in the *ekklesia* (or assembly). However, we ought to distinguish, as Foucault does, between an equal freedom to speak (*isegoria*), which does not necessarily imply saying whatever you want, and speaking your mind freely (*parrhesia*), which does. As Foucault observes, the 'one who uses *parrhesia*, the *parrhesiastes*, is someone who says everything he has in mind: he does not hide anything, but opens his heart and mind completely to other people through his discourse' (Foucault 2001: 12, and 22, 72–4; see also Stone 1988: 15–24 and Momigliano 1973: II, 260). The *parrhesiastes* believes 'he' is in possession of the truth, which 'he' must tell as fully and clearly as possible – indeed, 'he' cannot but speak the truth. This commitment to the unvarnished truth obviously places the parrhesiast in opposition to the professional rhetorician. But if we ask what distinguishes the parrhesiast from someone like, say, a teacher, who is professionally committed to telling the truth, the answer is the element of personal danger – and hence courage – involved. For a philosopher to tell a tyrant he is unjust is clearly not the same as for a teacher to correct a student. This is because *parrhesia*, as Foucault insists, 'is a form of criticism' spoken by one who

> is in a position of inferiority with respect to the interlocutor. The *parrhesiastes* is always less powerful than the one to whom he speaks. The *parrhesia* comes from 'below,' as it were, and is directed towards 'above'. This is why an ancient Greek would not say that a teacher or father who criticizes a child uses *parrhesia*. But when a philosopher criticizes a tyrant, when a citizen criticizes the majority, when a pupil criticizes his teacher, then such speakers may be using *parrhesia*.
>
> (Foucault 2001: 17–18)

Parrhesia is, in short, telling the truth to power.

Although the rhetoric of opposition in the advice-to-a-painter poems would appear to be amenable to analysis in just these terms, there is an obvious complication in that, as we have already seen, *parrhesia* is (or ought to be) inherently anti-rhetorical. The opposition between *parrhesia* and rhetoric is axiomatic because speaking boldly or plainly, or voicing the naked truth, just *is* to speak without resorting to rhetorical devices and ornamentation. In so far as *parrhesia* can be incorporated within the field of rhetoric at all, according to Foucault, it must be as a kind of 'natural exclamation', a rhetorical figure without figure, the 'zero degree of those rhetorical figures which intensify the emotions of the audience'. Nevertheless, even Foucault implies that *parrhesia* is susceptible to some degree of formalisation when he sets out the ground rules for what he calls the 'parrhesiastic game' or the 'parrhesiastic contract'. The parties to the contract are, respectively, 'the one who has power but lacks the truth' and 'the one who has the truth but lacks power' (for example, a king and a messenger or herald) in which the former undertakes not to punish the latter for telling the truth (Foucault 2001: 21, 32).

Scenes in which the terms and conditions of the parrhesiastic contract are negotiated were a staple feature of early modern drama. But in staging these often formulaic exchanges, the dramatists were merely following in the footsteps of the Roman rhetoricians and their followers, who had assimilated *parrhesia* (or, in Latin, *licentia*) to their various schemes of figures.[4] According to Henry Peacham, in the second edition of *The Garden of Eloquence*, *parrhesia* is a figure that

> serueth to insinuate, admonish, and reprehend, and may fitly be called the Herald or Ambassador of speech, which is the onely forme that boldly deliuereth to great dignities and most high degrees of man, the message of iustice and equitie, sparing neither magistrates that peruert lawes, nor Princes that do abuse their kingdoms.
>
> (Peacham 1593: R1v–2r)

Here Peacham registers in full the importance of speaking truth to power. Initially, however, he had struck a much more cautious note when stressing the way in which the figure ought ordinarily to be used:

> Parrhesia, is a forme of speech by which the Orator speaking before those whom he feareth, or ought to reuerence, & hauing somewhat to say that may either touch themselues, or those whom they fauour, preuenteth the displeasure and offence that might be taken, as by crauing pardon afore hand, and by shewing the necessitie of free speech in that behalfe, or by some other like forme of humble submission and modest insinuation.
>
> (Peacham 1593: R1r)

Parrhesia now unexpectedly acquires ambivalence as a figure, slipping from the act of speaking out itself to an apology for speaking out.

Even more surprisingly, as David Colclough has pointed out in a brilliant essay, the figure was from the start paradoxically associated with a capacity for dissimulation. The pseudo-Ciceronian rhetorical manual *Ad herennium*, for example, moves smoothly from discussing frankness to discussing a 'frankness effect':

> There is also a certain kind of frankness in speaking which is achieved by a craftier device, when we remonstrate with the hearers as they wish us to remonstrate with them, or when we say 'we fear how the audience may take' something which we know they all will hear with acceptance, 'yet the truth moves us to say it none the less'.
>
> (*Rhetorica Ad Herennium*, 4.37.49; quoted in Colclough 1999: 85)

So the spectrum of possibilities is being stretched further still, from telling the truth and nothing but the truth, to apologising for telling it, to telling only the 'truth' that your interlocutors wish to hear while promoting the charade that it is not to their taste.

Among early modern writers, it was again Shakespeare who grasped most fully the implications of the problematisation of *parrhesia* in plays such as *Coriolanus, Timon of Athens* and *King Lear* (see Graham 1994). Although *King Lear* ends with Edgar's declaration that we should 'Speak what we feel, not what we ought to say' (Shakespeare 1974: 5.3.325), for much of the play this has been shown to be next to impossible without dire consequences for the speaker, not least of course in the case of Cordelia (see Zitner 1975). Kent may say "tis my occupation to be plain' (2.2.92), but Cornwall at once places a sinister construction upon his claim to be a parrhesiast:

> This is some fellow
> Who, having been prais'd for bluntness, doth affect
> A saucy roughness, and constrains the garb
> Quite from his nature. He cannot flatter, he,
> An honest mind and plain, he must speak truth!
> And they will take['t], so; if not, he's plain.
> These kind of knaves I know, which in this plainness
> Harbor more craft and more corrupter ends
> Than twenty silly-ducking observants
> That stretch their duties nicely.
> (Shakespeare 1974: 2.2.95–104)

In fact, Cornwall's redescription stands *parrhesia* on its head: truth-telling becomes the most refined form of duplicity (and Kent is, after all, disguised in the 'garb' of Caius at the time). Even – or perhaps especially – Cordelia can become in some accounts an example of 'how discourses that affect a plain and candid opposition to rhetoric[al] ornament are in themselves a subtle and deceitful form of rhetoric'. And given that, as Valesio argues, anti-rhetoric has a rhetoric all of its own, the 'cleansing of speech from all hypocrisy' must remain a utopian fantasy (Valesio 1980: 46, 57). There can be little doubt that Marvell too was fully aware of the problematics of truth-telling. On the one hand, the poet excoriates the counsellors who have failed to live up to the terms of their parrhesiastic contract by not telling the King the truth even though they would be protected from the consequences of doing so. On the other hand, he himself finds it difficult to tell the truth in the envoy without resorting to the antithesis of *parrhesia*, flattery, to sugar the pill.

> To the King
> Great Prince, and so much greater as more wise,
> Sweet as our life, and dearer than our eyes:
> What servants will conceal, and couns'llors spare
> To tell, the painter and the poet dare;
> And the assistance of an heav'nly muse
> And pencil represents the crimes abstruse.
> Here needs no sword, no fleet, no foreign foe;
> Only let vice be damned, and justice flow.
> Shake but like Jove thy locks divine, and frown;
> Thy sceptre will suffice to guard thy crown.
> Hark to Cassandra's song, ere Fate destroy,
> By thy own navy's wooden horse, thy Troy.
> Us our Apollo, from the tumult's wave,
> And gentle gales, though but in oars, will save.
>   So Philomel her sad embroid'ry strung,
> And vocal silks with her needle's tongue.
> (The picture dumb, in colours loud, revealed
> The tragedies of court so long concealed.)
> But, when restored to voice, increased with wings,
> To woods and groves, what once she painted, sings.
>   (Marvell 2003a: 353–4, ll. 437–56)

The statement of parrhesiastic intent about daring to tell the truth is embedded in fulsome praise of the 'Great Prince' who can dispense with armed force and, Jove-like, needs only shake his 'locks divine, and frown' to safeguard his throne. The combination of defiant and obsequious tones makes the envoy exceptionally hard to decipher, but the difficulty does not arise so much from any wavering of purpose on the poet's part as from the prior problematisation of the conditions of truth-telling. It may therefore be significant that the envoy ostentatiously introduces two thwarted female parrhesiasts: Cassandra, whose prophecies were dismissed as the ravings of a madwoman, and Philomela, whose tongue was cut out to prevent her from revealing vocally the facts of her rape. They are there to serve as a reminder of how easily the ideal of free and transparent utterance can be compromised, to hint at the existence of other 'tragedies of court, so long concealed' and, perhaps, to extenuate the poet's own relative lack of outspokenness. As Philomela's successful resort to a visual medium suggests, however, the implication is also that the truth will out one way or another.

We are now in a position to address the question which is central to our understanding of *The Third Advice*; why does Marvell hand over half the poem to be ventriloquised by a female speaker, the very definitely non-mythological Duchess of Albemarle? Her function in the poem has been a matter of controversy from the very beginning. Late in July 1667, William Burden testified that the radical printer Francis Smith

> came to this Examinants house, & askt him, if He would let John-son (a Printer living in the Examinants house) Print 2 or 3 sheets of Verses, wch He called <u>The Second & Third Advice to a Painter;</u> for wch He should be well payd. This Examinant then ask't him what kind of Verses they were? & $^{\wedge upon}$ what Subject? If they did not reflect upon y^e State? Smith's Answer was, <u>Yes,</u> They did reflect upon my Lord Chancellor, The Dutchess of <u>Albemarle, & Others of y^e Court.</u> & if He would undertake y^e Thing; if He would come to his house, He should hear y^e worst on't.[5]
>
> (National Archives, SP 29/211/13 (*Calendar of State Papers Domestic* 1667, 330))

As far as Smith was concerned, the representation of the Duchess was such that she was included in rather than somehow exempt from the satirical thrust of the poem. In some ways, this is still the view of modern critics such as John M. Wallace: the Duchess, he says, 'is presented as so lewd and ignorant a woman that her hostile narrative about the government might appear to be discredited before it began' (Wallace 1968: 154). That is to say, while she may voice a critique of the government, her actual function is to undermine that critique, although it is hard to see why Marvell should engage in such a self-defeating exercise. While Marvell's most recent editor, Nigel Smith, sees her as offering cogent criticism of the regime, he argues that the joke is nevertheless 'complicated and works at the expense of Clarendon and the Presbyterians, of whom the Duchess was one'. (The path to the Restoration had been smoothed by a rapprochement between Clarendon and royalist-leaning Presbyterians, chief among them General George Monck.) In particular, since the Duchess was known for her meanness and financial improprieties, 'her calls for integrity in the administration of the navy would have seemed not merely hypocritical, but also incredible' (Marvell 2003a: 343). But even this more nuanced account still leaves us with the interpretative problem of how to respond to the genuinely contradictory way in which the figure of the Duchess is constructed, appropriately enough for a woman who began her life as a seamstress and ended it as a member of the aristocracy.

These contradictions are laid out in the crucial passage introducing the Duchess, and it rapidly becomes clear that she is at least as complex a figure as the nymph or the nun. Immediately after denouncing the 'lie of state' (l. 167) and, by implication, promising the truth, the poet's last instruction to the painter is to bring the Duchess into being; the rest can be left to her – making visible the mechanics of ventriloquisation:

> Seest not the monkey Duchess, all undressed?
> Paint thou but her, and she will paint the rest.
>   The sad tale found her in her outer room,
> Nailing up hangings not of Persian loom,
> Liker chaste Penelope that ne'er did roam,
> But made all fine against her George come home.
> Upon a ladder, in her coat much shorter,
> She stood with groom and porter for supporter,
> And careless what they saw or what they thought,
> With Hony pensy honestly she wrought.
> For in the gen'ral's britch, none could (she knows)
> Carry away the piece with eyes or nose.
> One tenter drove, to lose no time nor place,
> At once the ladder they remove and Grace.
> While thus they her translate from north to east,
> In posture just of a four-footed beast,
> She heard the news; but altered yet no more
> Than what was behind she turned before;

> Nor would come down; but with an hankercher,
> Which pocket foul did to her neck prefer,
> She dried no tears, for she was too viraginous:
> But only snuffling her trunk cartilaginous
> From scaling ladder she began a story,
> Worthy to be had in me(mento) mori.
> Arraigning past and present and futuri;
> With a prophetic (if not spirit) fury.
> Her hair began to creep, her belly sound,
> Her eyes to startle, and her udder bound.
> Half witch, half prophet, thus she-Albermarle,
> Like Presbyterian sibyl, out did snarl.
> 'Traitors[. . .]
>
>   (Marvell 2003a: 348, ll. 171–201)

From the start, the Duchess is figured in animalistic terms: she is a 'monkey' but also a 'four-footed beast' with an elephantine 'trunk cartilaginous', a ruminant with an 'udder' but also a wolf (as implied in the phrase 'she-Albermarle'). She is a grotesque composite beast or, perhaps more to the point, simply non-human and thus automatically excluded from the all-too-human corruption of the court. And this exclusion means that she herself cannot be implicated in what she criticises. At the same time, although she is 'undressed', she paradoxically becomes a figure of marital chastity, as signalled by the allusion to the faithful Penelope, the weaver to whom the Duchess is further connected by her needlework and the hangings. But what of the lewdness noted by Wallace? After all, she does expose herself fully to view: borne on the ladder by the groom and porter, her 'posture' on all fours – 'posture' itself being a term replete with pornographic resonance in the later seventeenth century – is such that they can hardly avoid looking up her short coat. However, this is strictly their problem (and ours), not hers, as the allusion to the motto of the Order of the Garter, of which her husband was a member, makes clear: *Honi soit qui mal y pense* ('evil be to him who evil thinks of this'). Her chastity – the 'She-Gen'rals britch' – remains invulnerable to the probing of 'eyes or nose' (l. 182).[6] The tone of these and similar lines is nonetheless undeniably bawdy. Thus line 188, 'what was behind she turn'd before', is ambivalent in an authentically Marvellian fashion: after the Duchess has been rotated through 180 degrees, with which end of her are we being confronted? Is she literally preposterous? The underlying point, however, is serious. For, as Marvell was well aware, the truth goes naked.[7]

The Duchess is of course also figured as a sibyl, joining the plethora of classical sibyls such as the Cumaean, Erythraean, Libyan, Persian and Phrygian, we now have a modern 'Presbyterian sibyl' (l. 200).[8] This endows her with a prophetic voice just as she launches into her massive speech of denunciation. However, the extent to which the description of her is geared to this sibylline identity has never been fully appreciated. In particular, it helps to explain the otherwise bizarre spectacle of the Duchess being held aloft on a ladder. The equation being made is between prophecy and physical elevation. It may therefore be that Marvell is here alluding to Trimalchio's famous account of the Cumaean Sibyl in Petronius's *Satyricon*: 'I myself with my eyes saw the Sibyl hanging in a cage' (Petronius 1925: 48).[9] The pseudo-Justin in his *Cohortatio ad Graecos* similarly describes a tour of Cumae in the third century that included the Sibyl's 'inmost Cell' where, 'when she had composed herself upon a high advanced seat, she uttered and gave forth Oracles'.[10] However, the figure uppermost in Marvell's mind seems to have been the Pythia, the priestess of the oracle at Delphi, who delivered her pronouncements in verse from a tripod or prophetic seat that supported her above a chasm in the earth from which the wind of inspiration – the *pneuma enthousiastikon* as Strabo called it – was thought to arise (Strabo 1961: 9.3.5).[11] The Duchess's ladder thus provides a platform, the equivalent of the Delphic tripod, from which she can pronounce in true sibylline fashion.

It is, however, true that the leading modern authority on the topic insists on drawing a sharp distinction between two forms of prophecy. Accordingly, we are told that 'the Pythia prophesied [. . .] in an ecstasy in which her own personality was completely submerged in that of Apollo', so that when she was speaking 'in the first person, it was the god himself who spoke'. This was not the case with the Sibyl: while she too was inspired by Apollo, she did 'not lose her personality' with the result that when she spoke 'in the first person, it [was] as the Sibyl herself' (Parke 1988: 9; see also 79, 111, 162). The difference is more or less that between a clairvoyante and a medium, and the complete supersession of the personality in the case of the latter has a significant bearing on our understanding of the role of the Duchess in Marvell's poem. Is she speaking as herself or is she possessed? And if she is possessed, then are we witnessing a kind of double ventriloquism whereby the poet's mouthpiece, drawn for him by the painter, has in turn been annexed as a channel for divine speech?

Marvell shows every sign of having considered these issues closely. On the one hand, that is, he carefully stipulates that the Duchess speaks 'With a prophetic (if not spirit) fury' (l. 196), implying that she is merely inspired by, rather than surrendering herself entirely to, the power of the divine. On the other hand, it is also clear that he wishes to present the Duchess as a conflation of the Sibyl and the Pythia. In doing so, he was following a well-trodden path. As sibyls proliferated in the ancient world, it had only been a matter of time before one was assigned to the oracle at Delphi, and a host of writers, including Heracleides of Pontus, Chrysippus, Diodorus Siculus, Varro, Plutarch and Pausanias, had testified to the existence of a Delphic sibyl (see Parke 1988: 10, 25–6, 33, 38–9, 110–17). When constructing the figure of the Duchess, Marvell could have found all the details he needed in these authors (particularly the hugely informative essays by Plutarch, who had served as a priest at Delphi) or in the famous literary accounts of the Cumaean Sibyl and the Pythia to be found in Book 6 of Virgil's *Aeneid* and Book 5 of Lucan's *Pharsalia* respectively.

The infectious jauntiness of the lines in which the prophetic fury comes upon the Duchess is no guide at all to their intertextual complexity. For example, when Marvell says that 'her belly' began to 'sound', this is to make literal the meaning of the Latin term ventriloquism, itself a translation of the Greek *engastrimuthos* (see Connor 2000: 49–52). In fact, there is no evidence that the utterances of the Pythia were ventriloquial, and in his essay on the obsolescence of oracles Plutarch indignantly dismisses the view that the god would enter the body in the manner of the *engastrimuthoi* or, as he disparagingly but nevertheless revealingly calls these ventriloquists, *Puthones* (Plutarch 1936: V, 377 [414E]).[12] Marvell, by contrast, has no hesitation in highlighting the physical nature of the process at the expense of the spiritual, thereby hinting at the possibility that the Duchess is merely an engastrimyth rather than a divinely-inspired prophetess. Similarly, his description of the other ways in which the Duchess's body is transfigured – 'Her hair began to creep [. . .] Her eyes to startle, and her udder bound' (ll. 198–9) – owes a good deal to Virgil. As Aeneas approaches the Sibyl at Cumae, we are told in John Ogilby's translation,

> her Colour straight did change, her Face,
> And flowing Tresses lost their former Grace,
> A growing Passion swells her troubled Breast.
> And Fury her distracted Soul possest.
> (Virgil 1668: 321)[13]

Marvell's version of these lines is again severely reductive as, for example, with the conversion of the 'troubled Breast' (*pectus anhelum*) into a bounding 'udder'. The corresponding episode in Lucan's *Pharsalia*, in which Appius Claudius Pulcher visits the oracle at Delphi and coerces the terrified Pythia, Phemonoë, into prophesying, is, arguably, already a parody of Virgil's account of Aeneas and the Cumaean Sibyl.[14] After Apollo has (in Thomas May's translation) 'possest / With a full spirit her vnaccustom'd brest', a total knowledge of the world floods into Phemonoë:

> all times are heapt
> Vp in one heape, and many ages crept into her wretched
>   breast[. . .]
> When the world ends, and when it shall begin
> The prophetesse can tell, and vnderstands.
>   (Lucan 1631: H3r)[15]

Marvell for his part simultaneously encapsulates the tenor of this passage in the line about the Duchess 'Arraigning past and present and futuri' (l. 195) and undercuts it by grossly distorting 'future' merely for the sake of the rhyme.

As well as speaking with the prophetic voice of a sibyl or pythia, the Duchess is also characterised as 'Half witch'. Since she has already been cast as Penelope at the start of the passage, this would seem to preclude her being identified with such Homeric enchantresses as Circe or the Sirens. Significantly, these figures were often associated with the magical allure and transformative power of speech by early modern critics of the art of rhetoric, and to associate the Duchess with them would obviously complicate any attempt to present her as a teller of unvarnished truths (see Rebhorn 1995: 137–43). But the alternatives are hardly more edifying. Given the context, one distinct possibility is that Marvell had in mind Erichtho, the gruesome Thessalian witch visited by Sextus Pompey in Book 6 of *Pharsalia* and who is presented by Lucan in strict parallel with the Pythia (see Ahl 1976: 130–1). Erichtho's necromantic mode of divination involves a displaced form of ventriloquism in which she reanimates the corpse of a recently-deceased soldier who can reveal the secrets of the underworld, though only after Erichtho has threatened the gods. The difference between the two consultations, as Connor points out, is that whereas the Pythia 'is entered by voice and becomes an agitated channel for utterance, Erichtho herself extorts speech' from the corpse (Connor 2000: 68–9). It is, however, hard to see how this scenario would work in relation to *The Third Advice*; arguably, it fits Marvell in his role as author rather better than it does the Duchess since it is he who, so to speak, conjures her up and forces her to prophesy.[16] In terms of literary tone, the passage as a whole is relatively uncomplicated. Marvell's brisk reworking of epic materials suggests that he was sympathetic to the anti-heroic ethos fashionable in the 1660s. The question of whether the epic or heroic poem was still a viable genre in a sceptical age had previously been aired by Sir William D'Avenant and Thomas Hobbes in a printed exchange of views in 1650. Marvell may have followed their debate, since we know he read the work they were discussing, D'Avenant's incomplete verse epic, *Gondibert* (1651). He may also have known Paul Scarron's parody of the *Aeneid*, entitled *Le Virgile Travesty* (1648–52), which Charles Cotton began to translate in 1664 as *Scarronides: Or, Le Virgile Travesty. A Mock-Poem. Being the First Book of Virgils Æneis in English, Burlésque*. And he certainly had a great deal of respect for the undoubted master of the genre, Samuel Butler, the first two parts of whose *Hudibras* appeared in 1662 and 1663 (see Marvell 2003b: I, 413). The name 'Hudibras' was taken from Edmund Spenser's *The Faerie Queene* (1596), while the pairing of a knight and a squire was modelled on the one in Cervantes' *Don Quixote* (1605). But whereas Cervantes' burlesque achieves its effects by elevating the low, Butler's method is to degrade whatever is elevated. The strategy appealed to Marvell, as did Butler's habit of combining colloquialisms with a recondite vocabulary and a taste for outrageous polysyllabic rhymes – hence, for example, the virtuoso rhyming of 'viraginous' with 'cartilaginous'. Indeed, it was presumably only the appearance of Milton's *Paradise Lost* in 1667 that gave Marvell pause for thought about the supposed obsolescence of epic. Composed the year before this transformation of the poetic landscape took place, Marvell's portrait of the Duchess was, literally, a travesty, the effect of which was to position her – notwithstanding her title and place at court – as an outsider and as someone who spoke from below and hence to constitute her as a parrhesiast.

To some extent, this resolves the puzzle about the logic underlying the highly discordant figurations of the Duchess. For Annabel Patterson, in an earlier assessment of *The Third Advice*, the most that could be said for the Duchess was that by the end of the poem her speech had, 'by revealing her basically admirable feelings and standards, cancelled the original portrait, based on externals only, of her introduction' (Patterson 1978: 156). In short, we should trust the speech more than what we are initially told of the speaker; what we hear is more reliable than what we see. More recently, Patterson has come round to the view that it is precisely the Duchess's coarseness and the fact that she is a grotesque that makes her appropriate for the task in hand (see Patterson 2000a: 94). The suggestion now is that the speaker and the speech are completely at one, an exercise in decorum which Steven N. Zwicker has analysed brilliantly:

> the curious and awkward internal rhymes, the multisyllabic couplets, the coarsening of voice and manner are calculated to define the prophetic voice. [. . .] Marvell chose to occupy a space not devoid of the heroic and prophetic, but he needed to reclaim those modes, to redefine the character of epic and prophetic rhetoric by cleansing such rhetoric of false identity.
>
> (Zwicker 1987: 240)

The Duchess's credentials as one who speaks the truth and nothing but the truth can only be established by these severely negative and deflationary means. For her to be attractive in any way would risk compromising her status as truth-teller. She is therefore a visibly anti-rhetorical construction: undressed, without shame, without self-consciousness, stripped of all artifice, raucous and ugly, she is the very embodiment of truth-telling, an authentic parrhesiast.

While there is much to recommend this analysis, it is not clear that it succeeds in accounting for all the contradictory elements in the description of the Duchess or that it exempts her as fully from the satire as some readers might wish. The main reason for this is that *parrhesia* itself, as we have seen, was a far from straightforward mode of speaking. Although avowedly anti-rhetorical, it had been assimilated by Roman and early modern rhetoricians in the guise of *licentia*, and had come to be seen as potentially lending itself to the most advanced forms of duplicity. Moreover, even Euripides and Plutarch had conceded that *parrhesia* could be taken in a pejorative sense to refer to speech that was scarcely distinguishable from mere babble: to speak in such a reckless or garrulous fashion was to be *athuroglossos*, like one whose mouth had a tongue but no door (see Foucault 2001: 62–7). Parrhesiastic speech could be frank and deceitful, plain and ornate, uncurbed and interminable.

This view of *parrhesia* as a paradoxical combination of traits certainly appears to be reflected in the description of the Duchess and the extraordinary performance she subsequently gives. It also helps to explain why Marvell chose a female speaker in the first place. This was because *parrhesia* (on this view of it) coincided more or less exactly with gendered assumptions about the relationship between truth and rhetorical ornament prevalent at the time. Quintilian had popularised the use of sexual metaphors in discussions of rhetoric when he observed that orators needed to clothe their argument in rhetorical colours if the naked truth was to be made attractive, but it was Tudor rhetoricians such as Puttenham who self-consciously elaborated the various ways in which women could be associated with *both* the truth on the one hand and abuses of speech on the other – hence, for example, Sir Philip Sidney's warning, in the course of an attack on Euphuism, that 'that hony-flowing Matrone *Eloquence*' should not be 'apparelled, or rather disguised, in a Courtisanlike painted affectation' (Skinner 1996: 196–7). It is hardly surprising therefore that, in representing the problematics of truth-telling, Marvell brought together such an imposing and diverse array of female speakers in the person of Anne, Duchess of Albemarle.

Acknowledgement

My thanks to Alison Thorne, Jennifer Richards, Nigel Smith and Nicholas von Maltzahn for their extremely helpful comments on an earlier draft of this essay.

Notes

1 On such stereotyping (and resistance to it), see Parker (1989).
2 The Duchess was the daughter of a farrier, John Clarges, and his wife, Anne Leaver. In February 1633 she married another farrier, Thomas Radford, though they eventually separated in 1649. However, John Aubrey reports that while George Monck was imprisoned in the Tower between July 1644 and November 1646, 'his semstress, Nan Clarges, a Blacksmith's daughter was kind to him; in a double capacity' and 'was gott with child. She was not at all handsome, nor cleanly' (Aubrey 1999: 205). Anne and George finally married in January 1653. Monck was created Duke of Albemarle in July 1660 in recognition of his crucial role as general of the northern army in the restoration of Charles II (see Hutton 2004). Nicholas von Maltzahn argues that Marvell was prompted by Christopher Wase's attack on *The Second Advice to a Painter* in his loyalist poem, 'Divination', and in particular by the 'complaint that 'the kind Duchess [of York] is forbid to mourn / When her lord parts, or joy at his return'" (35–3) to which Marvell responded in *The Third Advice* 'by then giving voice to another duchess, Albemarle's wife' (Maltzahn 2005: 92).
3 On the question of Marvell's authorship, see now Patterson (2000b) and Burrows (2005).
4 See Colclough (1999), an excellent account and store of examples to which I am deeply indebted in the following two paragraphs.
5 For further details, see Dzelzainis, 'Andrew Marvell and the Restoration Literary Underground: Printing the Painter Poems', in *Imaginaires*, Université de Reims, forthcoming.

6 Nigel Smith's text has 'the gen'ral's britch', which he interprets as an allusion to the Duke's buttocks ('britch' as a variant of *OED* n.4a 'breech' = 'buttocks, posteriors, rump, seat'), while *Poems on Affairs of State: Augustan Satirical Verse, 1660–1714*, has 'the Gen'ral's breech' (Lord 1963–75: I, 75). But in the case of either formulation it would surely be possible to interpret the 'britch' or 'breech' as being not the Duke's but the Duchess's which is, in terms of sexual availability, the 'Gen'ral's' alone. Bodleian Library, MS Eng. poet d. 49 has 'She-Gen'ralls britch' from the transcription of *The Second Advice* and *Third Advice* in Patterson (2000a: 159–78 [at 172]), while *The Second, and Third Advice to a Painter* ('A. Breda', 1667: B4r) has 'she Gen'rals breech'. Both these latter formulations make it clear – correctly in my view – that it is the Duchess's body which is being referred to, with 'she-general' functioning as a variant on 'she-Albermarle'.

7 Truth was often depicted as naked by iconographers; see, for example, Ripa, *Iconologia* (1603) (my thanks to Mike Bath and Alison Thorne for this reference) and 'Fidei Symbolum' in Alciato, *Livret des emblemes* (Paris, 1536), Emblem IX, available online at <http://www.emblems.arts.gla.ac.uk/>. When Marvell wrote *Mr. Smirke: Or, the Divine in Mode* (1676) in defence of Bishop Herbert Croft's *The Naked Truth: Or, the True State of the Primitive Church* (1675), he underlined this commonplace on the title page with an Horatian epigraph (cf. Odes 1.24.6) to the effect that the naked truth will prevail and by adopting as a pseudonym the Latinised name of the Protestant theologian, Andreas Rivetus, which he then proceeds to anagrammatise: 'Res Nudas Veritas' – the naked truth itself.

8 For a comprehensive contemporary listing, see Blondel (1661: 19–23 [I.VIII]). Blondel (1591–1655) was an ecclesiastical historian who studied theology at Geneva and in 1650 succeeded Vossius in his chair at Amsterdam. Suspicious of all forms of enthusiasm, he wrote *Des Sibylles* (1649) expressly to demonstrate that 'the *Sibyls* [. . .] neither were, nor could be [. . .] the communications of the Spirit of God; to whose Glory, and Worship, those Divinations were directly opposite' (Blondel 1661: 55 [I.XXI]). For the most authoritative recent study of sibyls, see Parke (1988).

9 'Nam ego ipse oculis meis vidi in ampulla pendere'.

10 [Justin], *Cohortatio ad Graecos*, 38; trans. Boys (1660: 43); cf. Parke (1988: 84).

11 For an excellent, theoretically-informed account of the oracle at Delphi, to which I am greatly indebted, see Connor (2000: 47–74). This interest in Delphi may have a bearing on Marvell's contested authorship of *A Dialogue between the Two Horses*. This satire is included in Marvell (1971: I, 208–13), but is excluded by Nigel Smith, presumably on the grounds that it is absent from Bodleian MS Eng. poet d. 49; see Marvell (2003a: xiv). Equestrian statues of Charles II and Charles I had been erected in London in 1672 and 1675 respectively (each individually the target of satires firmly attributed to Marvell), and the *Dialogue* imagines a conversation between the two after their royal riders have dismounted for the night. Although Charles I's mount warns of the dangers of *parrhesia* ('Wee ought to be wary and Bridle our Tongue; / Bold speaking hath done both man and beast wrong', ll. 99–100), this does not prevent a fiercely republican exchange of views. The 'Conclusion' of the poem returns once more to

the themes of divination and prophecy, in terms very close to those of *The Third Advice*. Although the *pneuma enthousiastikon* is replaced by a different kind of wind, it stills issues in an authentically parrhesiastic utterance (ll. 163–74).

> If Speech from Brute Animals in Romes first age
> Prodigious events did surely presage,
> That shall come to pass all mankind may swear
> Which two inanimate Horses declare.
> But I should have told you, before the Jades parted,
> Both Gallopt to Whitehall, and there Horribly farted,
> Which Monarchys downfall portended much more
> Than all that the beasts had spoken before.
> If the Delphick Sybills oracular speeches
> As learned men say, came out of their breeches,
> Why might not our Horses, since words are but wind,
> Have the spirit of Prophecy likewise behind?

12 The practice of referring to engastrimyths as *puthones* may have reflected the attempts of charlatans to associate themselves with the prestige of the oracle; see Connor (2000: 52).

13 'non color unus, / non comptae mansere comae; sed pectus anhelum, / et rabie fera corda tument' (ll. 47–9).

14 For an illuminating discussion, see Ahl (1976: 121–30); see also Dick (1965).

15 'venit aetas omnis in unam / congeriem: miserumque premunt tot saecula pectus [. . .] non prima dies, non ultima mundi [. . .] ' (ll. 177–8, 181).

16 Cf. *The Rehearsal Transpros'd* (1672) where Marvell accuses his adversary, Samuel Parker, who had posthumously published a work by Bishop John Bramhall, of being a necromancer like Erichtho or, in this case, the Witch of Endor: 'whereas the old Bishop was at rest, and had under his last Pillow laid by all cares and contests of this lower World; you by your *Necromancy* have disturb'd him, and rais'd his Ghost' (Marvell 2003b: I, 80).

7 Exemplarity, women and political rhetoric

Susan Wiseman

With praising: dispraising used.

Thomas Wilson, *Arte of Rhetorique*, p. 268

The question of women's relationship to politics has been discussed by political theorists most substantially in terms of contract theory with its attendant analysis of the domestic. The integration of women into political history through examination of political theory has been fruitful, but its success is qualified by restriction of the terrain of argument to the narrow canon of political theory. This chapter argues that we need to ask slightly different questions. What evidence is likely to reveal women's relationship to politics in seventeenth-century England? What methods are helpful in interpreting this evidence?

This chapter addresses these questions by exploring the significance of the example as it discloses women's relationship to political rhetoric in earlier seventeenth-century England. The example has been productively studied as an aspect of rhetoric per se (Lyons 1989, Hampton 1990). There have also been detailed investigations of a single example including analysis of the gendering of examples, especially female examples, such as Lucretia (Donaldson 1982, Wayne 1987). However, studies of rhetoric have tended to focus on the sixteenth century, and studies of particular examples have tended to explore either a particular figure through time or in a particular text. In investigating the place of the example in political rhetoric this chapter responds to these approaches, considering what is lost in isolating an example from the immediate context. The example was a rhetorical resource widely available to male and female writers of all ranks – differentially available, but available nonetheless. What follows, therefore, canvasses the example's role in shaping women's relationship to the political sphere in early seventeenth-century England. Underpinned by the assumption that in this period women's theoretical exclusion from the political sphere generated not silence but highly developed linguistic and often figurative responses, the chapter examines example's role in the discursive negotiation of women's involvement in politics. The oblique nature of example's place in thinking about politics, while it has perhaps been a factor in inhibiting critical discussion and particularly discussion within political theory, is also one reason why attention to the specific relationship between women and politics can be fruitful. The chapter opens by asking what is suggested by the uses of four examples: Arria, Cornelia, Esther and Lucretia. The central section examines a broader range of examples and particularly the dynamic of exemplarity in Aemilia Lanyer's poem, *Salve deus rex judaeorum* (1611) (Lanyer 1993). In the light of these two studies I return to the question of what exemplarity can disclose about the relationship of women to early modern political discourse.

Examples: Arria, Cornelia, Esther, Lucretia

> The end of so admirable a vertue was this. Her husband *Paetus* wanting the courage to doe himselfe to death, unto which the Emperor's cruelty reserved him; one day, having first employed discourses and exhortations, shee tooke a Dagger that her husband wore, and holding it outright in her hand, for the period of her exhortation: Doe thus *Paetus* (said she) and at that instant, stabbing her selfe mortally to the heart, and presently pulling the dagger out againe she reached the same unto her husband, and so yielded up the ghost, uttering this noble, generous and immortall speech, *Paete non dolet*, she had not the leasure to pronounce other than these three wordes, in substance materiall and worthy her selfe, *Holde*, Paetus, *it hath done me no hurt.*
>
> (Montaigne 1910: 477)

This is how the classical matron, Arria, appears in Montaigne's essay 'Three Good Women'. Having described the well-known horrors of marriage for men and the joys of widows, Montaigne counterposes three classical good wives, one low-born and the other two 'noble and rich' (Montaigne 1910: 476). Arria, the wife of Cecinna Paetus, is one of these. When, on the defeat of Scribonianus's 'faction' which he supported, Paetus had been taken prisoner by the soldiers of the Emperor

Claudius, his wife Arria followed his boat to Rome. Accosted by Scribonianus's widow, Arria responded 'What [. . .] shall I speak to thee [. . .]
? Thou, in whose lappe *Scribonianus* thy husband was slaine, and thou
yet livest? and thou breathest?' (Montaigne 1910: 476). And soon, as
we see, she has killed herself and prompted her husband to suicide.

What can we make of this particular example? Even as it claims
the function of a moral exemplar it complicates such a designation.
Arria's suicide can be registered as virtuous within a stoic frame.
If Arria's virtue shines, as Montaigne's use implies that it does, it
does so by contrast with her husband for it is the example of her
suicide which prompts his own, implicitly delayed, action. Critical
interpretation of the essay differs. As M. A. Screech reminds us,
this essay follows up Montaigne's discussion of history and Stoic
philosophy in Essay 10, 'Of Bookes', and shows the author at his
most stoic in his praise of suicide (Screech 1993: 843, Hampton 1990:
174). Taking a step back from the example, it is evident that whatever
interpretation is chosen, this particular example works by putting
women in relation to politics. Entering the dangerous terrain of
supplication with its implicit attempt to influence political outcomes
even while taking action only upon the self, as a classical example
Arria is complicatedly analogous with early modern feminine political
action, both acknowledged and denied as political. However, for all
that Montaigne's essays are a *locus classicus* for the exploration of
example, commentators do not note that Arria, though not as often
used as the death of Socrates, does have an exemplary existence at
least after Montaigne's text and one that consistently focuses the
reader's attention on female political virtue.

Thomas Heywood reuses Montaigne's essay in his history of women
where he also mentions one of the two Cornelias (Heywood 1657:
221, 172). Heywood's agenda in writing a history of women bears a
complex and incoherent relation to the question of their relationship
to the political (Cornelia and Arria mediate reactions to politics as
'wives'). However, the presence of the Roman matron as a figure of
political virtue mediating women's relationship to the political world
is, perhaps perforce, recognised amongst women of other virtues.
Thomas Wilson, in his *Arte of Rhetorique* (1553), recognises the other
Cornelia's bravery and her acknowledgement of the priority of the
political world. Wilson carefully turns his example to illuminate the
combined political and maternal virtue of his patron:

> But because your grace is a woman, I will shewe you an example of
> a noble woman, in whom appered wonderfull pacience. Cornelia,

a worthy ladie in Rome, being comforted for the loss of her two children, Tiberius and Caius Gracchus, bothe valiaunt jentle men, although bothe not the most honerst menne, which died not in their beddes, but violently were slain in Civill battaill, their bodies lying naked and unburied, when one emongst other said: Oh unhappie woman, that ever thou shouldest se this daie. Naie quod she, I will never thinke my self otherwise, then most happy, that I ever brought further these two Gracchions. If this noble lady, could thinke her self happie, being mother to these twoo valiaunt jentlemen, yet both rebelles, and therefore justly slain: How much more may your grace, thynke youre self most happie, that ever you brought further two suche Brandons, not onely by natural birth, but also by most godly education.

(Wilson 1982: 175)

Arria and Cornelia clearly put women's virtue in relation to the world of politics. They do not do so by making women political agents, but by using them as indices of political virtue. As Wilson's usage of Roman matrons suggests, stories of the virtues of Roman matrons were pressed to the needs of the moment. While the nature of retelling clearly suggests *what* the matrons are used to say about the political, in part because of the close relationship between classical history and political myth and in part because of the contours of the stories themselves, the relationship between women and politics *is* in question. So, if Arria shows us some of the stability with which one example is used to put women in relation to politics, the example of Esther shows us example as something debated by contemporaries, potentially and actually by women.

The story of Esther can be summarised as follows. Chosen from amongst the palace virgins to be the wife of King Ahasuerus, Esther exposes Haman's decision to destroy the Jews. So, notwithstanding that the King only sees those he calls for, Esther goes before Ahasuerus. When he asks, 'What is thy petition?' Esther invites him and Haman to a banquet the next day. At the banquet the King again asks Esther her petition. Esther explains Haman's plan against the Jews. Haman is hanged from the high gallows he intended for Mordecai and – this is the foundation of the feast of Purim – Ahasuerus appoints a day on which the Jews can take revenge on those who plot against them. Esther's story is a story of female transgressive supplication forgiven, a story of invited and successful petitioning, and a story of a reversal of fortune; it might also be seen, though, as an account of feminine counsel to a misdirected governor and, of course, of a double revenge.

The story of Esther or Hester is found everywhere in early modern writing. Aemilia Lanyer uses Hester as an example of a woman given 'power' to 'bring down' proud and arrogant detractors (Lanyer 1993: 49). Significantly, the pseudonym 'Ester Sowernam' graced a key essay in the Jacobean controversy over the nature of women: *Ester hath hang'd Haman* (Ester Sowernam pseud. 1617). In 1640, with Deborah and Judith, Esther was one of Heywood's exemplary Jewish women, though she is presented ambiguously. In France the complexity of her story was acknowledged when she became the subject of one of Racine's religious tragedies (Heywood 1640: 44). However, Esther did acquire particular and deepened significances during the mid-century crisis, becoming virtually a patron saint of Civil War women's petitions (Higgins 1973: 178–222). Finally, in Lucy Hutchinson's meditation on the Christian religion we find a use of Esther which is significant in relation to this: the soul longing for grace is 'Like Queene Hester, who, comming before the greate King, was not satisfied when the scepter of grace was held forth with that first favour, for which she fainted, too, before she had it; but entreats a further'. She continues, '[s]o the soule which setts God before its eies, and comes trembling into his presence, encouraged by his grace' (Hutchinson 1817: 121). Esther's story is here taken away from the political arena of transgressive petitioning back to the supplicatory realm where she exemplifies the soul importuning God for a sparkle of grace. In Hutchinson's use of Esther as a figure for the desire for grace we can see a tension about whether female use of petition falls into the realm of supplication or something closer to the exercising of the subject's political right. This is one of many instances of the way in which exemplarity suggests the ambiguous relation of women to the political sphere – as virtuous actors within the circumscribed realm of female claims to virtue or martyrdom.

The textual use and reinterpretation of Esther discloses part of a debate on the nature of women's political action. Generally excising her coercive relations with Mordecai, her teacher and governor, mid-century retellings outline a drama of 'petition' as kingly power and feminine bravery. Here a woman acts (almost) like a political subject as Esther (almost) appropriates for herself a mantle of citizenship while also – as the story emphasises – trembling before the overwhelming authority of the king. Putting before the reader the question of women's political action, the story withholds comment on the exact status or logical implications of Esther's actions. Thus, we find in the petitions that Esther 'enterprised this duty', 'did adventure her life to petition' – the emphasis is on risk and enterprise, on justice and duty, and also on public good, but not on the rights of women. Put to use in the political debates of the Civil War, Esther is, perhaps, a justified transgressor but not one who demands political right. Esther's power as an example is as one who, without asserting rights, perhaps, acts like a political subject and is certainly a resource for political identity. Given Esther's appearance in petitions we might take into account the ambiguous nature of her story when assessing the political implications of the women's petitions: are these demands for citizenship or supplications that offer feminine transgression as contingently justified? Lucy Hutchinson's use of petition makes clear that Esther could, certainly, be used in a religious sphere in which, of course, the point about the soul's relationship with God's grace is that God has *all* the power. Though it differs from the stories of the Roman matrons, Esther's story explicitly puts women in relation to politics. Esther, then, expresses the ambiguous and contradictory potential of women's political action and was repeatedly used to explore that issue.

The complexity of the exemplary figure is illuminated by the best known of the examples discussed here – Lucretia. '[O]ne of the hinges in which the history of Rome turns', this story of virtue and republic certainly puts women in relation to politics (Donaldson 1982: 8). That even the earliest telling of the story, Livy's, is a *re*telling makes Lucretia a *locus classicus* of the example: her existence and significance is in her continual rededication (Livy 1971: 100–3; Matthes 2000: 23–50). Lucretia had a significant visual presence in early modern England. Artemesia Gentileschi's paintings of Lucretia may have been added to Charles I's collection in 1633 and 1639 (Garrard 1989: 110, 201, 514; cf. Haskell 1989: 211). The Lucretia we find amongst the embroideries of the Virtues at Hardwick Hall, the seat of Elizabeth, Countess of Shrewsbury, has on her right Chastity, symbolised by a unicorn, on her left Liberality (Levey 1998: 69). She is connected to, and as importantly, connects the two aspects of feminine virtue. The literary archive is vast, embracing Thomas Heywood's *The Rape of Lucrece* (acted at the Red Bull in Clerkenwell in 1608, 1630, 1638) as well as Shakespeare's *Lucrece* which was republished under the Protectorate in 1655 with John Quarles's *The Banishment of Tarquin: or, the Reward of Lust* (Shakespeare and Quarles 1655). These texts are politically enigmatic: far from being pro-republican texts, what these share is that each uses Lucretia as an empathetic focus. Early modern presentations of Lucretia are sharply aware of the power of the name and the power of the myth, but also of its instability. If examples are oblique and contradictory, we can note the strangely static organisation of Lucretia in Shakespeare's poem – a supplicator, political, sexual and yet stable. In considering the potential of Lucretia to signal opposite qualities, we can remember also Machiavelli's uses of her to exemplify chastity in the *Discourses* and adulterous desire in *La Mandragola* where she tells us, 'I'm sweating with excitement' (Machiavelli 1979a: 477, Machiavelli 1979b: 459).

If early modern uses of Lucretia were ambiguous, late modern writing on Lucretia in the early modern period has been contrastingly taxonomic. Even as he acknowledges that the story of Lucretia is 'closely intertwined' with a range of other myths, Ian Donaldson responds to the sheer volume of representations of Lucretia by splitting recensions of the story into those concerned with sexual and political issues (Donaldson 1982: v–vi, 28). Yet, it is Lucretia's potential to draw on both strands of representation that make her a key example. For an early modern reader, to pause on Lucretia was, certainly, to think of women and politics in the same moment. It was not, of course, to imagine women as legitimate actors in a public sphere. If Lucretia is an important instance of the example working to put women and politics into communication, the range of ways the example is used also suggests that those connections were diverse and, above all, contingent. Lucretia's ambiguous or dual quality indicates the example's complex workings, particularly in putting women in relation to politics. While the name 'Lucretia' puts before the reader the authority and troubling presence of the story of Rome, it is also an example of the tension that Timothy Hampton hints at between a proper name and the stories that name calls up. The example of Lucretia is a point at which model melds into myth: 'Lucretia' names a place of departure for a web, indeed a *mise en abyme* of association.

If Lucretia is a complex example, that is because her use in political theory and popular texts was complex and differently inflected; we cannot tell what the example means from the simple fact that it is often and ubiquitously used, we need to trace contexts of writing and circulation more specifically. Clearly, however, in a wide range of texts, by men and women, the retelling of this story did put women in relation to politics, and reading with attention to example means that we find this story everywhere, find everywhere the question of women's political virtue. Repetition and instability characterise the frequent early modern uses of Lucretia. However, the sexualised, affective significance of the story and the questions it raises about political action, women and the public good are at the heart of each retelling. It would be a rash modern commentator on the example of Lucretia who discounted the significance of exemplary reading, yet each telling of the story has its own logic. Writers and readers recognise the example of Lucretia as generating contradictory, moving, troubling, sexual and political thoughts in a reader; in seventeenth-century England, philosophical, political and erotic interpretations of Lucretia were intertwined. Indeed, the term 'Iconaes' was of course used of martyrs as well as classical figures. The relationship between biblical and classical exemplarity was, again, particularly intense though not uniquely so in the period from which I have chosen many of my examples.

The study of these examples does, clearly, reveal that particular examples put women in relation to politics. However, although the study of particular examples reveals patterns in their use, as a method it has evident limits in that by tracing one figure the actual force and occasion of the use of example is at times elided. It is clear that, while it is possible to trace the histories specific to exemplary figures, they were used and interpreted intertextually and as the context of reading invited. These examples put women in relation to politics but the how and why, always the key issues, are determined by the contexts of writing, publication and reading. Exemplarity offers us evidence of a deep engagement with political issues both expressed in terms of gendered dramas – the rape of Lucretia, her suicide, that of Arria, Esther's brave and transgressive appearance before the king – and, just as significantly, as examples that inflect the question of female political virtue. In each case, the exemplary figure has meanings generated by the history of usage – and in each case discussed the history puts women in relation to politics. At the same time, both in terms of the writer's prowess and the particular conjuncture, the specific usage is what lends the example its power. Therefore, in order to track exemplarity more closely, let us turn to the study of a single text, in this case Aemilia Lanyer's *Salve deus rex judaeorum.* In discussing exemplarity in *Salve deus* I will not be examining her use of these particular examples (though Lanyer does use Hester and Lucretia) but examining the way exemplarity puts women in relation to politics in a particular text.

'Thou fair example': Aemilia Lanyer's *Salve deus rex judaeorum*

In September 1597, Simon Forman wrote:

> She hath bin favored moch of her mati[majesty] and of mani noble men & hath had gret gifts & bin moch made of. and a noble man that is dead hath Loved her well & kept her and did maintain her Long. but her husband hath delte hardly wth her

and spent and consumed her goods and she is nowe very nedy and in debte & it seams for Lucrese sake will be a good fellow for necessity doth co[m]pell.

(Woods 1999: 24–5)

Forman was describing the poet, Aemilia Lanyer, who had consulted him. Forman's use of Lucretia as a shorthand example of a woman sexually available through necessity is both familiar and particular. Leaving aside Forman and Lanyer's later associations, it may well be significant that she had consulted him for advice on how she would fare at court, as one issue emphasised in Lanyer's later poem, *Salve deus rex judaeorum* (entered in the Stationer's Register 2 October 1610), seems to be her understanding of court relationships and hierarchies (Lanyer 1993: xlvii–xlviii). So, if Lanyer was described by example, she also used example to articulate her own understanding of her world. The use of example in her poem *Salve deus* introduces us to a more diverse politics of the example than we have encountered so far.

In Lanyer's text we encounter a use of exemplarity where a politics of praise of virtue is complexly articulated with patronage and hierarchy. Much critical attention has been paid to the use of rhetoric in the poem and Lanyer's access to it (Hutson 1992: 13–38, 20–3, Woods 1999: *passim*, Bennett 2004: *passim*). Critics have taken very different views on the extent to which *Salve deus* is 'conceived as a Book of Good Women' in which Lanyer builds a 'female community' (Lanyer 1993: xxxi, Coiro 1993: 357–76, Goldberg 1997: 16–41, Lewalski 1998: 49). There has been little specific discussion of the volume's use of example beyond the question of the praise of patrons. However, Lanyer addressed her poem to a range of selected aristocratic women (famously editing and tailoring individual copies), and she uses Pilate's wife and Eve as examples of good women. The poem is evidently exemplary in offering to the reader and patron Christ as a pattern for the Christian life, in offering the patron as an example to the reader and in its consistent use of comparison illuminating the patron's virtue.

Exemplarity in *Salve deus* does invite discussion. It is important in the main poem itself, in the dedicatory materials, and in 'To Cookeham', but how far the three are to be considered as linked is unclear. While Lanyer's apparent policy of adapting the volume's dedicatory epistles according to the patron to whom she was sending the particular copy makes it problematic to read the poems as a sequence, there may nevertheless be a patterning of examples similar to the rest of the poem (Lanyer 1993: xlvii–li). For example, the Queen is associated with Cynthia, Phoebe, Apollo, and, before shifting to an advertisement of her poem's defence of Eve, Lanyer notes that the 'royal' virtues include 'The natural, the moral and divine' ('To the Queen's Most Excellent Majesty', ll. 19–31 p. 4; l. 68, p. 6). The second poem, 'To All Virtuous Ladies in General', makes the shift from classical to Christian. 'To Cookeham', following the main poem, is the promised place poem for the Countess that *Salve deus* is not. The examples in 'To Cookeham', as in the dedicatory poems, follow a similar pattern to the main poem – moving from classical examples (here Philomela is mentioned and Phoebus) to the idea of the women at Cookham walking and talking with Christ and his apostles (ll. 81–2) and Old Testament figures such as Moses and David (ll. 85–8). The use of classical figures and the repeated move from classical to Christian time establishes connections amongst the three sections of the collection, as does the way each replays questions of faith and truth. We can explore, then, the exemplary patterning of the main poem and a part of the prefatory material which, in reflecting on the poems' collective concern with faith and true speech, also reflects on the nature of exemplarity.

The opening of *Salve deus* itself returns to the departed Cynthia, replacing Elizabeth with the poem's presiding genius, Margaret, Countess Dowager of Cumberland – 'wonder of our wanton age' (l. 169), 'faire example' (l. 177). Taking up the question of false, deceptive, outer versus inner beauty and virtuous interpretation, the poem compares the Countess favourably to classical women:

> 'Twas Beautie bred in *Troy* the ten yeares strife,
> And carried Hellen from her lawfull Lord;
> Twas Beautie made chaste *Lucrece* loose her life,
> For which proud *Tarquins* fact was so abhorr'd;
> Beautie the cause *Antonius* wrong'd his wife,
> Which could not be decided but by sword;
> > Great *Cleopatra's* Beautie and defects
> > Did work *Octaviaes* wrongs, and his neglects.
> > > (ll. 209–16)

Following this, historical women (the problematic Rosamund and Matilda) are offered as those who have suffered and caused suffering through beauty. The poem then moves to the question of Lanyer's own muse, likening it to Icarus before turning to the *'Passion of Christ'*, the 'very Night our Saviour was betrayed' (l. 329). Tracing the story of

Gethsemane and Christ's trial, Lanyer works a slightly different furrow in comparing Christ's 'harmlesse tongue' (l. 699) with the 'trothlesse tongues' (l. 639) of 'False Witnesses' (l. 638) when 'The Jewish wolves' attack 'our Saviour' (l. 685). Judas is used to carry forward the poem's testing of truth and virtue, as well as feeding into the question of the gendering of Christ's oppressors when he is contrasted with Pilate's 'most worthy wife' (l. 751).

Pilate's wife, situated before the introduction of Eve, serves to remind the reader that as in the case of the fall, Christ's death issues in the potential of redemption, as W. Gardener Campbell argues (Campbell 1995: 1–13). In Lanyer's use of Pilate's wife – particularly in her introduction of that figure *before* the promised apology of Eve, and in her work to make the figure, who is elsewhere understood as problematic, a positive example of female eloquence – we can see a non-typological use of sequencing. Moreover, as suggested by the particular uses discussed in the preceding section, Jacobean readers would be alert to such a deliberate inflection of a particular example. The text makes its major exemplary innovation on the subject of Eve. From Christ's passion and Pilate's wife the poem moves to the Old Testament to make its crucial recuperation of the example of Eve who acts as 'simply good' (l. 765) in comparison to Adam:

> Her fault though great, yet hee was most too blame;
> What Weaknesse offerd, strength might have refusde,
> Being Lord of all, the greater was his shame;
> Although the Serpents craft had her abusde,
> God's holy word ought all his actions frame,
>   For he was Lord and King of all the earth,
>   Before poor *Eve* had either life or breath.
>
> (ll. 777–84)

Having heavily weighted the gendering of fault, the poem makes the briefest mention of the promised section on 'The teares of the daughters of Jerusalem', of how 'the women cri'd' (l. 968), before moving to the 'blessed Virgin' (l. 1081).

As critics have noted, following Christ's passion, death and resurrection, the poet turns, or returns, to the virtues of her patron. The Countess is compared to 'famous women elder times have knowne' (l. 1465) including those whose armies have overthrown men. Examples start with the problematic, complex life and death of Cleopatra (again, ll. 1409–48), followed by heroines of the Old Testament: Deborah,

Judith, Hester – Esther – '*Joachims* wife' (l. 1529), Susanna and ending with the Queen of Sheba journeying to exchange wisdom with Solomon (ll. 1569–84). Exceeding Solomon (l. 1698), the Countess's Christian devotion is praised and she is exhorted to make an explicitly exemplary interpretation: 'Loe Madame, heere you take a view of those, / Whose worthy steps you doe desire to tread' (ll. 1825–6). Because of her own exemplary status, indeed, the Countess must measure herself against Christ's best followers, those '*Confessors & Martirs*' who bear Christ's colours (l. 1838).

Besides the comparative rhetoric testing the patron, the poem constantly invokes the authorising and suppliant figure of the poet addressing the patron. The two central issues of the poem are articulated most fully in its closing stanzas. First, Lanyer addresses the tailoring of the creation myth and the story of the passion in terms of a sequence of good and bad examples. Second, the final stanza of the volume's main poem, in part returning to the question of the poet's muse, addresses the creative interplay of poet and patron – a patron, 'Whose excellence hath rais'd my sprites to write' (l. 1833) and who remains 'the Arcticke Starre that guides my hand; / All what I am, I rest at your command' (ll. 1839–40).

Thus, the poem repeatedly provokes the patron to evaluate her response to Christ's passion as evoked by the poem. This is the ultimate example, and so test, for the Countess of Cumberland as Christian reader. The Countess is also tested against examples which she exceeds either easily (Cleopatra), or by access to superlative virtue (the Queen of Sheba). Both strategies of praise entangle the reader in a recursive return to the power of the poet to praise and so to dispraise. Yet, significantly, a discursive separation of the questions of poetic intention, failure and ambition is signalled by a sequence of gestures in which the poet steps out of the poem to address its object, or one of its objects: the patron.

These points are characterised by a shift from the testing of virtue and overt comparative rhetoric to articulation of the poet's asserted, ostensible, failures: failure to write on the subject proposed by the patron, failure to conclude discussion of the passion. The most marked instance is her turn from passion to patron which begins, 'Ah! Give me leave (good Lady) now to leave / This taske of Beauty which I tooke in hand' (ll. 1321–2). However, this address echoes an earlier one found at the start of *Salve deus*: 'And pardon (Madame) though I do not write / Those praisefull lines of that delightful place, / As you commaunded me in that faire night' (ll. 17–19). That the turn from beauty echoes an earlier turn reinforces poetic authority;

taken together, these assertions emphasise poetic control and, to an extent, separate it from the authority of patronage. Evidently, even as they separate discussion of poetic endeavour from the comparative discourse of the poem, such moments also link poetic will to the selection of objects of praise and – potentially – dispraise. Thus, we see that at key moments *Salve deus* switches address from comparative praise to direct address to the patroness, keeping in play the question of the poet's power to select the subject of praise.

In the same part of the volume in which Lanyer discusses exemplar-ity – the prose dedication 'To the Vertuous Reader' – the question of dispraise as an aspect of praise is discussed, and a partial attempt to defuse the potential to see dispraise in the strategy of comparison is made. Preceding a highly emulatory poem – one very strongly marked by desire for and competition with the patron – Lanyer addresses emulation and exemplarity:

> Often have I heard, that it is the property of some women, not only to emulate the virtues and perfections of the rest, but also by all their powers of ill-speaking, to eclipse the brightness of their deserved fame: now contrary to this custome, which men I hope unjustly lay to their charge, I have written this small volume, or little booke, for the generall use of all virtuous Ladies and Gentlewomen of this kingdome; and in commendation of some particular persons of our owne sexe.
>
> (Lanyer 1993: 48)

Whether readers are true and 'virtuous' is at issue. Attributing to another ('[o]ften have I heard'), and then to men, the charge that for women emulation and slander are twinned impulses, Lanyer cites her own work's intention as (first) being for the use of 'all virtuous ladies and gentlewomen' and (perhaps significantly, second) an example of praise disentangled from blame in 'commendation' of particular women. She contrasts the enterprise of praise with 'some [who] forgetting they are themselves' condemn other women and 'fall into so great an errour, as to speake unadvisedly against the rest of their sexe' (Lanyer 1993: 48). However, it is significant that even as she signs up on the side of praise Lanyer evokes a circuit of gossip and condemnation against which her own 'pure' praise is to be set. Lanyer's invocation of dispraise, slander and ill-speaking initiates a discussion of praise and blame; blame (of course) exposes the blamer. Christ is the exemplar of praise for and good treatment of women – unlike male slanderers he remembers physical and emotional ties. And so, through praise of Christ for remembering women, Lanyer is able to associate slanderers of women with those 'that dishonoured Christ, his apostles and prophets, putting them to shameful deaths'. Slander and martyrdom are linked; by contrast, God has given women the power to 'bring down [. . .] pride and arrogance': 'As was cruel Caesarius by the discreet counsel of noble Deborah, [. . .] and resolution of Jael, [. . .] wicked Haman by the divine prayers and prudent proceedings of beautifull Hester'. The '[m]any other examples' of virtuous women the poet 'could allege' must be seen in the context of the power of praise to also blame. This prose meditation on ill- and well-speaking addresses the potential for the example to involve, as we have seen, both praise and blame. Addressed to readers, it tests the virtue of readers by their response to the poem, but also offers an awareness of the potential of praise to become reversed.

Given Lanyer's careful tailoring of at least some of the presentation copies, the omission of 'To the Vertuous Reader' in several extant copies was probably deliberate. As Suzanne Woods says, the 'prose piece may have been kept in the volume to Prince Henry out of respect for his reputation as an intellectual', but complicating such a supposition is the possibility that this copy, though it went to him, was intended, as Woods notes, for the Countess of Cumberland herself (Lanyer 1993: xlviii–xlix). However, for the purposes of the current argument, it is significant that the person preparing the texts – probably Lanyer – thought it appropriate for some and not others. Exemplarity was a crucial means by which praise could address specific women and men, and so access the hierarchy of patronage. Exemplarity allows ambition and praise to be synchronised in inflating poem and patron simultaneously, even as the poet (as Ann Baines Coiro acutely notes) deals with her own status (Coiro 1993: 365 and *passim*). At the same time, though, the particular way *Salve deus* plays out its use of example – as a repeated test of patron against example – indicates the complex tension between ambition and obedience. Lanyer's invocation of not only Christ's passion but also other comparable women enhances the patron by setting tests which she is then seen to pass. While this means, of course, that it is in a sense the poet that decides how and where the patron is to become the star in the hierarchical firmament, it is perhaps truer to say that the poem offers the reader a tense game of exemplarity in which the question is not whether, but *how*, the patron is to be installed by the poet's skill in the hierarchy of virtue. For all the poem's concentration on loss, examples and pastoral are both used to restore the patron's position as redeemed Christian and chief star. For poet, and patron too, much is mutable and melancholy: Elizabeth is gone, praise may become dispraise, Christ is dead, Cookeham is lost. Examination of exemplarity in *Salve deus*, then, suggests that it puts its chief patron in relation to the exigencies of loss attendant on the Jacobean hierarchy by constantly testing and ultimately restoring her.

Salve deus tests men against women in a systematic way noticed by all its commentators. At the same time, it tests patrons against poets. Concentration on exemplarity in *Salve deus* illuminates the way the poem both uses rhetoric and meditates on ways of using it. The poem articulates the power and problems inherent in using exemplarity to evidence the *poet's* power of praise. At the same time it illuminates (and tests) the true virtue of both patron and good or bad classical, biblical or 'historical' examples. In Thomas Wilson's *Arte of Rhetorique*, which it is at least possible that Lanyer knew, Wilson concisely summarises a significant dynamic of exemplarity, 'With praising: dispraising used' (Wilson 1982: 268). If there are to be 'good' women and men there must also be bad and Lanyer's use of exemplarity instantiates not so much community as a competitive dynamic with complex, if not fully worked through, implications for hierarchy. How, then, should we understand Lanyer's text, and specifically her examples, as putting women in relation to politics? First, the choice of examples suggests a renovatory politics in terms of both the gender and political hierarchy. Obviously enough, if Lanyer's reading of Eve's crime is accepted, it invites a renovation of the gender hierarchy – and so of the wider political world. Second, the circle of women that Lanyer invokes as her patrons is suggestive in terms of both the Elizabethan and Jacobean court politics. The elegiac note of 'To Cooke-ham' is unmistakable and Lanyer explicitly invokes the death of Elizabeth. Even as the editions are individualised, then, perhaps the choice of patrons in itself suggests a regrouping or reworking of the politics of patronage with which Lanyer had grown up. Examining *Salve deus* in terms of exemplarity suggests some of the specific ways in which use of the example articulates the poem's politicised intervention. Third, though Lanyer's text might appear to use exemplarity to express what some critics have identified as a specifically feminist politics, albeit in complex ways, it is also clear that this is only one aspect of the volume's politics of exemplarity. The use of examples also articulates an understanding of politics in terms of patron–poet relations, wealth and biblical hierarchy. There is also the question of the poet's status. While, clearly, the particular exemplary figures do, in Lanyer's text, put women in relation to politics, examination of an individual text indicates the way such uses are contingent rather than stable.

Politics, Rhetoric, Analysis

Having considered particular examples and traced the politics of exemplarity in a single text, we come to two larger questions. What are the implications of the exemplary reading practices of the early modern period for the way examples put women in relation to politics? Why has example not been considered as one of the significant ways in which politics was gendered? This discussion of exemplarity comes into being where three approaches to the question of gender and politics fail to meet. First, the centrality of rhetoric to early modern culture is indeed recognised, and current critical historicist work makes clear the centrality of gender to the textual operations of rhetoric. Critics have examined the gender politics of rhetoric – and the distributive role of rhetoric in itself shaping gendered (and sexualised) knowledge of the world. Even the highly formal work in this field, particularly that within a comparative framework, could be described as scrupulously historicist in its desire to recognise discursive disjunctures as change rather than progress and in its suspicion of paradigms of development. Even so, there remain fewer studies of exemplarity that engage with political readings and gender.

Second, within political theory the case is very different. For all the fruitful current emphasis on studies of rhetoric and contextualisation in political theory (obviously the work of Quentin Skinner is important here), the gendering of politics in sixteenth- and seventeenth-century England has received little treatment (e.g., Skinner 1978: I, ix; see also the essays in Skinner and Phillipson 1993). The place of gender in political theory has, of course, received extensive and incisive treatments in the work of Carole Pateman, Susan Moller Oiken, Diana Coole (Pateman 1988: 3, Pateman 1991: 53–73, 66; Oiken 1979: 197–9, Coole 1988: 88–9) and more recently by the historicist study of Victoria Kahn (Kahn, 2004: 1–2 and *passim*). With the exception of Kahn, this important body of scholarship concentrates on the emergence and development of modernity. Accordingly, the significance of seventeenth-century contract theory in this debate is, quite properly in its own terms, oriented towards modernity. While it traces contract theory and contract thinking from Hobbes, marginally in Filmer, through Locke on to the late twentieth century, other seventeenth-century material (particularly less rigorous formulations of contract or other conceptualisations of politics) are not germane to this argument directed towards the emergence of modernity. In contrast to the synchronic and diachronic approach of rhetoric studies, the history of political theory, and this debate specifically, is teleological: for this debate, the past is useful in relation to modernity (compare Weil 1999: 3–4).

Third, the feminist study of women writers has tended to take the question of what women thought about women as its starting place. Much literary and historical work exists analysing women and men writing on the emergence of feminism (Jordan 1990, Kelly 1999: 21–47). But it is also clear that this was not the only way in which women (like the men with whom they shared lives and categories) came to politics. As we know, substantial debate about political rights organised by categories of sex (debates about, for example, the franchise) did not become established until much later. How, then, is gender politics to be related to politics more widely in this period? It would be an over-reading of pro- and anti-women writing to see it as organising women as a political group. As we see in Lanyer's analysis, only at times do claims for women imply consideration of wider political questions. It is, I think, problematic to use gender not only as a founding category for analysis but *as though it was at the time the foundation of a political discourse* – for to do so captures only a tiny fraction of the way in which politics was gendered for contemporaries.

These approaches, fruitful as they are, leave the terrain of women's relationship to the political sphere – in the writings of both men and women – only partly canvassed. Analysis of the rhetorical placing of women in relation to politics allows a different approach from the narrowly focussed understanding of political texts as found in the Skinnerian 'expanded' canon of political theory or the progressive or developmental inflection of feminist political theorists such as Carole Pateman. Rather than return to the debates over the representation of femininity in the linear triad of Hobbes, Filmer and Locke, we can find that women's relationship to politics is also concretely disclosed by the techniques of writing that organise that relationship across a wide range of discourses and do so by the use, amongst other techniques, of examples. We can remember that the prohibition against women's participation in the political arena that characterises the early modern period (as opposed to the modern), rather than meaning that women had no relationship to the political arena, set the terms of their relationship to it. Recalling this oblique way in which political meaning was made, it becomes evident that the teleological analysis of political theory and the feminist emphasis on feminist writing leave very specific terrain unassessed – that of the ways in which women's relationship to politics was expressed and read by men and women in the early modern period.

To revisit my question, what evidence is likely to reveal women's relationship to politics in seventeenth-century England, what method is helpful in interpreting this evidence? In response I want to make three points. Methodologically, the discipline of political theory has dominated discussion of women's relationship to politics. Restricting itself to a narrow canon of texts, sometimes literalising figure as argument, invested in a developmental teleology of modernity, the work in this field can take account of only some of the texts, some of the ways in which politics and women are related. If, first, we turn to a wider range of texts from early modern England than are studied by political theorists and, second, take women's participation in political discourse to include material we might understand as proto-feminist but also acknowledge their claims on other political questions, the picture can look rather different.

If we assess a wider range of early modern texts than those discussed by the political theorists, it becomes clear that women and politics are put in relation to each other by male and female writers in a range of ways. Both the use of exemplarity (including, momentarily, the biblical example and type) and particular examples were part of the textual features which made such connections. Obviously they do so according to textual contingency; a companion paper would examine the use of examples in specific texts and circumstances. It is also clear that while women are not assigned a singular position in exemplarity – we need not, for example, think of exemplary women locked always into positions of mediation between men but as diverse in their implications – their use can be simultaneously misogynistic and political. More significantly, consideration of examples does reveal that there was a repertoire of these which signalled to a reader a discussion of politics. A reader encountering Arria, Lucretia and Esther would anticipate the emergence of a political point and the same can be said of Jael, Judith, Medea and Antigone.

However, the identification of a repertoire of examples that put women into politics does not mean that exemplarity and examples worked in a stable way. As we have seen, exemplarity involved complex dynamics of praise and dispraise even as it tends to tie its subject to public life. If the example of Lucretia suggests the emergence of the Roman republic, it also suggests, at the least, sexual subjection and perhaps sexual guilt: readers of the example can hardly know of the one without the other. Lucretia is arguably an extreme example of the instability of example in opening politics to women, but it nevertheless reminds us of the discriminations and problems examples posed for readers. Esther, an example that seems to operate within perhaps a more schematic set of options, alerts us in a different way to the part such examples played in reading and – crucially – to the different ways in which feminine petition might be understood in relation to politics.

The paths early modern readers were expected to take through texts is indicated by early modern indexing and by, for instance, lists of biblical exempla used with page numbers. In each case the basic apparatus of reading reminds us of what the rhetoric books tell us of the use of example. As Puttenham writes of 'historicall Poesie':

> There is nothing in man of all the potential parts of his mind (reason and will except) more noble or more necessary to the active life than memory: because it maketh most to a sound judgement and perfect worldly wisedom, examining and comparing the times past with the present, and by them both considering the time to come [. . .]. and yet experience is no more than a masse of memories assembled, that is, such trials as man hath made in time before. Right so no kind of argument in all the Oratorie craft, doth better perswade and more universally satisfie then example, which is but the representation of old memories, and like successes happened in times past.
>
> (Puttenham 1936: 39; see also Mack 2002: 91)

In action, comparison is more troubling and generates more kinds of interpretation than Puttenham seems keen to acknowledge. Examples require the reader to negotiate between taking the proper name as an incantation or in using the name to unlock thoughts on the life. At times, indeed, as with many uses of Lucretia, there seems to be a display of virtuosity involved in the author's ability to balance positive and negative versions of the example. And all unpackings are hazardous; where should the reader stop reading into an example? As much as being a clearing or clarification, the example is a complicating addition – a sign that is an addition to explanation. Its evocation of a parallel narrative simultaneously calls attention to the way it is an artful, potentially dangerous, supplement to argument.

The examples discussed in this essay remind us of the example's own undoing by the reader – an undoing that is, of course, its coming into being. Example is a form of proof of which if one can say one thing one can say its opposite: does an example illustrate or complicate a text? However, in the early modern period and up to the mid-seventeenth century, example, not always used sophisticatedly, was a basic method of argument; indeed, for all his attack on examples, Hobbes finds himself using them, and exemplarity continued to be used long into the eighteenth century in some circles (against example and figure more generally see Hobbes 1991: 31; also Locke 1975: 490–508, Schochet 1988: xxv). Exemplarity – however complicated and self-disassembling, or, on the other hand, didactic and simplistic – clearly remained a building block of interpretation, supplying a framework for reading. One of the things attention to exemplarity discloses, as we have seen, is some of the ways in which it puts women in relation to politics.

In sum, the way examples permit the coexistence of what elsewhere appear as contradictions makes them a primary location for closely contextual study as well as the tracing of a single example. Exemplarity is part of writing, but its effect is part of reading. Examples, therefore, are dual and ambiguous: if exemplarity invites a reader to use reason, it also provokes empathy and identification. Exemplarity apparently stabilises the text in giving a concrete example, but in doing so, in Derrida's terms, offers a destabilising 'supplement' (Derrida 1977: 144). In the writing of a text, the same example can be positively or negatively inflected; writers and readers, too, needed to make decisions about whether or not to agree to an example's force as illustrative and ideal (Jeanneret 1998: 565–79). Apparently the property of humanist and post-humanist learning, exemplarity is also bound to Protestant typological exegesis; exemplarity has both Christian and classical histories of use. For all these reasons, one of exemplarity's many significances is in putting women in relation to politics and – from the point of view of the contemporary scholar – in helping us to trace some of those connections made in a very different political vocabulary and rhetorical ethos from our own. To use the lens of exemplarity to examine, as this essay has, legends and dynamics of good and bad women is not, as Jonathan Goldberg has argued, to reproduce the value system found there (Goldberg 1997: 4–6). Rather, as the evidence given here suggests, in the use and reading of exemplarity, values are as much contingent to purpose and negotiated between reader and text as obvious and given. Exemplary reading is something that reminds us that the early modern world grouped things differently, read differently and that exemplary reading was a significant – and complicated – part of the way in which women and politics were connected.

8 The rhetoric of (in)fertility

Shifting responses to Elizabeth I's childlessness

Helen Hackett

It has often been noticed that Elizabeth I was represented during her reign as a symbolic mother to her people (see, for instance Orlin 1995: 84–110, Coch 2003: 134–61). Numerous examples may be cited. A farewell oration written for Elizabeth's departure from Norwich in 1578 spoke of the townspeople's filial grief: 'How lamentable a thing is it, to pul away sucking babes from the breastes and bosomes of their most louing mothers?'. Elizabeth was claimed as 'the mother and nurse of this whole Common welth, and Countrie' (Garter 1578: F3v–4r). Decades later, at Elizabeth's death in 1603, an elegy by Thomas Byng mourned that God had 'reft away / The aged mother of these orphane lands' (Byng 1603: 10–11).[1] This chapter aims to explore why this particular topos was so persistent throughout Elizabeth's long reign, and how its use shifted over that period. In particular, it will examine competing and even opposing deployments of the motif by Elizabeth and her subjects; how use of the motif varied according to shifting political circumstances; and, in particular, how it was affected by Elizabeth's transition into irrevocable childlessness following the unsuccessful Anjou courtship of 1579–82.

The maternal metaphor is, of course, part of a larger figuration of the state as a family, with the monarch as its parental head. David Norbrook, among others, has shown how such natural analogies – whereby stability and hierarchy in the state were justified by comparison with hierarchies in nature, such as in the cosmos, the family or the human body – were less a static and shared belief system than a self-conscious and defensive rhetorical construct (Dollimore 1984). Such analogies therefore need to be read 'rhetorically, as strategies of persuasion with very palpable designs, and hence open to challenge [. . .] analogies from nature were at once common in political discourse and liable to be treated with scepticism [. . .] analogies would always be advanced in the full awareness that they could be mustered in a different cause' (Norbrook 1994: 140, 143).

As we shall see, the image of Elizabeth as mother of the nation was used both to bolster her authority and to challenge it. The period from her accession in 1558 to the early 1580s was the period of her marriage negotiations, and through these years we find maternal imagery extensively used in deliberative rhetoric, to put the case for and against her possible marriage and biological motherhood. However, once this period had passed and physical maternity was out of the question, the maternal metaphor occurs increasingly in epideictic rhetoric, where it is not only a means of celebrating Elizabeth's gifts to her people of supposed peace and prosperity, but also a means of covering up and compensating for her perceived political and physiological deficiencies.[2]

Early years

The imagery of maternity surrounded Elizabeth right from the beginning of her reign. Much of it was generated by a crucial biblical text, Isaiah 49:23: 'And Kings shalbe thy nourcing fathers, and Quenes shalbe thy nources'. The Geneva Bible glossed this as follows: 'meaning, that Kings shalbe conuerted to the Gospel and bestow their power, & autoritie for the preseruation of the Church'.[3] This image of nurturing motherhood was thereby freighted with theological and political significance: it became a rallying cry for Protestant monarchs to take control of the church in their territories and defy the Pope.

It was also a text much cited in the aftermath of John Knox's attack on female rule in his *First Blast of the Trumpet against the Monstrous Regiment of Women* (1558). When Knox, a Calvinist, launched his polemical onslaught, all the queens in Europe were Catholic, but the ascent to the English throne of Protestant Elizabeth just a few months later meant that it misfired badly. In 1559, Calvin himself tried to reconcile the Genevan church with the new Protestant English regime, assuring William Cecil in a letter that he had remonstrated with Knox 'that God promised by the mouth of Isaiah that queens should be the nursing mothers of the church, which clearly distinguished such persons from private women' (Calvin 1980: 212). The image of a *nursing* mother is striking. It could mean simply a parent giving tender care and protection to her children; after all, in Isaiah, kings too could be nursing fathers. However, a more specific meaning of 'to nurse' was and is 'to breastfeed', so that the nursing mother image when invoked alone also conjured up quite a graphic physical image of a mother suckling her child at the breast.[4] Calvin's deployment of the image at once acknowledges Elizabeth's authority as God's chosen agent and implies her obligation to advance the true Protestant faith and show beneficence towards her people.

During the post-Knox furore, John Aylmer, a Marian exile who returned to become Bishop of London under Elizabeth, published *An Harborowe for Faithfull and Trew Subiectes*. Its purpose was both to improve relations between Elizabeth and the Calvinist camp and to encourage Protestant loyalty to the new queen. Aylmer stressed the advantages of having a woman ruler, who would practise maternal clemency: 'She commeth in lyke a lambe, and not lyke a Lyon, lyke a mother, and not lyke a stepdam' (Aylmer 1559: N4v). The wicked stepmother that he had in mind was no doubt Elizabeth's sister Mary, her heretic-burning predecessor on the English throne. Elizabeth is presented as her diametrical opposite, a good, true, caring mother: she is 'a louing Quene and mother to raigne ouer vs' (Aylmer 1559: Q3v). The text culminates with an example of *prosopopoeia*, a speech by Mother England, who is distinct from Elizabeth but also closely allied with her: 'You can not be my children, if you be not her subiectes' (Aylmer 1559: R2r). If the people carry out their duty towards Elizabeth, which is to 'obey hir, honour hir, and loue hir' as they would a parent, then Mother England will reward them with her cornucopian 'good frutes' of peace and plenty, 'as corne and cattell, lande and pasture, wull and cloth, lead and tynne, fleshe and fishe, gold and siluer, and all my other treasures' (Aylmer 1559: R1v–2r).

These instances of maternal imagery from the beginning of the reign responded to a set of topical problems. Calvin's concern was to forge ties between the new English regime and the Calvinist Protestant church, whose interests had been damaged by Knox's polemic against female rule; Aylmer shared this concern, while also persuading the English people to welcome a female ruler, especially after their traumatic experience of Mary I. Motherhood therefore served from the outset as a problem-solving rhetoric, a comforting iconography that soothed and mollified. At the same time, these uses of the maternal image had forceful subtexts that sought to shape the new queen as a benign and Protestant monarch.[5] This coercive aspect of the rhetoric of motherhood came increasingly to the fore in exhortations to Elizabeth to marry and become not merely metaphorical mother of the nation but a biological mother. In fact, at first this was less a matter of exhortation or persuasion than simple expectation. Aylmer urged loyal subjects to pray for God 'to guide hir harte in the choise of hir husbande, and to make hir frutefull, and the mother of manye chyldren [. . .] That oure chyldren and posterite may see hirs occupying hir throne' (1559: I2r–v). Any vulnerability to this vision of the future arose less from the fear that Elizabeth would refuse to marry than the fear that, like her sister, her attempts to become a mother might not bear fruit.

Early parliaments: rhetorical conflict over motherhood

One of the first things parliament did following Elizabeth's accession was to petition her to marry. Different versions exist of her reply, which was her first speech to parliament. Camden's account, published after her death, contains the memorable moment when Elizabeth reputedly held out her hand, wearing her coronation ring, and asserted her marriage to the nation, declaring 'reproach me so no more [. . .] that I have no children: for every one of you, and as many as are English, are my children and kinsfolks' (Elizabeth I 2000: 59). Manuscript sources closer to the event confirm that Elizabeth undertook to care for the realm 'as a good mother of my country' (Elizabeth I 2000: 58 n.9). In 1563, when parliament petitioned her about marriage again, she replied evasively, but concluded: 'though after my death you may have many stepdames, yet shall you never have any a more natural mother than I mean to be unto you all', again invoking that almost folklorish image of a wicked stepmother for the kind of bad queen from whom she wished to distinguish herself (Elizabeth I 2000: 72).

Elizabeth, then, right from the outset was using the role of mother rhetorically as a mode of self-defence, apparently to deflect attention away from her reluctance to become an actual mother. After all, she also said in her first speech to parliament, 'in the end this shall be for me sufficient: that a marble stone shall declare that a queen, having reigned such a time, lived and died a virgin' (Elizabeth I 2000: 58). What ensued was a rhetorical contest between the Queen and her subjects through the 1560s, as they persistently and strenuously put forward the case for biological motherhood. Sir Nicholas Bacon, the Lord Keeper of the Great Seal, wrote to her wheedlingly in 1563: 'If your Highness could conceive or imagine the comfort, surety and delight that should happen to yourself by beholding an imp of your own' (Neale 1953: I, 112). In 1565 her progress took her through Coventry, where the Recorder delivered an oration which wished that:

> like as you are a mother to your kingdom, and to the subjects of
> the same, by justice and motherly care and clemency, so you may,
> by God's goodness and justice, be a natural mother, and, having

blest issue of your princely body, may live to see your children, unto the third and fourth generation.

(Nichols 1823: I, 197)

Elizabeth's reaction to this is not recorded, but it *is* reported that when the Public Orator of Cambridge University delivered to her a speech in praise of virginity in 1564, she responded 'God's blessing of thyne heart; there continue' (Nichols 1823: I, 161).

Thus, through the 1560s tension increased between the wishes of Elizabeth's subjects for her to become a mother physically and her apparent resistance to doing so. Each side used maternal imagery as a form of deliberative rhetoric, each attempting to drive policy in an opposite direction. Maternal imagery rapidly ceased to be a soothing, pacifying device and became instead a set of contested terms and ideas: what would it mean for the Queen to be a true mother to the nation? In fact, in parliament the issue of the succession came to be equated with the whole fraught issue of freedom of speech, as Elizabeth tried to suppress discussion of the subject. During the turbulent parliament of 1566, a petition to the Queen was composed, though never delivered, which asserted the rights of parliament to liberty of speech. It concluded with a wish to be 'your faithful, lowly subjects, honouring and obeying you, like children, for duty, reverence, and love, without the burden of any unnecessary, unaccustomed, or undeserved yoke of commandment' (Neale 1953: I, 156). This asserts a fealty to Elizabeth which is as natural as that of a child to a mother, and therefore needs no excessive discipline or regulation. At the same parliament, a speaker asserted that if Elizabeth would remove the peril to her people of an unsettled succession, 'then doth she declare herself to be a deare mother and tender nource over them', but if not, she 'will [. . .] coole the heate of love in any, how fervent so ever it be' (Hartley 1981: I, 138). To be a good political and symbolic mother to the nation, then, Elizabeth has to become a mother literally and biologically. The ground of argument may be shifting slightly, however: this same speech proposed that Elizabeth should nominate an heir and pass a bill of succession, acknowledging, after eight years of fierce debate and little progress towards her marriage, that an heir of her body might not be forthcoming and a successor might have to be identified by other means.

In 1569, at the end of a decade of turbulent debate, a document summarising 'the Queen's Proceedings since her Reign' was ordered to be read in parish churches throughout England. Elizabeth stated that she desired

> all persons to understand, that of our own natural disposition, through God's goodness, we have been always desirous to have the obedience of all our subjects of all sorts, both high and low, by love and not compulsion, by their own yielding and not by our exacting, allowing that which was well said by a wise prince of the Greeks: 'That king to be in most surety that so ruled over his subjects as a father over the children'.
>
> (Orlin 1995: 92)

It is striking here how a shift of gender allows Elizabeth to claim patriarchal authority over her subjects, while prefacing this with emphasis upon her maternal tenderness and compassion. As Lena Cowen Orlin has put it, Elizabeth used parental – usually maternal – metaphors 'to make demands of her people – even if only, as in her first use of the analogy, to ask that the people not make demands of marriage and childbirth upon her' (Orlin 1995: 91). Maternal imagery continued to be a site of rhetorical contestation as the reign proceeded, but changing circumstances, and especially the changing state of the Queen's body – from potential fertility to uncertain fertility to conclusive infertility – led to shifts and even inversions in how it was deployed.[6]

The Anjou courtship, 1578–82

Exhortations for Elizabeth to marry continued well into the 1570s; that is, well into her forties. An unperformed masque composed for the 'Princely Pleasures' at Kenilworth in 1575, often seen as the Earl of Leicester's last-ditch attempt to become Elizabeth's husband, urged her:

> How necessarie were
>   for worthy Queenes to wed,
> That know you wel, whose life alwaies
>   in learning hath been led.
> The country craves consent,
>   your virtues vaunt themselfe,
> And Jove in Heaven would smile to see
>   Diana set on shelfe.
>
> (Nichols 1823: I, 514–15)

As her last serious foreign marriage negotiation unfolded, however, in the late 1570s, maternal imagery began to be used in exactly the opposite way, to attempt to *dissuade* Elizabeth from marriage.

Francis, Duke of Anjou (formerly Duke of Alençon), the youngest son of Catherine de Medici, was more than twenty years Elizabeth's junior. His interest in marriage to the Queen of England was largely to advance his military campaign against Spain in the Netherlands. England's interest was to use Anjou to fight her battles in the Netherlands for her and to prevent France and Spain from combining against England; and, of course, all being well, to gain a child of the Queen's body and thereby secure the succession. In September 1578 Elizabeth turned forty-five, so that a key question in the debate about the Anjou courtship was whether she *could* now physically become a mother or, if she did, at what possible risk of her own death and/or that of the child.

Despite their previous exhortations to Elizabeth to marry, many of her subjects were now hostile towards the prospect of her marriage to a French Catholic prince. Popular ballads and Latin verses appeared expressing this antipathy, including two pasquins which were posted on the Lord Mayor of London's door. One of them declared: 'The kinge of ffrance shall not advance his shippes in English sande / Ne shall his brother ffrancis have the Ruleng of the lande' (Doran 1996: 164). The image of French ships advancing their prows in English sand has distinctly sexual connotations, alluding to Petrarch's image of his unrequited desire for the chaste Laura as a ship guided endlessly through the oceans by the star of her virtue.[7] The implication is that the ship's arrival in dock would equate to sexual consummation;[8] the pasquin thus maps Elizabeth's body onto the intact island nation of England and rebuffs France's attempted penetration of both. The rhetoric of the marriage debate is shifting to put increasing emphasis on the Queen's female body, at once virginal and maternal, which lies at risk of violation.

Opposition to the Anjou marriage was most stridently voiced by John Stubbs, a lawyer, who in August 1579 published *The Discoverie of a Gaping Gvlf whereinto England is like to be swallovved by an other French mariage, if the Lord forbid not the banes, by letting her Maiestie see the sin and punishment thereof.* This work was viewed as so seditious by Elizabeth and her government that not only did the Privy Council attempt to call in all copies, but Stubbs, and William Page who distributed the book, had their right hands cut off on a public scaffold. Stubbs's main objection to the Anjou marriage was the risk that it would convert Elizabeth, as 'the weaker vessel' (Stubbs 1968: 11), and therefore the English church and nation, to Catholicism. He puts his case by means of a shifting iconography of the female body. Right at the opening of the text, he claims that the French are infected with Turkish and Italian political practices which are ungodly and contagious: 'This sickness of mind have the French drawn from those eastern parts of the world, as they did that other horrible disease of the body, and having already too far westward communicated the one contagion, do now seek notably to infect our minds with the other' (Stubbs 1968: 3). Anjou was widely suspected by his enemies of having syphilis; Stubbs here conflates this with the idea of his carrying a metaphorical, moral and political syphilis. The horrifying implication that Anjou will infect the symbolic mother of the nation with venereal disease is compounded by the iconography of the Fall: 'They have sent us hither, not Satan in body of a serpent, but the old serpent in shape of a man, whose sting is in his mouth, and who doth his endeavour to seduce our Eve, that she and we may lose this English paradise' (Stubbs 1968: 3–4). Elizabeth in this account is a frail mother figure, vulnerable to fatal seduction and corruption.

Stubbs assigns symbolic female roles to Elizabeth in diverse and even contradictory ways. At an early stage he personifies the English church as a mother: 'mild though she be, without all gall in her heart and have no words in her mouth but of a most loving mother', yet she would reprove those disloyal children who seek the French marriage. The match 'is offered her with shameful dishonour to her spouse, [and] with the separating her from her Lord God' (Stubbs 1968: 5–6). Elizabeth seems here to be identified with the church as mother of the nation and bride of Christ. Shortly afterwards, however, in Stubbs's unstable iconography, she is named as merely first among the church's children: the church will not part with 'her dear daughter, her daughter of highest honour' but 'hold her fast in her loving arms as being loath to give her to a stranger' (Stubbs 1968: 8). A few pages on Elizabeth is 'the goodwife of England', whose threatened corruption puts the whole household, that is the whole nation, at risk (Stubbs 1968: 15). Then she is assigned a maternal role again: 'The infant churches in the Low Countries shall lose a nurse of us; the elder churches in Germany a sister of strength' (Stubbs 1968: 20). At this point, the promoters of the marriage are set up in opposition as 'unkind mothers', who 'put (as it were) their own child, the Church of England, to be nursed of a French enemy' (Stubbs 1968: 20). Another specific bad mother is pitted against the good mother Elizabeth throughout the text, namely Catherine de Medici, who is variously a hollow shell manipulated by the Pope, a spider twisting the cords of her children's fateful marriages and a Machiavellian poisoner and schemer (Stubbs 1968: 22–6, 87).

As well as merging Elizabeth as mother with the English church as mother, Stubbs identifies Elizabeth with the commonwealth, also personified as a woman. The advocates of the French marriage want to let her blood from her largest vein, or want her to throw herself into the sea (Stubbs 1968: 68). At the same time her subjects must be like parents advising a beloved daughter on her marriage (Stubbs 1980: 69–70). Thus, Elizabeth's symbolic female roles in Stubbs's iconography are constantly mutating between mother, wife and daughter of the nation, but throughout, while venerating her as 'our most precious treasure, our Elizabeth' (Stubbs 1968: 37), he tends to deploy female iconography to emphasise her vulnerability, the jeopardy in which this places the nation and the consequent need for her to take good counsel from her subjects.

Stubbs tests the boundaries of free speech not only by seeking to direct Elizabeth's political decisions, but also by speculating frankly about her gynaecological health. The female body is at the centre of his text, and the centre of the Anjou debate, not only in metaphorical forms that personify the church and commonwealth, but also in the literal and essential form of Elizabeth's ageing body natural – what Stubbs calls 'her very self or self self' (Stubbs 1968: 68). Stubbs introduces the subject of 'her children of her body' with the loaded phrase 'if any there be' (Stubbs 1968: 8). Even if she is fertile, a child born of the French marriage would be 'a babe yet unborn whose shape we see not' (Stubbs 1968: 11): literally, a mixed-faith child; figuratively, a mixed-faith church and nation; by implication, a monstrous and deformed progeny. Stubbs challenges Elizabeth to ask her physicians to tell her honestly, 'how exceedingly dangerous they find it by their learning for Her Majesty at these years to have her first child, yea, how fearful the expectation of death is to mother and child; I fear to say what will be their answer' (Stubbs 1968: 51). Stubbs accuses the French of actively seeking Elizabeth's death in childbirth, and the death of the child too, laying England open to foreign invasion and civil war: theirs is 'a very French love to our Queen and land' (Stubbs 1968: 51–2).

Stubbs turned against Elizabeth her own reluctance to marry, now assumed to be a generally known fact. He wrote that godly men had 'hitherto dutifully sought her marriage whilst hope of issue was' and had 'continually [. . .] taken every good occasion to persuade you to marriage, hanging upon your skirts (as it were) and lying at your feet for to win you to marriage' (Stubbs 1968: 31–2, 51), but that she had displayed 'her constant dislike and indisposed mind to marriage from the flower of her youth' (Stubbs 1968: 69). Sir Philip Sidney, in a manuscript letter to Elizabeth written shortly after the *Gaping Gulf* and also putting the case against the Anjou marriage, used the same rhetorical strategy, but inflected with the personal familiarity of one who moved in inner circles at court: 'Often have I heard you with protestation say, "No private pleasure nor self affection could lead you unto it"' (Sidney 1973: 51). Previous roles were now entirely inverted, and Elizabeth found herself no longer resisting marriage and motherhood, but its leading advocate. Just as her opponents made rhetorical use of her previous reluctance against her, so she now turned their previous enthusiasm against them. A proclamation issued in response to the *Gaping Gulf* voiced the Queen's surprise, after all her subjects' solicitations for her to marry, that some should now take the opposite view (Stubbs 1968: 150). More than ever, the image of Elizabeth as mother of the nation was at the centre of a heated rhetorical battle.

Elizabeth's biological clock

It is impossible to distinguish how far Elizabeth's interest in the Anjou match was merely political, and how far it was intensified by the urgent ticking of her biological clock. Some of her statements at this time might seem to imply a strong last-minute desire to have children. In October 1579, responding to the objections of her council to the marriage, she asked 'whether there could be any more surety for her and her realm than to have her marry and have a child of her own body to inherit, and so to continue the line of Henry the Eighth' (Stubbs 1968: xvii). She upbraided Sir Francis Knollys that 'it was a fine way to show his attachment to her; who might desire, like others, to have children' (Stubbs 1968: xvii).

Certainly some modern historians have read Elizabeth's enthusiasm for marriage to Anjou as evidence that she was under the sway of hormonal as well as political influences. Conyers Read in 1960 wrote that Elizabeth

> was approaching, if she had not already reached, what the sixteenth century would have called her climacteric, and we would call menopause. With many women this period is accompanied by great emotional instability, particularly in matters sexual [. . .] Much of Elizabeth's extraordinary behaviour during the protracted Alençon [i.e., Anjou] courtship is explicable in these

terms [. . .] her behaviour [. . .] was, to say the least, unbecoming
both to the woman and to the Queen.

(Read 1960: 207)

J. E. Neale, in his highly influential biography of Elizabeth, regarded
the matter somewhat more sentimentally. Recounting Elizabeth's
apparent grief at Anjou's death in 1584, he wrote, 'He had been her
last hope of children. She wept for herself' (Neale 1960: 259). Susan
Doran, however, returning to the origins of the marriage negotiation
in 1578–9, is more analytical and circumspect:

> The likelihood is that Elizabeth was influenced by her head first
> and her heart second. After all, political considerations had led
> her to initiate the courtship and the events of the summer and
> autumn of 1579 [which brought several Spanish- and French-
> backed threats to English security] gave her strong reason to
> continue it.
>
> (Doran 1996: 163)

The great question which lay behind the national debate in 1579,
and which continues to lie behind modern interpretations of it, is
whether Elizabeth was indeed still capable of having a child. The most
fervent supporter of the Anjou match, aside from Elizabeth herself,
was her chief minister, William Cecil, Lord Burghley. He believed that
she was able to conceive, and we can be confident that he would have
made it his business to be well informed on the subject. He wrote in a
memorandum of 27 March 1579:

> considering the proportion of her body, having no impediment
> of smallness in stature, of largeness in body, nor no sickness, nor
> lack of natural functions in those things that properly belong
> to the procreation of children, but contrarywise, by judgment of
> physicians that know her estate in those things and by the opinion
> of women, being most acquainted with her Majesty's body in such
> things as properly appertain, to show probability of her aptness
> to have children, even at this day.
>
> (Read 1960: 210–11)

The 'number of her years' are 'not so many but by common course of
nature it is generally adjudged that not only she but all other women of
her age may have children for the space of v or vi years and sometimes
after the same term' (Read 1960: 210–11). Burghley's memorandum,

penned as it is by one who probably had the most accurate information on this subject, is a salutary reminder that Stubbs and those historians who have been influenced by his arguments may well have been hurrying Elizabeth into her menopause before her time. Even by Burghley's optimistic estimate, however, only five or six years of fertility were left, and this too was very much to the forefront of his mind. At some point during the turbulent year of 1579 he wrote the Queen a letter full of resonant imagery of timeliness and seasonality whose purpose is to persuade her to stop delaying:

> The clock that stond so long hath now so weighty plummets of favour and courage put on that it striketh still, a clock not to tell how this day passeth only, but how days and time passeth like river streams, whose waves return no more [. . .] if your majesty tarry till all clocks strike and agree of one hour, or tarry till all the oars row the barge, you shall never point the time and you may slip the tide that yet patiently tarryeth for you.
>
> (Elizabeth I 2000: 240)

Burghley deploys natural analogies to put the case that time is running out – the tide is turning, not only on Elizabeth's fertility, but also on her more general health. He goes on:

> In the beginning, the morning of your time, your majesty hath taken the sweet dew of pleasure and delight, the temperate air of a quiet and a calm, contented mind [. . .] It is not enough then your majesty reign and to be queen still, but to reign and rule honoured, pleased and contented; and to have the morning dew all the whole day of your life [. . .] your majesty still in your old state to sit sure and rule singly as you did, could you yet then think it morning still? Have you the sweet dew and the temperate air so agreeable and necessary to your nature? No.
>
> (Elizabeth I 2000: 240–1)

His tone here is tactful and discreet and his meaning is far from explicit, but it is illuminated by that same memorandum which he wrote in March. There he stated that:

> it may be by good reasons maintained that by forbearing from marriage her Majesty's own person shall daily be subject to such dolours and infirmities as all physicians do usually impute to womankind for lack of marriage, and specially to such women as

naturally have their bodies apt to conceive and procreate children. And to this end were to be remembered the likelihood of her Majesty's pains in her cheek and face to come only of lack of the use of marriage, a thing meeter by physicians to be advertised to her Majesty than otherwise to be set down in writing.

(Read 1960: 211)

Burghley is referring here to the Elizabethan medical doctrine that abstention from sex rendered a woman vulnerable to disorders of the womb, disorders that could have far-reaching bodily and emotional symptoms. A similar point had been raised back in the early 1560s, in a *Dialogue on the Queen's Marriage* by Sir Thomas Smith, which circulated widely in manuscript. Smith asserted that childbirth would improve Elizabeth's health: 'I think that bringing forth of children doth not only preserve women from many diseases, and other inconveniences, but it doth also clear their bodies, amend the colour, prolong their youth' (Doran 1996: 197). Burghley and Smith were applying widely held early modern views on the necessity of sexual activity and procreation to women's health. *De Secretis Mulierum*, for instance, a popular and influential book on women's health, maintained that women who abstain from sex suffer suffocation of the womb: it becomes congested with stale menses and may become displaced in the body, causing disorders in other organs (Lemay 1992: 131–5). Edward Jorden published a study of the condition in 1603, entitled *A Briefe Discourse of a Disease Called the Suffocation of the Mother*. He explained that if the womb was deprived of the health-giving moisture derived from sexual intercourse, it would rise up in the body, producing choking, breathing difficulties, vomiting and spasms (Rousseau 1993: 118). The barren womb generated vapours that affected the mind and imagination. John Sadler, in *The Sick Woman's Private Looking Glass* (1636), wrote that when he researched and considered all diseases of women, 'I found none more frequent, none more perilous than the ill affected wombe [. . .] there is no disease so ill but may procede from the evill quality of it' (Sadler 1636: A4v–5r). The symptoms of womb-sickness, or hysteria, could include garrulity, excessive desire for coitus, lovesickness, melancholia, listlessness and irrational behaviour (Maclean 1980: 42). G. S. Rousseau, in his study of hysteria in the early modern world, has found the widespread belief that 'Female seed constantly retained, whether through lack of sexual intercourse or excessive female masturbation, contained the source of anatomical imbalance and led to derangement' (1993: 112).

Elizabeth's continuing virginity, then, had more far-reaching consequences than just the nation's lack of an heir of her body. Opponents of the Anjou marriage such as Stubbs and Sidney assumed that if she did not marry, everything would go on as it was; that the rule of the Virgin Queen, to which her subjects had grown accustomed after twenty years, would simply continue as before. Indeed, Sidney warned Elizabeth against change: 'as in bodies natural any sudden change is not without peril, so in this body politic, whereof you are the only head, it is so much the more' (Sidney 1973: 49). Burghley's concern, however, was that change was coming anyway. Elizabeth would shortly, inevitably, become a post-menopausal woman. If she did not marry and use her body's potential fertility before it was too late, England would find itself with a queen whose body natural was in a state of womb-sickness, with all the potential effects on mind and body that this implied. In short, England would find itself ruled by a hysteric. For this reason, as Elizabeth indeed passed beyond the possibility of child-bearing, her infertility became an even more complex issue and generated increasingly complex and diverse rhetorical strategies.

The triumph of metaphor

As we have seen, Elizabeth's body, and its fertility or otherwise, was a political and rhetorical battleground in the period 1579–82. To express belief in the Queen's potential to bear children was to express allegiance to the Crown. Thus, Henry Howard, Earl of Northampton, retorted to Stubbs that nature 'promiseth Her Majesty the procreation of many children', and her marriage would produce 'the fruit of her Majesty's body' (Stubbs 1968: 165). George Puttenham's *Partheniades*, a manuscript cycle of poems presented to Elizabeth as a New Year's gift in 1579, wished her 'the twoo ioys shee doth misse / A Cesar to her husband, a kinge to her so[n]ne / What lackt her highnes then to all erthly blisse' (Puttenham 1579: 169v). John Lyly's *Euphues and his England*, 1580, expressed the hope

> that as she hath liued fortie yeares a virgin in great maiestie, so she may lyue fourescore yeares a mother, with great ioye, that as with hir we haue long time hadde peace and plentie, so by hir we may euer haue quietnesse and abundance, wishing this euen from the bottome of a heart that wisheth well to England.
>
> (Lyly 1902: 212)

Yet at the same time as he loyally envisaged Elizabeth's motherhood, Lyly's use of hyperbole – the wish that she should 'lyue fourescore yeares a mother' – indicated a transition into unreality. Acceptance was developing, even among the most ardent supporters of the Anjou match, that as time passed, Elizabeth's maternity was a waning possibility. Sidney, in his letter to Elizabeth about the projected marriage, sought to make his arguments palatable to her by diplomatically 'assum[ing] throughout that the Queen really will marry and have children', but his modern editors observe that 'It is doubtful whether he really believed this. Even six years earlier [. . .] he described the Queen [. . .] as old and ripe for death' (Sidney 1973: 37).

Much of the literature of 1579–82 is poised on this cusp. Alongside his wishes for Elizabeth's fertility, Lyly also contributes to the increasing mythologisation of her virginity. He stresses the long peace that England has enjoyed, neither 'molested with broyles in their owne bosomes, nor threatned with blasts of other borderers', and identifies this temperate self-government and resistance to invasion with the intactness of Elizabeth's virgin body: 'This is the onely myracle that virginitie euer wrought' (Lyly 1902: 209–10). Paradoxically and mystically, Elizabeth's virginity has had the result that the whole nation is fruitful and abundant: 'Their fieldes haue beene sowne with corne [. . .] they haue their men reaping their haruest [. . .] their barnes [are] full' (Lyly 1902: 209–11). Thus, the cornucopian imagery applied to Aylmer's figure of Mother England returns with a vengeance just at the point when Elizabeth's physical fertility is coming to an end.

Fears of alternatives to Elizabeth's motherhood were often expressed through imagery of the failure of natural growth and fertility. In Puttenham's *Partheniades*, a plant with three buds was used as an emblem of the Tudor dynasty:

> Twoo blossoms falne, the thirde began to fade
> So as with in the compas of an houre
> Sore withered was this noble deintye flowre
> That noe soyle bredd, nor lande shall loose the like
> Ne no seazon or soone or soking showre
> Can reare agayne for prayer ne for meede.
> Woe and alas, the people crye and shrike
> Why fades this flower, and leaues noe fruit nor seede.
>   (Puttenham 1579: 172v–173r)

Complementing this, wishes for Elizabeth to procreate were also expressed in images of natural fertility: Lyly prayed for her to be 'fruitfull in hir age lyke the Uyne' (Lyly 1902: 119). Yet as the recognition grew that she would not bear fruit, this natural, pastoral imagery, instead of receding, became ever more prominent and prevalent. We can observe a shift taking place in the genre of rhetoric in which maternal imagery was deployed. During Elizabeth's potentially fertile years, the maternal topos was used in a deliberative rhetoric which was self-consciously time-bound, seeking to change policy and looking to the future. Now it began to be increasingly used in epideictic rhetoric, praising Elizabeth as a timeless icon of eternal, ideal, symbolic motherhood.

A crucial instance of this was Spenser's 'Aprill Eclogue' in the *Shepheardes Calender* of 1579. Spenser carefully avoids Stubbs's fate by expressing the hope that Elizabeth will not suffer the childlessness of Niobe and gesturing graciously towards the possibility of the Anjou match. Amid the poem's catalogue of flowers, 'The pretie Pawnce, / And the Chevisaunce, / Shall match with the fayre flowre Delice', the fleur-de-lis, the emblem of France.[9] Yet, as Stubbs pointed out, Elizabeth already bore the the fleur-de-lis in her coat of arms, as rightful monarch of France; although Anjou's family occupied the French throne, they bore the fleur-de-lis as usurpers (Stubbs 1968: 67). Read in these terms, Spenser is looking forward to a future match between 'chevisaunce', that is, chivalry, and the fleur-de-lis – perhaps a future return of France to rightful and virtuous English rule. Elizabeth, in effect, is being invited to match with herself. In fact, the whole poem creates for her use and for that of Spenser's fellow panegyrists an iconography of her perpetual virginity, frozen in an iconic moment of bridal fertility expressed by means of the litany of flowers:

> Bring hether the pincke and purple cullambine,
>   With gelliflowres;
> Bring coronations, and sops in wine,
>   Worne of paramours;
> Strowe me the ground with daffadowndillies,
> And cowslips, and kingcups, and loved lilies.
>   (Spenser 1999: 65, ll. 136–44)

These teeming flowers of spring indicate that Elizabeth does not need to marry and bear children to achieve fertility; indeed, it is by her very avoidance of marriage, by her preservation of her intact virginity, that she brings peace and plenty to the nation and achieves a mystical, symbolic fertility.

Probably some time during the Anjou courtship, Elizabeth wrote out in her own hand a prayer book adorned with miniatures of herself and her suitor. It includes a French prayer which reverts to the image from Isaiah of queens as nursing mothers of the Church: 'My God and Father, I render Thee everlasting thanks that Thou hast given me the honour of being mother and nurse of thy dear children [. . .] Preserve therefore the mother and the children whom thou hast given her' (Elizabeth I 2000: 314–15). It was an image that also continued to be popular among loyal Protestant subjects: Thomas Bentley in 1582 described Elizabeth as 'the most naturall mother and noble nursse' of the Church (Bentley 1582: I, dedication). Elizabeth's people had grown accustomed to the idea of her as their symbolic mother, and it remained unaltered by the passing of her capacity for biological motherhood. In fact, if anything, it was reinforced by it.

Later years

The iconography of natural fertility took hold and was predominant for the rest of the reign. Lyly again, in his play *Endymion*, performed before the Queen in 1588, presented Elizabeth as Cynthia, the moon goddess, and praised her as a nature goddess of fruitfulness and harvest: 'know you not [. . .] that Cynthia governeth all things? Your grapes would be but dry husks, your corn but chaff, and all your virtues vain, were it not Cynthia that preserveth the one in the bud and nourisheth the other in the blade, and by her influence [. . .] comforteth all things' (Lyly 1996: 1.2.29–34). A song from Elizabeth's visit to Elvetham in 1591 also celebrated her as a kind of spring goddess:

> Now earth, with verdure newly dight,
> Giues perfect signe of her delight [. . .]
> Now euerie thing that nature breeds,
> Doth clad itself in pleasant weeds.
> (Wilson 1980: 96–118)

Even as late as 1603, *The Triumphs of Oriana* imitated the 'Aprill Eclogue' by showing Elizabeth dressed in 'gaudy green' and surrounded by flowers.[10]

The language of pastoral and of natural fertility thus became ever more established the further Elizabeth receded from biological fertility. Frances Yates accounts for this by reference to Elizabeth's role in some panegyric as Astraea, the virgin goddess of justice who presided over a perpetual golden age, where spring and harvest combined (Yates 1947: 27–82). While accepting this, we may also detect in the efflorescence of this pastoral iconography a reaction to, and compensation for, Elizabeth's physical infertility. Menstrual blood was commonly termed 'flowers', as James Rueff's *The Expert Midwife* explained:

> The Germans do name this Purgation, Flowers; because even as the trees which doe not blossome and send forth flowers either through age or corruption of Nature, doe not fructifie, nor bring forth fruit: so also euery woman deprived of these Flowers, I say, of this purging in her due season, by the course of Nature, can neither conceive, nor ingender.
>
> (Rueff 1637: Part 1, 11)

The ceasing of Elizabeth's 'flowers' paradoxically produced ever more floral imagery in panegyric.

Medical books of the period customarily used analogies drawn from the cultivation of fruits and crops to discuss the functions and malfunctions of the female generative organs. Eucharius Roesslin's *The Birth of Mankind*, also known as *The Woman's Book*, was the earliest printed midwifery textbook in English; first published in 1513, it went through thirteen editions up to 1654. It explicitly compared human conception to 'the sowing of Corne, and all other maner of seede', and compared human infertility to the sowing of corn 'in ouer cold places [. . .] where the sunne doth not shine' (Roesslin 1598: 186–7, 189). Similarly *The Expert Midwife* opened:

> We observe the naturall Procreation of man, to be altogether such, as we perceive the Generation & beginning of Plants, or Herbes, of every kinde to be. For as they, every one of them from the seede of his kinde, cast into the wombe of the earth, doe bud, or increase, and doe naturally grow to the perfect form of his proper Nature: So man also, being a reasonable creature, according to the quality of his body, doth naturally draw his originall & beginning from the Sperme, and Seede of man, projected and cast forth into the wombe of woman, as into a field.
>
> (Rueff 1637: Part 1, 1–2)

The modern historian of childbirth, Jacques Gélis, summarises, 'The woman's body was like a field, cultivated earth opening to receive the seed of the child' (Gélis 1991: 36). We are familiar with this use of images of seed and harvest for human procreation from poetry and drama. Shakespeare, in Sonnet 3, asks, 'where is she so fair whose uneared womb / Disdains the tillage of thy husbandry?' (Shakespeare 1974: ll. 5–6). In *Measure for Measure*, Lucio speaks thus of Juliet's pregnancy:

> as blossoming time
> That from the seedness the bare fallow brings
> To teeming foison, even so her plenteous womb
> Expresseth his full tilth and husbandry.
> (Shakespeare 1974: 1.4.41–4)

In *Antony and Cleopatra*, Agrippa gives a succinct description of Cleopatra's relationship with Julius Caesar: 'He ploughed her, and she cropp'd' (Shakespeare 1974: 2.2.228).

To continue associating Elizabeth with fruit and flowers, then, was to assert the flourishing health of both her body natural and the body politic. The alternative is depicted in *A Midsummer Night's Dream*, in the childless marriage of Titania and Oberon:

> The ox hath therefore stretch'd his yoke in vain,
> The ploughman lost his sweat, and the green corn
> Hath rotted ere his youth attained a beard.
> The fold stands empty in the drownèd field,
> And crows are fatted with the murrion flock.
> (Shakespeare 1974: 2.1.93–7)

Many scholars have read this passage as a topical allusion to the bad summers and failed harvests of the mid-1590s. We may also read it as an Ovidian aetiological myth, with Oberon and Titania as nature deities whose emotional battles explain cosmic disorder and the disruption of the seasons; and we can read it as Titania speaking metaphorically about her grief over her own failed fertility. The speech ends with imagery of procreation gone wrong:

> the spring, the summer,
> The childing autumn, angry winter change
> Their wonted liveries, and the mazèd world,
> By their increase, now knows not which is which.
> And this same progeny of evils comes
> From our debate, from our dissension;
> We are their parents and original.
> (2.1.111–17)

Shakespeare is careful to make Titania both suggestively like Elizabeth, as Fairy Queen, and safely unlike her, as a married woman. At that safe distance, Titania may well be speaking here, in encoded form, both of Elizabeth's responsibility for the social hardships of the 1590s, and of the sterility and stasis in which Elizabeth as ageing heirless monarch was felt to be holding the nation suspended.[11]

In fact, underneath all the celebratory iconography of fertility of Elizabeth's later years may be detected that anxiety that Burghley voiced back in 1579, the anxiety that England was being ruled by a hysteric. Elizabeth became increasingly notorious among her courtiers for her volatility and unpredictability, for her rages and unreasonableness. A constant theme of courtiers' letters was the difficulty of managing the Queen. Leicester received a letter from his brother in 1586 about his conduct of the Spanish campaign: 'Our mistress's extreme rage doth increase rather than any way diminish, and giveth out great threatening words against you. Therefore make the best assurance you can for yourself, and trust not her oath, for that her malice is great and unquenchable, in the wisest of their opinions here' (Haigh 1988: 132). In 1598, notoriously, she boxed Essex's ears in Council (Neale 1960: 354). Sir John Harington, looking back on Elizabeth's reign after her death, had recourse to natural analogy again, but this time to represent not her maternal love and abundance, but her tempestuousness: 'When she smiled, it was a pure sunshine that everyone did choose to bask in if they could; but anon came a storm from a hidden gathering of clouds, and the thunder fell in wondrous manner on all alike' (Neale 1960: 222).

Hence the underside of the rhetoric of fertility which dominated late Elizabethan panegyric was a rhetoric of infertility that could be readily deployed to depict the unhealthy state of the body politic. This infertility was in turn associated with the unseasonal and untimely, and with the distorting and destructive effects of time. This was the mode deployed by Ralegh in his complaint poem *The Ocean to Cynthia*, probably composed in the early 1590s:

> When shee that from the soonn reves poure and light
> Did but decline her beames as discontented
> Convertinge sweetest days to saddest night
> All droopes, all dyes, all troden under dust
> The person, place, and passages forgotten
> The hardest steele eaten with softest ruste
> The firme and sollide tree both rent and rotten.

This is very like Titania's speech quoted above, but here it is explicitly Elizabeth who is associated with rottenness, with a cold dampness that decays and blights, and which seems to have its origins in her femaleness: 'So hath perfection which begatt her mynde / Added therto a change of fantasye / And left her the affections of her kynde'.[12] Whereas earlier it was Elizabeth's intact body that was identified with the nation, now it seems that her hysteria has infected the body politic. While loyal panegyric propounded the myth that by her virginity Elizabeth had elevated herself above time, dissenting texts such as this accentuated the supposedly disturbing effects of time upon the female body.

This rhetoric of infertility is the shadow side of late Elizabethan panegyric and exposes the hollowness of the increasingly extravagant terms of poetry celebrating the Queen. Her supporters represented her virginity as a mystical paradox, endowing her with miraculous powers of political abundance, and in the competition to devise new hyperboles they began to appropriate motifs from Catholic veneration of the Virgin Mary, as in a poem about Elizabeth written for Christmas 1602:

> This Sacred Nimphe, because noe mortall wight
> Deserved to Lincke with her in chaines of Love,
> Unto the god of soules her faith hath plight,
> And vowde her self to him without remove.
> Thus doth this brid[e] tenn thowsand children breed,
> And virgins milke the Church of god doth feed.[13]

Mariological iconography facilitated the conversion of infertility into mystical fertility.

Meanwhile, in public debate, the maternal metaphor did not disappear from deliberative rhetoric, as the rhetorical contest between the authority of a mother and the rights of her children persisted right to the end of the reign. The Puritan parliamentarian Peter Wentworth, a fervent exponent of freedom of speech, wrote a pamphlet in 1598 urging Elizabeth to follow the wishes of her subjects in naming her successor, which asserted that Mary Tudor would 'have had this Island to have become a dwelling for strangers: much like unto an unnatural nurse', whereas Elizabeth had preserved England 'in peace and prosperity, most like unto a natural nursing mother, for the use of the ancient inhabitants thereof' (Wentworth 1598: F6r–v, quoted in Orlin 1995: 91). On the government side, the epideictic rhetoric of Elizabeth as ideal mother – which was, of course, ideologically motivated – could readily shade into deliberative rhetoric, as during the tempestuous parliament of 1601. The Queen pacified her audience and defused their discontent about grants of monopolies with her so-called 'Golden Speech', in which she declared, 'this I count the glory of my crown: that I have reigned with your loves [. . .] though you have had and may have princes more mighty and wise sitting in this seat, yet you never had or shall have any that shall be more careful and loving' (Elizabeth I 2000: 337, 340). Our survey of the reign suggests that this imaginary mother–child relationship was often less like that of a baby calmly suckling at the breast, and more like that of a rebellious adolescent who thinks his mother is past it.

Conclusion

It is easy to see why Elizabeth and her supporters seized on the role of symbolic mother for its many rhetorical advantages at different phases in her long reign. However, it had disadvantages too, in that it was a rhetoric that bound her to her female body, and to processes of time and ageing, and could thereby be used against her as well as for her. In the marriage debate of the early years of the reign, her attempts to suppress demands for her biological motherhood by invoking her symbolic motherhood were countered with claims that a truly loving mother would show more tolerance and care to her children, and with aggressive assertions of those 'children's' rights. At the time of the Anjou courtship, her female body, at once virginal and maternal, was identified with the body politic and lay at the centre of the fraught political debate. After the conclusive passing of her fertility, maternal rhetoric became ever more abundant and elaborate as a compensation for her actual childlessness, while an undertow of dissent was expressed by means of a rhetoric of infertility, hysteria, and decay.

Jacques Gélis, in his *History of Childbirth*, discusses the extensive use in early modern culture of analogies between crop cycles and human fertility and sums up: 'A barren woman turns her back on nature' (Gélis 1991: 16). It was Elizabeth's very 'unnaturalness' that produced her representation as England's mother, a mystical paradox designed to inspire wondering assent; yet the very paradoxicality of this image, and a persistent consciousness that it was merely an image, meant that it was always at the centre of rhetorical contestation between different interest groups throughout the reign.

Acknowledgement

I am grateful to Alison Thorne and Jennifer Richards for their extremely helpful comments on this essay.

Notes

1 For more examples of the persistent maternal image, see Orlin (1995: 90).
2 For the distinction between deliberative rhetoric, which seeks to persuade or dissuade in relation to a policy or course of action, and epideictic rhetoric, which is concerned with praise or blame, see Dixon (1971: 22–3), Vickers (1989: 20–3, 26, 53–62), Aristotle (1991: 47–50).
3 *The Geneva Bible* (1969), 1560 facsimile, intro. L. E. Berry, Madison, Wisc.: University of Wisconsin Press.
4 *OED* nurse v., 3.a. trans. For further examples of the 'nursing mother' image from throughout the reign, see Orlin (1995: 91).
5 See Orlin (1995: 91), for a discussion of parental metaphors as expressing both a monarch's obligation to his/her people, and *vice versa*.
6 Coch (2003: 136, 160) asserts that Elizabeth herself did not use the maternal metaphor after about 1563. This may be true in Parliament, where the metaphor was increasingly turned against her, but there are instances from other sources, as quoted in the present essay.
7 Petrarch, *Rime Sparse*, 189, 235. For imitation, see for instance Spenser, *Amoretti* XXXIIII (1999: 404).
8 As in *Amoretti* LXIII, in Spenser (1999: 419).
9 Spenser (1999: 60–71), ll. 86–90, E. K.'s note on ll. 86–7, ll. 142–4. The 'Pawnce' is the pansy; the 'Chevisaunce' is a flower-name invented by Spenser.
10 Fellowes (1967: 158–66, nos. XI, XIII).
11 For a fuller discussion, see Hackett (2003: 338–57).
12 Sir Walter Ralegh, *The 21ˢᵗ: and last booke of the Ocean to Scinthia*, in Norbrook and Woudhuysen (eds) (1992: 102–16).
13 'Verses of the Queene', 1602, in Davies (1975: 307). For a full discussion of the relation between panegyric of Elizabeth and the iconography of the Virgin Mary, see Hackett (1995).

9 Women's letters of recommendation and the rhetoric of friendship in sixteenth-century England

James Daybell

In recent years, scholarly attention has increasingly focused on the relations between gender and rhetoric.[1] One important strand of work by early modernists researching in this area has attended to women's marginalisation from formal classical rhetorical traditions, with the obvious exception of a small handful of humanistically educated individuals, and has explored the diverse strategies women used to negotiate their silencing.[2] Conventionally, rhetorical training has been viewed by both sixteenth-century educational theorists and modern-day scholars as a male preserve; women, it was thought, had no requirement for the kinds of persuasive linguistic skills that became the prerequisite for men destined for public office, since the locus of their activity was restricted to the household or domestic sphere. Indeed, Juan Luis Vives in his *De institutione feminae Christianae* (1523), which was penned for Catherine of Aragon as an educational guide for her daughter Princess Mary, intoned 'As for eloquence, I have no great care, nor a women needeth it not, but she needeth goodness and wisdom' (Watson 1912: 54). The general assumption that women were excluded from rhetoric has, however, received slight modification by Catherine Eskin in her survey of educational and rhetorical manuals, in which she observes the range of views of male writers on the advisability of teaching girls rhetoric (Eskin 1999: 100–32; cf. Donawerth 1995). Whilst conservative sixteenth-century texts by Giovanni Michele Bruto and Thomas Salter denied women access to rhetorical training, at the other end of the spectrum the educationalist Richard Mulcaster argued that girls should be endowed 'with some *Logicall* helpe to chop, and some *Rhetoricke* to brave' (Mulcaster 1581: 182; Bruto 1598; Salter 1579). Alternatively, other scholars have attempted to overcome the intractability of women's exclusion from restrictive classical definitions of education by adopting a broader, more flexible and inclusive definition of rhetoric, one that recognises a variety of female discourses, both spoken and written, as constituting forms of 'rhetorical' activity.[3] Operating parallel to the democratisation of this approach, early modern social historians have highlighted the innate, yet untrained, rhetorical qualities contained within women's oral testimony. Natalie Zemon Davis, for example, has examined the devices utilised in women's pardon tales in sixteenth-century France; Tim Stretton has studied the rhetorical nature of pleading strategies of women in the Elizabethan Court of Requests; and Laura Gowing has emphasised the degree of linguistic facility of ordinary female deponents brought before the London consistitory courts on charges of sexual slander, who manipulated language and narratives for political ends (Davis 1987: Chapter 3, Gowing 1996: 201, 235–9, Stretton 1998: Chapter 8). These different approaches work to expose the disjuncture between informal rhetorical practices and the kinds of classical rhetorical principles that were promulgated in England by sixteenth-century humanists, and raise thorny questions relating to the definitions and acquisition of women's rhetorical skills.

Whilst a rethinking of the definition of what encompasses rhetorical activity permits scholars on one level to incorporate women better into the study of rhetoric, the concern of some rhetoricians remains the critical quality of these categories. In light of this scholarly rupture in terms of approaches and methodologies, this essay seeks to reconcile the apparent division between formal, institutional and professional rhetorical traditions and informal and non-traditional rhetorical modes. A study of women's letters of recommendation, it will be argued, highlights female mastery of formal rhetorical skills, and women's adoption of a classical language of political 'friendship'. Indeed, read for rhetoric – in terms of structure, language and strategies – women's letters of recommendation, intercession and mediation clearly conform to traditional rhetorical models, demonstrating female conversance with the formal conventions of the epistolary genre. Excluded from the kinds of male-dominated educational institutions – schools, universities and inns of court – that provided official rhetorical training, women gleaned their knowledge of rhetoric less from formal tuition than from vernacular letter-writing manuals that transmitted classical epistolary models to a wider non-Latinate audience and, perhaps more commonly, from practical contact with the everyday form. Furthermore, women's letters of commendation and intercession display a rich vocabulary of patronage, favour and 'political friendship'. Female letter-writers employed a Senecan language of mutual benefits: they promised repayment of favours in kind, assured the friendship of themselves and husbands and mobilised alliances of family and 'friends'. Such usage presumably derived less from knowledge of classical texts than the fact that this Senecan language soaked the very social and cultural world in which they operated. Although highly ritualised, women's easy familiarity with and utilisation of a language of favour and reciprocity – a language typically seen as predominantly male – is suggestive of the high degree of confidence and authority with which many women wrote and intervened in the political arena. In terms of social status, it was mainly upper-class women who composed commendations, and a significant percentage of these were court ladies. Thus, the majority of female writers of this type of letter were well connected and of high birth, operating within a relatively wide social ambit, though a small proportion of letters derived from women of the professional and middling classes, the wives and widows of lawyers and merchants. It is, therefore, highly likely that many women were acquainted with the officials to whom they corresponded and in a position to exert influence. The actions of these female letter writers were not unusual or extraordinary for women of their status, but a normal and necessary part of the social duties incumbent upon upper-class women as family members, mistresses of households, landowners and patrons in their own right. In this analysis, the rhetoric of women's letters differs very little from that of the letters of their male counterparts, which followed similar social hierarchies based on rank and social position; this contrasts with the calculated use of negative female gender assumptions in letters of deference of female suitors.

Concomitantly, viewed as historical documents, letters of recommendation permit an examination of female involvement in Tudor patronage and politics, delineating the scope and nature of female activity, in order better to integrate women into traditional narratives of political history. Such letters (over 700 examples of which survive for the Elizabethan period alone) were written on behalf of family, dependants and other social groups, including 'friends', neighbours and clients, and conveyed a broad range of patronage suits.[4] The range and nature of requests made by women elucidates female intervention in the dispensing of crown, ecclesiastical and more local forms of patronage. Acting as intermediaries, 'brokers' and patrons in their own right, noblewomen and gentlewomen wrote concerning the preferment of suitors to offices; the bestowing of titles and honours; to procure grants of land, wardships, pensions and annuities; to secure justice and release from imprisonment; and, more nebulously, they wrote to acquire influence and advice. Margaret, Countess of Pembroke preferred a 'poore' servant to Sir Julius Caesar in his capacity as Master of the Court of Requests; Alice, Countess of Derby, sponsored one John Owen for a military post to be in charge of troops levied in Northamptonshire for dispatch to Ireland.[5] Muriel Knyvett wrote to her cousin Sir Bassingbourne Gawdy on behalf of one William Chartery: 'Good cosen this bearer has ernestly entreated me to wryght 3 or 4 lynes on his behalf requiring your favour to him for a certain benefice w[hi]ch is in your power to present'.[6] Anne Lady Bacon, preferring one Mr Holmes to Burghley, wrote that the advancement of the former would be for 'the great benefit of o[u]r land & specially of the adva[n]cem[en]t of the gospell herin'.[7] Letters of recommendation thus illustrate the ways in which elite women performed many of the same patronage functions as men. Moreover, the *politics* of letter-writing was at the heart of women's interventions, and study of form and genre thus highlights the need to extend the category of the 'political' in order to facilitate the accommodation of women's discursive or rhetorical activities.

Rhetorical models

Historians working on early modern literature have long been alert to the need to read the writings of the period with attention to form as well as content, though this attention to rhetoric and structure rarely extends to documents such as letters, which themselves conform to generic conventions, following epistolary and rhetorical exemplars.[8] Numerous printed manuals were produced during the sixteenth century offering instructions and models that laid out the rules governing letter-writing. Writers and publishers were responding partly to an increasingly receptive audience among upper- and middling-status groups. The medieval *ars dictaminis* and early sixteenth-century Latin formularies, such as Erasmus' *Conficiendarum epistolarum formula* (1521) and his influential *De conscribendis epistolis* (1522), aimed largely at students of rhetoric, were modified for an increasingly receptive gentry and mercantile audience (Henderson 1983 and 1993, Gibson 2000). William Fulwood dedicated *The Enemie of Idlenesse* (1568) to the Merchant Taylors of London: 'I meane not I / the cunning clerks to teach / But rather the unlearned sort / a few precepts to preach' (Fullwood 1568: A3v). Similarly, Angel Day's *The English Secretary* (1586), Abraham Fleming's *A Panoplie of Epistles* (1576) and John Browne's *The Merchants' Avizo* (1589) were written for wider public readership, including women.[9] Epistolographies of this kind outlined the art of letter-writing, mapping the generic boundaries of the early modern letter (Guillén 1986). In his epistolary manual *De conscribendis epistolis*, Erasmus, following classical oratorical lines, adopted a tripartite division of epistles into deliberative, demonstrative and judicial writing. To the three main classical rhetorical types of epistle Erasmus added a new fourth category – the familiar letter. The latter, according to Erasmus, included letters that narrated events, provided news both 'public' and 'private', contained congratulations and complaints, proffered advice or help, gave praise or were written merely to amuse (Erasmus 1985: 71).[10] This fourfold Erasmian method of epistolary classification was adopted by other authors, such as Angel Day. In this manner, vernacular letter-writing manuals contributed to the broader dissemination of classical rhetorical techniques (Day 1586: 41–2).

Letters of recommendation were classed as a sub-genre of letter, grouped by Erasmus in the deliberative and demonstrative class, and closely related to the petitionary form or 'letter of request', 'for when we recommend someone, we are really making a request in another's name' (Erasmus 1985: 181–2). Following the Dutch humanist, Day emphasises the similarities between letters of petition and recommendation; yet in his treatment of 'epistles commendatorie' he amplifies on the innate differences between the two types of letter occasioned by the act of writing on behalf of another. Whereas letters of petition should employ a deferential language of 'humilitie and entreatie' and 'pleasures or courtesie', letters of recommendation required use of a strategy of 'supposal and assurance', the request formulated in the manner of a 'courteous demaunde':

> Now besides these hereby already deliuered, ther are letters also might besuted vnder this form, which from noble men or others, are many times written in fauour of sondry persons, containing requestes in their behalfes to be perfourmed, which notwithstanding the difference of estates, in that the same doe for the most part passe vnto their inferiours, yet seemeth the nature thereof to be *Petitorie*, but in a different order of these to be altogeather pursued. Insomuch as neither agreeth it, to vse lyke circumstaunces of humilitie and entreatie, nor of pleasures or courtesie, as in the other are required: but rather a necessarie supposall and assuraunce of their demaundes to be hearkned vnto, in respect that of their honours, reputations, or credites, it is intended they will require nothing, but what with reasonable tolleration may be liked of. But in truth hold the vse of such kind

of directions in choice of both, rather pertinent vnto the title *Commendatorie*, for that whatsoeuer is therein written in fauour either of the person or of the cause, maye in respect of the honor or reputation from whom they come, be better deemed in sort of a courteous demaunde, to recommend the regard of the partie or thing spoken of, then by the submissiue title of a matter craued, or by any order of humilitie otherwise to be sought for [. . .]

(Day 1586: 184–5)

The structure of letters of recommendation was based on five main rhetorical parts which were commonly employed in early modern epistles. These could be adapted according to requirements: *exordium* (introduction), *narratio* or *propositio* (declaration of the substance of the letter), *confirmatio* (amplification), *confutatio* (refutation of objections) and *peroratio* (conclusion). Thus, Day's example of 'An Epistle Commendatorie from a noble man, in preferment of his seruant' begins with *narratio*, followed by a 'recommendation' and *propositio*; the servant's suit is then presented (*petitio*), and the nobleman promises requital of the favour should his request prevail ('remuneration'), before concluding with salutations (*peroratio*) (Day 1586: 191–2).

Female conversance with the formal rhetorical structure of letters – a conversance gained, as suggested above, less through formal tuition than via readership of early modern printed epistolographies and exemplars in manuscript miscellanies, or perhaps more commonly from regular practical contact with the form[11] – is demonstrated by an examination of examples of women's letters of recommendation, which themselves reflect the arguments and instructions outlined in early modern epistolary manuals (Mack 2002: 114–16). A letter to Sir Julius Caesar from Frances, Countess of Kildare follows a standard rhetorical structure, beginning by entreating his 'fauor' on behalf of two Irish merchants who had a suit before him in the Court of Admiralty. The Countess explained that the men were her neighbours and that she would be glad to procure them what friendship she might in their 'just and honest cause'. She then offered thanks, expressing her readyness to 'requite' the favour 'by any good meane', before leaving the men and their cause to Caesar's 'goode and fauorable consideration'.[12] In another letter to Caesar, Cicely, Countess of Dorset pressed the suit of a 'poore gentlewoman'. After offering her 'hartie commendacions', and stating her relationship to the supplicant, the Countess detailed the woman's request, stressing the injustices she faced and her need for Caesar's 'lawful fauour and kindnes towards her'.[13] The letter then promises that the woman, her husband and children will be bound to pray for him, and the Countess binds herself to 'yield [. . .] manie thanks in this behaulf'. The letter ends with remembrances to Caesar's wife and well wishes to him and all his family. Following a similar format, Joyce Wrotesley wrote to her cousin Walter Bagot preferring suits for two men – the letter-bearer and her neighbour John Smyth – both of whom wished to keep their posts under Bagot as High Sherrif of Staffordshire. In both instances, the suit of each man is recommended, his honesty and ability to 'discharge' the post praised. The letter ends with the writer's commendations, with no mention of requital of favours rendered. The absence of an offer to repay the favour might explain the postscript to the letter penned by Walter Wrotesley, in which he endorses his wife's support for the bearer and promises reciprocation in kind should the favour be granted.[14] In each case, the formality of the letter is perhaps reflective of the nature of the social situation of request-making. Indeed, the rhetorician Peter Mack argues in the case of letters of recommendation (and consolation) that 'by following well established norms' writers 'conveyed a sense of order and reassurance', adding that 'originality in letters of this type would be a sign of anxiety, of uncertain or inappropriate sentiments on the part of the writer' (Mack 2002: 116). By contrast, women's 'familiar' letters to family and friends, beyond the use of conventional opening, closing and salutory forms, display a greater degree of freedom in terms of subject matter and organisation of the body of the letter that is absent from recommendatory epistles.

Although letters of recommendation are indeed formulaic, both structurally and linguistically, choice and adaptation of, and deviation from, conventional forms indicate more personal elements of women's business correspondence. The example of a letter written by Katherine, Duchess of Suffolk in 1550 to William Cecil illustrates the flexibility possible in letters of recommendation. An accomplished letter writer, the Duchess was fully aware of the structural conventions of the letter form; her letter to Cecil betrays a playful, even artful self-consciousness of the act of letter-writing and of the function of letters. 'This letter must serve you for many purposes' she informed the newly appointed Secretary Cecil. 'First, you shall hereby find you be not forgotten, but amongst the biggest remembered, and farther, you shall hereby take occasion not to be idle, but to be occupied by me'. With remembrances delivered, the letter then expands upon the business of the suit that would 'occupy' Cecil, in short that he intercede in '[William] Naunton's cause', a matter about which she had written to him on a previous occasion. Where next there should be a promise of favour reciprocated, the letter moves rather to a discussion of friendship. The letter then reiterates the suit, 'I pray you save them innocent from being condemned', before knowingly closing with a more formulaic salutation: 'And thus, two parts being played, the third is to bid you farewell with my hearty commendations to mistress Mildred and yourself'.[15] The originality of the letter, and the Duchess's deliberate deviation from epistolary norms, exhibits her practised dexterity as a letter writer and is also symptomatic of her high social standing and the close relationship with Cecil.

The rhetoric of friendship

Sixteenth-century letters of recommendation highlight not only women's adherence to and manipulation of the rhetorical structure of correspondence, but also their easy familiarity in using a highly rhetorical language of patronage, favour and 'political friendship' – a language of equality traditionally seen as exclusively male (James 1986: 330–2, Bray 1990: 3–8, Hutson 1994, Tadmor 2001). The basis upon which women laid claim to this language was founded in large part on material power, social status and influence. Indeed, recent scholarship has stressed the breadth of aristocratic women's political and patronage roles at varying levels, within the family, locality and sometimes on the wider political stage.[16] Although excluded from official, formal and direct forms of power – in most cases, for example, they could not hold office[17] – women exerted significant influence through unofficial and indirect channels, such as family and court networks, playing key roles in the sustaining of vital kinship and patronage networks. Court posts and landownership likewise bequeathed status and influence. Furthermore, the fact women were approached to write in the first place in support of suitors indicates underlying assumptions about their abilities to intercede effectively. Women's choice of language is thus reflective of social standing and position. And yet language constructs as well as reflects reality. There is a sense, therefore, that women's selection of a language of political friendship, and the dexterity with which they deployed this rhetoric, is in itself instrumental in constructing an image of their authority and equality with the addressee.

The language of political friendship infuses women's letters of recommendation. Female letter writers frequently invoked the friendship of the addressee: Agnes Stubbings asked Julius Ferrers to continue her 'friend'.[18] Philadelphia, Lady Scrope asked Sir Julius Caesar to show his 'friendly favour' to the letter-bearer her cousin Morgan, who was to come before Caesar concerning a farm lease.[19] Letters also evidence female involvement in 'friendship' networks: women are represented as situated within groups of friends and establishing useful political contacts. Writing to his wife from London, Thomas Lord Paget informed her that several of her 'friends at court' had asked after her.[20] Joan Bradborne informed her brother-in-law Sir Humphrey Ferrers that she would take advice from her 'frendes' about her jointure.[21] In many of the instances cited in the essay, women are shown calling on other women to intercede on their behalf, suggesting that they had access to female friendship networks. The uncovering of early modern women's alliances offers a plausible alternative to the narrative of women 'identified with and serving men and male interests', yet female networks did not exist in isolation but, as Barbara Harris has shown, 'coexisted' and were compatible with primary loyalties to the patrilineages of women's marital families (Harris 2004; Frye and Robertson 1999). Female alliances, while not exclusive, were useful to women in numerous ways, and many women assiduously maintained links, sustaining these 'horizontal' ties through letters, visits and the exchange of favours and gifts. Female contacts were useful in placing girls either at court or in aristocratic households and in arranging marriages. In the case of appointments to Maids of Honour, which was in many ways a female domain, women rather than men were seen as influential in distributing positions (Harris 1990: 276). Thus, John Husee counselled his mistress Lady Lisle to refrain from writing to Cromwell or Francis Bryan in order to place her daughters for service in Jane Seymour's household: 'for it is thought by my Lady Sussex and other your Ladyship's very friends that it is no meet suit for any man to move such matters, but for such ladies and woman as be your friends' (Byrne 1981: IV, 896). In this sense, the category of the 'political' should not only be extended to include women but also redefined to incorporate a gendered dynamic of power and influence.

The meaning of the term 'friend' is slippery for the early modern period and was used to refer to family (even between husbands and wives), as well as more broadly to cover persons unrelated by blood or marriage, where 'friendship' assumes political connotations. In relation to early modern marriage, Diana O'Hara shows how the term 'friends' referred to family and kinship groups, both 'biological' and 'fictive'; groups that were simultaneously advantageous (as a source of counsel, advice and support) and constraining for the individual (in that their 'goodwill' often needed to be sought) (O'Hara 1991). Furthermore, the meaning of friendship as a concept, as Lorna Hutson has argued, itself changed over the course of the sixteenth century with the impact of humanism 'from that of a code of "faith-fulness" assured by acts of hospitality and the circulation of gifts through the family and its allies, to that of an instrumental and affec-tive relationship which might be generated, even between strangers, through emotionally persuasive communication' (Hutson 1994: 2–3). This model of friendship derives from a form of exchange between humanistically educated men. The extent to which it achieved more widespread epistolary currency is uneven – late medieval social and cultural modes survived well into the Tudor period – but in general terms late Elizabethan business letters (specifically, letters of recom-mendation and intercession), in contrast to early Tudor examples such as the Lisle letters, follow more closely humanistic models that rely on a greater degree of rhetorical persuasion. Furthermore, at the heart of this humanistic conceptualisation of friendship lies the suggestion that rhetorical skill is in fact capable of engendering friend-ships, not merely mobilising existing networks, a conceptualisation that needs to be extended to include women. Women's conducting of correspondence was central to oiling the wheels of kinship and patronage networks and to cultivating useful contacts that could be called upon for future assistance. Indeed, it was Lady Anne Newdigate rather than her husband who kept up regular correspondence with kin and court contacts (Larminie 1995: 10–17).

In it simplest practical form, 'friends' could be understood as 'allies', 'supporters' or 'well-wishers'. Such was the meaning of Alice Mervyn when she informed her daughter Elizabeth Bourne after her split from her violent wastrel husband, 'I will wryte to make suche frends as I can for the fauor of yo[u]r cause'.[22] In a reply, Elizabeth Bourne asked her mother to thank Lady Conway for her efforts on her behalf and in particular for writing to the countesses of Warwick and Sussex to garner their support. Friends here are defined in opposition to 'enemies', groups of people who sought to cause one 'harm'. In the same letter to her mother, Elizabeth Bourne complained of the 'many enemyes' set against her, bemoaning her 'evell fortun and wante of good frendes'.[23] Whilst friends could be called upon by women for advice and support, friendship worked both ways, and women frequently promoted the suits of persons described as 'friends'. Interventions on behalf of 'friends' outside of family and household groups were common: Lady Southwell preferred Dr Some to the bishopric of Exeter 'at the request of a friend'; Lucy, Marchioness of Winchester wrote to her uncle Robert Cecil on behalf of her 'own friend' Mr Philpot, the bearer of her letter, requesting that his son be granted leave to travel to France; Magdalen Lady Montagu petitioned her godson Sir Julius Caesar 'on the behalfe of a speciall friende'.[24] Frances Brooke, Lady Cobham informed Lady Paget that she had been approached by her 'verie friends' 'to intreate' her ladyship to commend to her husband the cause of one Mr Paramore who was at Westminster embroiled in a land dispute.[25]

The language of friendship was ultimately one of reciprocity, a Senecan language of mutual benefits that pervaded early modern patronage relations (Salmon 1991). In their letters, women commonly extended offers of 'friendship' – either their own friendship or, in the case of married women, generally their husbands' as well. Joan Wincombe, in a letter to the Earl of Essex, excused her husband's absence because of illness and assured him of both their friendships.[26] For the early Tudor period, Barbara Harris has noted the 'regularity' with which wives 'offered to return favours "with a like pleasure"', which she argues 'suggests that they had some voice in how their husbands distributed their patronage' (Harris 1990: 270). In other instances, women offered their own friendship: Mary, Countess of Shrewsbury assured Cecil that she and all her friends would 'w[i]t[h]out all ceremony remen your most thankeful and constant frendes for euer'.[27] Letters of recommendation were thus largely devoid of the humility tropes that characterise women's letters of petition: without elaborate supplications, business is often dealt with very directly, reminiscent of gentlewomen's authoritarian letters to male servants. Mary Scudamore, writing to Caesar concerning a case before him in the Court of Requests, for example, omitted both greeting and commendation, opening by stating the concern of her letter: 'Sonne Ceasar wheras I did write vnto yo[u] the laste terme in the behalfe of my good frend m[r] John Pettus concerning a suite depending before yo[u] in your courte of Requestes'.[28] Such confidence and authority is more commonly detected in letters to men of inferior rank or standing.[29]

Closing modes of address are similarly imbued with a language of friendship; many women of high social standing frequently signed themselves as 'friends', which was symbolic of their influence and worth. Elizabeth, Marchioness of Northampton signed her letter to William More prefaced by the words 'by your frynd'.[30] Typically, letters to Sir Julius Caesar, for example, commonly conclude with declarations of friendship: 'your assured frend', 'your assured good frend', 'your loving frend'. Anne Glemham, daughter of Thomas Sackville, the Lord Treasurer, habitually signed her letters to Caesar as his 'assured', 'faithful' or 'loving' 'frind';[31] in other letters she ended, perhaps more tellingly, with phraseology testifying to the mutuality of their practical friendship: 'such to you as accometh me', and 'your vnfained frind so purchaced by your desart'.[32] Contrastingly, correspondence to Lord Burghley (Caesar's social superior after his peerage in 1571), for instance, evokes the language of service: letters were often concluded 'your lordships assured and most bounde', 'your lordships as I am bounde', 'your lordships humbly to command'. The closural phrases used in writing to Caesar, whilst assuring a woman's loyalty, articulate a greater equality in relationship between sender and recipient than is implied in Burghley's correspondence. The language of friendship is generally only used among equals, which suggests the degree of confidence with which women dealt with government officials (James 1986: 330–2). In this sense, it is social rank rather than gender that underwrites the language of 'supposal and assurance' utilised by female letter writers and is the main determinant of stylistic register.

In general, suits on behalf of others were often couched in personal terms. At the request of a 'speciall frind', Lady Anne Glemham petitioned Sir Julius Caesar on behalf of a 'poore woman' and her imprisoned husband, expressing her desire to the Master of Requests, 'that you doe vouchsafe to consider [the suit] for my sake'.[33] Lady Frances Wilkes asked William Wallop, Mayor of Southampton to show special favour to her poor kinsman 'rather of myne instance'.[34] Elizabeth, Countess of Shrewsbury hoped that Lord Paget would support her son Henry Cavendish in a dispute, writing 'Thus hoping that at my request you will stand the more his friend.'[35] She also wrote to her cousin Henry Foljambe to use 'frendly consideration' and 'well handling' towards the widow, Elizabeth Flint, adding that she would 'loath' to see her 'wronged' and was in no doubt of his 'forwardness' and 'favour' to her cause. The letter added that she would 'take' his kind offices 'in very thankful thought' and 'not be found unmindful in anything that may do' him 'pleasure'.[36] Anne Dudley, Countess of Warwick approaching Caesar on behalf of a former servant embroiled in a land dispute wrote:

> I doe therefore praie yo[w] acordinge to the uprightnes and equitie of the cause, to afford him [her servant] all the lawfull favour yo[w] maie, and the rather for my sake for w[hi]ch you shall finde him verie thankfull, and beinge a good cause I hope yo[w] will helpe him to a more speedie ende for w[hi]ch I shall allso (doinge it at my request) thinke my selfe more behouldinge vnto yo[w].[37]

In these examples, the suitability or merits of the beneficiaries of letters of commendation were typically not described, except in broad terms, assuring that, in the case of male suitors, they were 'honourable', 'worthy' or of 'good repute'; female suitors were more commonly presented as objects of pity or charity. The performance of a request for a suitor was thus normally presented as a favour for the noblewoman herself, a favour that it was promised would be returned in kind. Frances Bridges, Lady Chandos assured Sir Julius Caesar that she would, be 'ever ready to requite' him 'in a greater matter when occasion shalbe offered'.[38]

The practice of reciprocal exchange evident in these letters was at the heart of sixteenth-century patronage relations, whether it be the exchange of favours in kind, the exchange of money (as in the example of clients' fees) or material gifts. In a letter to Thomas Fanshawe, Rembrancer of the Exchequer, Lady Abigail Digby wrote on behalf of a servant, John Cowp, and a neighbour, one Butler, against whom a process had been issued. The letter made clear that she undertook to pay the debt that the two men owed, asking Fanshawe to 'frend the poor' men, and to 'pleasure' her

> so much as you may effect my request therein, which I am assured resteth much in you to perform. In requittal thereof I will do you or any friend of yours any curtesie I may either by my self or any frend I have. Here or where as occasion shall serve.

The letter then moves to literal exchange, as Lady Digby acknowledges her debt of a brace of Bucks which Fanshawe 'deserved' for his 'former frendlyness', promising to perform the same this season if he let her know 'when or where they may pleasure you'.[39] Furthermore, some women appear to have received payment for their services as political intermediaries and letter writers (Wright 1987: 161–2). There is evidence that Lady Anne Glemham received money from clients to approach her father the Lord Treasurer. In 1603, Robert Cecil wrote to Michael Hickes his secretary, directing him to give Lady Glemham 'a purse' of 100 pounds to deal directly with her father, the Lord Treasurer.[40] Thomas Lichfield 'delivered' to Lady Gerrard two 'silver saltes' for Mrs Julian Penn to intercede with Hickes, her son, to obtain a grant; in his letter he requested that these be 'redeliver[ed]' since his suit was not granted.[41] Elizabeth Bourne implored Mrs Morgan to be 'earnest' with Blanche Parry, a gentlewomen of Elizabeth I's bedchamber, concerning repayment of a 1,000 pound debt to the Queen. In the event that Blanche Parry could persuade the Queen to allow repayment of the debt at 100 pounds per annum, Elizabeth Bourne promised to pay Mistress Morgan 200 marks; if, however, the amount of repayment had to be increased to 1,200 pounds in order to be able to repay at 100 pounds a year, then she would pay only 100 pounds.[42] More broadly, the language of exchange permeated the political scene, and is imbued in a letter from Katherine Ashley, a gentlewoman of the Elizabethan Privy Chamber, to the Countess of Bath, thanking her for a token; the letter indicated that she was 'sory' to take any 'thynge' from her since she claimed to be unable to do her 'any pleasuer'.[43] There is a strong sense that the act of receiving, albeit a token, formed an obligation to requite a favour. Letters in themselves were part of this form of exchange.

In adopting this vocabulary of 'friendship', mutual exchange and reciprocity, women were borrowing conventional forms available in letter-writing manuals of the period. Yet these were not empty rhetorical gestures. What is significant here, however, is that women chose to employ these epistolary forms for the purposes for which they were writing. In so doing, women asserted their own influence and capabilities, conscious that they were indeed able to repay political favours in kind, operating through family and kinship connections, through court and county contacts and in their own right as landowners and patrons. It also further demonstrates the legitimacy with which women involved themselves in patronage activities. Thus, in this sense, there is a correlation between a woman's language and her self-perception of her power; the authority invoked by women in their letters might be interpreted as much as an act of rhetorical self-presentation as a reflection of actual status (Magnusson 2004). In contrast to the images of female weakness and fragility that characterise women's letters of petition, many women in their letters of recommendation adopted the persona of a patron.[44] Acting in her capacity as patroness of the benefice of Horton in Buckinghamshire, Lady Abigail Digby wrote to her cousin John Fortescue at the Exchequer on behalf of the incumbent of the benefice, Mr Wickham, Chaplain to the Bishop of Lincoln. In her letter she asked Fortescue to support Wickham's promise to compound the first fruits and tenths subsidies to the crown for payment of his debts, 'the rather because I am patronesse of the benefice in question & knowe the promises to be true'.[45]

Women who wrote letters of petition on behalf of family members, servants, neighbours, 'friends' and clients were conforming to the unwritten rules that governed the pursuit of patronage. Whilst both men and women did petition for favour themselves, it was generally regarded as more acceptable to get someone else to sue on one's behalf; to refuse a supplicant directly was difficult or awkward for a patron. Thus, Castiglione advised in *Il Cortegiano* that 'very sildome or (in maner) never shall he [the courtier] crave any thinge of his Lorde for himselfe, least the lorde having respect to denie it him for him selfe should happen to graunte it him with dyspleasure, which is farr worse (Castiglione 1994: 121). In addition, a person could express certain matters more easily in a letter on somebody else's behalf, than for themselves. Bacon's essay 'Of Friendship' discusses the way that one friend might pursue a suit for another, writing:

> How many things are there which a man cannot, with any face or comeliness, say or do himself! A man can scarce allege his own merits or modesty, much less extol them; a man cannot sometimes brook to supplicate or beg; and a number of the like. But all these things are graceful in a friend's mouth, which are blushing in a man's own.
>
> (Bacon 1994: 86)

In practice, some suitors preferred indirect modes of approach, considering it unseemly themselves to write. Thus, Elizabeth Nunne wrote to her nephew Sir Bassingbourne Gawdy on behalf of her nephew Cressmor because as she explained 'he [her nephew] fearethe youe should thinke hime ouer boulde he hathe desirede me to breake the mattere vnto you'.[46]

The obligations that noblewomen had towards neighbours, 'friends' or clients who sought their advocacy in patronage matters are clearly visible in their letters. Dorothy, Countess of Northumberland, preferring a gentleman to her brother the Earl of Essex wrote that 'I can not deny him my letter to intreat you'; Mary Wriothesley, Dowager Countess of Southampton wrote to her son the earl that, 'I am desyred by my La[dy] Cutts (whom you knowe I may not deny) to commend a kynsman of hers [. . .] to your favo[u]r'; and writing to Sir Robert Cecil, Lady Elizabeth Hoby described how 'this afternone my neighbor, Mr John Borlase, earnestly entreated me if ever I woold do eny thing for him to be a suter for him to yow' which 'have made me thowghe most unwillingly to satisfie his request'.[47] It was also incumbent upon upper-class women as mistresses of the household to further the interests of servants and retainers, to mediate in their affairs and to forward their suits. Such duties are expressed in many noblewomen's letters. Lady Penelope Rich writing to her brother the Earl of Essex declared with barely disguised lack of enthusiasm her obligation to forward the suit of a male servant: 'my sarvant Geralde make[s] me troble you with an other letter'.[48] Furthermore, bound by duty to further the interests of servants, noblewomen did not even need to know the precise details of a suit in order to promote it. This is well illustrated in a letter from Katherine Bertie, Duchess of Suffolk to William Cecil, written on behalf of her gardener, whose brother was involved in a dispute in Jersey:

> I most dessere you good master Cyssell to showe yo[u]r frendship to thys poor berar in a sortten suite that won off jarrsey hathe agenst his brother his reqwyst is but that it wely plyese my lorde of Somersett ether to derycte hys letter or eles to commande his undercapeten in Jarrsey to cal the matter befor hym & to make some honest ende of it for otherwyes the poor soly [soul] is lyke to be undon but watt this matter is I am nott ably to tell you & I pray god the poor soly him selfe be ably to do it but if he can I pray you than to helpe him even for charytes sake & w[i]th the more spyde [speed] that he may the soner retorne to his gardyn at hom for I can have no saleds tel he retorne nyther shal the[re] be of swytt erbes [herbs] if you helpe him not w[i]t[h] his suit & so I commytt him w[i]t[h] al his elve [evil] englyshe to you & you to god.[49]

As a man of Jersey, the gardener almost certainly spoke Norman French, which may account for his 'evil' attempt to convey to the Duchess the matter of his suit.

The responsibility owed to dependants, social inferiors and acquaintances explains why noblewomen petitioned on their behalves; it also explains why they were first approached. The strong expectation of the exercise of beneficence generated by client–patron and servant–master relationships clearly extended to include noblewomen and mistresses of households.[50] Francis Bacon in his essay 'Of Suitors' stated that, 'nothing is thought so easy a request to a great person as his letter' (Bacon 1994: 149). To write on behalf of a suitor was to fulfil one's obligation and with less exertion of effort than through dispensing more material forms of patronage. By acting in this capacity women were concerned with personal and family reputation within a wider community of honour. For many, the commending of suitors formed a significant and powerful part of their sense of social responsibility. Elizabeth Bourne valued her role as intermediary, promising her future son-in-law Edward Conway that: 'yf the travel of my pen wyth the reste of my body could brynge you the fauour of the hyer powers or the welth of an emproure [emperor] then you showld se I would make no spare of them'.[51] Writing to her son Anthony, Anne Lady Bacon expressed the importance she attached to commending one of her servants for an office in her own person: 'he is my man

& therfore have I written'.[52] Lady Bacon appears to have considered the act a matter of personal dignity; she therefore cautioned her son not to interfere on the man's behalf. This illustrates the dual sense of obligation and self-worth felt by women and the degree to which they internalised honour codes relating to nobility, rank and duty towards suitors usually associated with male patrons and nobles.

In conclusion, analysis of sixteenth-century women's letters of recommendation offers direct evidence that women were by no means excluded from classical rhetorical traditions. Viewed as texts, the commendatory and intercessory correspondence penned by female letter writers indicates the sophistication, flexibility and range of women's epistolary and rhetorical skills. It demonstrates the extent of women's knowledge – either through readership of early modern letter-writing manuals, formal tuition or contact with the form – of conventional epistolary forms relating to structure, opening and closing modes of address and salutations and the ways in which letters, letter-writing practices and the deployment of rhetoric were central to the trade of courtiership. Moreover, the fact that elite women appropriated these 'powerful' rhetorical forms, especially in employing a Senecan language of favour and political 'friendship' with its attendant promise of reciprocal benefits in kind, asserts the high degree of confidence and authority with which many operated within the realm of patronage and politics, an arena often depicted as exclusively male. As such, the study of women's epistolary rhetoric as manifested in letters of recommendation contributes towards an increasing recognition among scholars that any attempt to reconfigure what constituted the category of 'political' during the early modern period should necessarily include women's discursive activities.

Notes

1 Exemplary of this work is Parker (1987), Bates (1992), Clarke and Clarke (2000).
2 Donovan (1980), Enterline (2000), Clarke (2001), Luckyj (2002). Cf. Sondergard (2002).
3 For general studies, see Lunsford (1995), Glenn (1997), Wertheimer (1997), Sutherland and Sutcliffe (1999).
4 Letters of recommendation survive in several main types of archive: among government state papers, legal and other institutional archives and in collections of family and individuals' papers.
5 British Library (BL), Additional MS, 12506, fol. 235: 1 June 1596; BL, Additional MS, 25079, fol. 53: [1600].
6 Norfolk Record Office (NRO), Norwich, Knyvett/Wilson Papers, KNY932/372/X6: 1602.

7 BL, Lansdowne MS, 79, fol. 79: 22 May 1595.
8 Whilst historians have generally ignored the rhetorical and generic conventions of letters, this is hardly true of literary critics: Whigham (1981),
   Lyall (1996), Carrington (1997), Van Houdt *et al.* (2002), Magnusson
   (2001, 2004). Cf. Wall (2001).
9 Robertson (1942: 7), Hornbeak (1934: 1). On letter-writing manuals
   aimed at women see Humiliata (1949–50), Mitchell (2003).
10 Familiar epistles by this definition encompassed a wide range of subjects and purposes; distinctions between sub-genres of letters, therefore,
   tended to be fluid. Indeed, the word 'familiari' according to Judith Rice
   Henderson (1993: 149, 151) is in many ways a catch-all term that 'can
   mean almost anything'.
11 For a more detailed discussion of women's contact with epistolary rhetorical models, see Daybell (2006a).
12 BL, Add. MS, 12506, fol. 258: 6 February 1592.
13 BL, Add. MS, 12506, fol. 207, 4 July 1604.
14 Folger Shakespeare Library, Washington, DC, Bagot Papers, L.a. 1000: 15
   May 1599.
15 National Archives (NA), Kew, SP 10/10/32, 18 September 1550. On the
   Duchess's patronage of William Naunton, her husband's second cousin,
   see Harris (2002: 199–200).
16 On early modern women's involvement in patronage see, for example, Kettering (1989), Harris (1990), Payne (2002), Daybell (2004).
17 An exception to the rule that women were not awarded crown offices is
   Lady Elizabeth Russell, who in 1589 was appointed Keeper of the Queen's
   Castle of Donnington and Bailiff of the Honour, Lordship, and Manor of
   Donnington. See Hatfield House, Hertfordshire, Cecil MS, 178, fol.132;
   106, fol. 39: 5 March 1600, 3 August 1602.
18 NA, SP46/18/164: 6 May 1598.
19 BL, Lansdowne MS, 158, fol. 30, 21 November 1596.
20 Staffordshire Record Office (SRO), Paget Papers, D603, K1/3/23, 2 May
   1572.
21 Folger, Tamworth MS, L.e.474, 4 November 1600.
22 BL, Add. MS, 23212, fol. 195, no date.
23 BL, Add. MS, 23212, fol. 180, no date.
24 Cecil MS, 58, fol. 57, August 1597; 59, fol. 84, 20 February 1599; BL, Add.
   MS, 12506, fol. 115, 20 March 1603.
25 SRO, Paget Papers, D603, K1/4/26, 4 March 1578.
26 Cecil MS, 81, fol. 85, September 1600.
27 Cecil MS, 86, fol. 32, 6 May 1601.
28 BL, Add. MS, 12506, fol. 481, 26 January 1599.
29 A similar absence of deference has been noted by Mendelson and Crawford (1998: 373) in advisory letters from court ladies, who 'engaged with
   men on some kind of equal terms'.
30 Folger, Loseley MS, L.b. 559, (c.1550).
31 See, for example, BL, Lansdowne MS, 158, fol. 4, April 1597; BL, Add.
   MS, 12506, fol. 365, 6 December 1597; BL, Lansdowne MS, 158, fol. 88,
   14 March 1598; BL, Lansdowne MS, 158, fol. 86, 24 January 1599.
32 BL, Lansdowne MS, 158, fol. 92, 26 March 1597; BL, Lansdowne MS, 158,
   fol. 76, August 1599.

33 BL, Lansdowne MS, 158, fol. 78, 6 October 1599.
34 Anderson (1921: 209–10), 4 December 1596.
35 SRO, Paget Papers, D603, K1/10/32, no date.
36 NA, SP46/24/35, no date.
37 BL, Add. MS, 12506, fol. 219, 22 January 1596.
38 BL, Add. MS, 12507, fol. 9, 10 March 1604.
39 NA, SP46/35/87, 1 July 1588.
40 BL, Lansdowne MS, 88, fol. 105.
41 BL, Lansdowne MS, 107, fol. 205, 20 September, no year.
42 BL, Add. MS, 23212, fol. 187, no date.
43 Cambridge University Library, Hengrave MS, 88/1, fol. 123, no date.
44 On the deferential tropes redolent in sixteenth-century women's letters of petition see Daybell (2006b: Chapter 9).
45 NA, SP46/38/76, 11 June 1591.
46 BL, Egerton MS, 2722, fol. 156, 4 August, no year.
47 Warwick County Record Office (WCRO), 'Essex Letter Book c. 1595–1600', MI 229, unfoliated, no date; Cecil MS, 70, fol. 35, 18 May 1599; NA, SP12/44/37, 8 November 1567.
48 WCRO, 'Essex Letter Book', June 1596.
49 NA, SP10/10/39, 2 October 1550.
50 On the expectations that patrons would be beneficent see MacCaffrey (1991: 21).
51 BL, Add. MS, 23212, fol. 184, 24 February, no year.
52 Lambeth Palace Library, Bacon MS, 653, fol. 248, no date.

10 Embodied rhetoric

Quaker public discourse in the 1650s

Hilary Hinds

In 1653, a year after George Fox's itinerant mission through northern England had transformed the nascent Quaker movement into an increasingly sizeable and potent force, Francis Higginson published *The Irreligion of the Northern Quakers*, a condemnation of this latest radical religious grouping. Higginson, a minister from Kirkby Stephen in Westmorland who claimed some first-hand knowledge of early Friends (Higginson 1653: 15), was troubled by many aspects of Quaker doctrine and practice, not least by the manner and circumstances of their speaking:[1]

> They have onely their own mode of speaking [. . .] which they do not call, but deny to be preaching; nor indeed doth it deserve that more honourable Name. [. . .] Their Speaker for the most part uses the posture of standing, or sitting with his hat on; his countenance severe, his face downward, his eyes fixed mostly towards the Earth, his hands and fingers expanded, continually striking gently on his breast; his beginning is without a Text, abrupt and sudden to his hearers, his Voice for the most part low, his Sentences incohærent, hanging together like Ropes of Sand, very frequently full of Impiety [. . .]. His admiring Auditors that are of his way, stand the while like men astonished, listening to every word, as though every word were oraculous; and so they believe them to be the very words and dictates of Christ speaking in him.
>
> Sometimes some of them, men, or women, will more like Phrantick people, then modest Teachers of the Gospell; or like the Prophets of *Munster*, or *John* of *Leydens* Apostles, run through, or stand in the streets, or Market-place, or get upon a stone, and cry Repent, Repent, woe, woe, the Judge of the World is come, Christ is in you all.
>
> (Higginson 1653: 11, 12)

The Quaker mode of preaching contravened so many of the conventions of orthodox sermonising that Higginson agreed with Friends that it ought not to go by that name. It was not only the words themselves to which he objected, though he found these incoherent and impious, but also the mode of delivery; the speakers' garb, posture and gesture, the vocal register, modulation and inflection were indicative of the impiety and incoherence of speech. His opposition was in part to do with what he perceived to be the inappropriateness and unorthodoxy of Quaker 'preaching' style: there was no biblical text; the speaker might be sitting, or wearing his hat; 'he' might even be female, for 'sometimes Girles are vocall in their Convents' (Higginson 1653: 11). Despite the Quaker belief that these utterances were 'the very words and dictates of Christ speaking in him', Higginson suspected the speaker of harvesting the words from a much more dubious source, as he looked 'downward, his eyes fixed mostly towards the Earth', his hand 'continually striking gently on his breast' as if to release the words lodged there.

Although explicitly challenging Quaker preaching on the grounds of its doctrinal errors, Higginson also implicitly criticises the preaching as a performance that beguiles listeners into an erroneous acceptance of the Quaker message. He notes the manifest and (to his mind) unwarranted effect the speaker has on 'his admiring Auditors', and is in particular disturbed by the quaking that characterised early meetings, when 'many of them, sometimes men, but more frequently Women and Children fall into quaking fits. [. . .] [They] fall suddenly down, as it were in a Swoon [. . .], and lye groveling on the Earth, and strugling as it were for life' (Higginson 1653: 15). What, Higginson wonders, is the cause of such behaviour? Is it genuine, or – as the repeated phrase 'as it were' suggests – pretended?

> It is an utter impossibility for any man, especially women, that never knew what belonged to Stage-playing, and young Children to feign such swounings, tremblings, palsie-motions, swelling, foaming, purging, such great and horrid screechings, and roarings; yea common Modesty would restrain any man, or woman that are themselves, from such uncleanly Excretions as do often accompany these sordid Trances. Surely it must needs bee some black Art that works so turbulently on mens Spirits or bodies, and conjures them into such Surprizes.
>
> (Higginson 1653: 16)

Higginson raises the possibility of the quaking being a deceit, a performance produced in imitation of the kinds of excesses to be found on the stage, but simultaneously rejects it, on two grounds: first, because people in remote parts of northern England would not have the knowledge of the conventions of stage-playing that would allow an imitation of them; and second, because the corporeal excesses that accompany the quaking are such that 'common Modesty' would restrain the voluntary execution of such acts; no one, he concludes, would wilfully choose to behave in this way. The authenticity of this reaction to Quaker speakers thus established by dint of its being neither a pretended nor a willed state, he concludes that 'some black Art' has worked on these auditors, an Art wrought by the speaker's words. Just as the speakers are 'more like Phrantick people, then modest Teachers of the Gospell', so, in a self-confirming cycle of cause and effect, the madness of the speakers engenders similar frantic behaviour in their hearers. Reinforcing this reading of Quaker preaching style as a kind of madness is an unease concerning the prominence of women, conventionally understood as the irrational sex, in the movement, whether as preachers or prophets or as converts. 'Sometimes Girles are vocall in their Convents', he writes, 'convents' evoking associations with witches' covens as well as Catholic sororities: early Quakers were often accused of both witchcraft and papism.[2] Furthermore, he notes the susceptibility of 'Women and Children [to] fall into quaking fits' (Higginson 1653: 11, 15). Higginson's unease is formed in significant part through his reading of the gendered politics and practices of the movement: for him, the problematics of Quaker preaching are articulated both through reference to its accommodation of female public speakers and for the way in which its rhetoric appeals to, and calls forth, the irrationalities of women and children.

The rhetorical power of Quaker public discourse was clearly recognised by Higginson and was a matter of significant concern to him. Indeed, it was the success of this rhetoric, as evinced by rapidly growing numbers of northern Friends in the wake of the itinerant missions of early Quaker leaders such as Fox and Nayler, that prompted him to write; Friends were proving all too successful in their bid to persuade their hearers of the doctrine of the indwelling Christ. Contrary to the predestinarian Calvinist doctrine of election and reprobation prevalent amongst most other radical religious groups at the time, such as the Independents and Particular Baptists, Quakers argued that salvation, turning to the inward light, was open to all and was something that could be freely chosen or wilfully refused.[3] The will, flawed and carnal as it was, needed to be engaged, such that its carnality gave way to that of God within – as Fox put it, he 'turned them to the light of Christ, the heavenly man, and to the spirit of God in their own hearts and where they might find God and Christ and his kingdom and know him their teacher' (Fox 1952: 120). The very notion of 'convincement', the Quaker term for conversion, registers the centrality of persuasion to the process of conversion; whilst this was a process of 'turning to the Light', converts needed to be 'convinced' to do so. For Friends, quaking itself might not be a willed and chosen act, but it testified to the capacity of the human subject to be moved by the Truth as manifested in the divinely inspired words of the speaker: as Richard Bauman put it, 'the minister's *speaking* moved the non-Quaker [. . .] subject into this [. . .] stage of the conversion process' (Bauman 1983: 81; my italics). If convincements, acts of persuasion, are lodged at the heart of Quaker practice, we can begin to think of a Quaker 'art' of persuasion, a distinctive Quaker rhetoric. To what extent can it be defined as a manner of speaking and behaving produced in opposition to what were seen as the ungodly modes of other Christian ministers, and to what extent does it share a set of common discursive concerns with them? And, in particular, to what extent can the particularities of Quaker rhetorical practice (rather than the theology itself) help explain the vehement hostility encountered by early Friends, and in what ways was the gendering of the early movement implicated in this hostility? To address these questions, I shall examine some indicative Quaker texts from the early years of the movement in relation to broader contemporary debates within and about sacred rhetoric and analyse the interrelation of the linguistic and extra-linguistic dimensions of Quaker rhetorical practice with regard to the reactions of their contemporaries.

Higginson might not have liked what he saw in the early Quaker movement, but even a brief examination of the writings of early Friends suggests that he did not radically misrepresent their preferred modes and locations of speaking. Fox's *Journal* records that he spoke not only in meetings of Friends, but proselytised on hilltops, in churchyards, private houses, streets, marketplaces, courtrooms and gaols. In 1653, for instance, he went into the 'steeplehouse' in Carlisle:

> and after the priest had done I spoke the truth to them and declared the word of life amongst the people. The magistrates desired me to go my ways and desired me not to speak; and the priest got away, but I still declared [. . .]. A dreadful power of the Lord there was amongst them in the steeplehouse that the people

trembled and shook: and they thought the very steeplehouse shook and thought it would have fallen down. The magistrates' wives were in a rage and tore and rent to have been at me, but the soldiers and friendly people stood thick about me.

(Fox 1952: 158)

Many of those who turned to the light also put their convictions into action by speaking the Quaker message in public places. Dorothy Waugh, a young servant and one of Fox's earliest converts, recorded how she spoke 'against all deceit and ungodly practices' in Carlisle marketplace; the mayor's officer then 'haled me off the Crosse, and put me in prison' (Waugh 1656: 29). There, a scold's bridle was placed on her head for three hours:

> so I stood their time with my hands bound behind me with the stone weight of Iron upon my head, and the bitt in my mouth to keep me from speaking. And the Mayor said he would make me an Example to all that should ever come in that name. And the people to see me so violently abused were broken into teares [. . .]. And the man that kept the prison-doore demanded two-pence of every one that came to see me while their bridle remained upon me; Afterwards it was taken off and they kept me in prison for a little season, and after a while the Mayor came up againe and caused it to be put on againe, and sent me out of the Cittie with it on [. . .] and charged the Officer to whip me out of the Towne, from Constable to Constable to send me, till I came to my owne home, when as they had not any thing to lay to my Charge.

(Waugh 1656: 30)

Fox's and Waugh's accounts represent important elements within Quaker writing from the outset of the movement: narratives recorded to register specific instances of the 'sounding of the day of the Lord', and of the persecutions suffered as a result. Fox's *Journal* became the iconic register and touchstone of early Quakerism on its publication following his death, whilst Waugh's account was just one of many such early Quaker narratives of their 'sufferings'. Neither account is exceptional; both are unapologetic, combative, partisan and dramatic, detailing events that were contrary to orthodox modes of preacherly behaviour: Fox interrupted a church service and harangued the priest; Waugh spoke her message in a marketplace. Both were lay people who assumed for themselves the authority of spiritual and religious rectitude, an audacity clearly exacerbated in Waugh's case by her sex and social rank, as is attested by the imposition of the quintessentially gendered and classed punishment of the scold's bridle: this was, after all, a punishment reserved for women of low social rank.[4] Both occasions were explicitly and confrontationally dialogic, drawing the priest, magistrate, congregation, mayor and people into their polemical and rhetorical ambit. As Higginson suggested, this was a mode of speaking that, in the enactment and expression of its theology and doctrine, apparently refused the conventions of Protestant preaching practice at every level.

Such a proposition supposes a uniformity and common purpose to orthodox Protestant preaching theory and practice against which Quaker practice can be set. Debora Shuger, however, has demonstrated that orthodox thinking about the rhetoric of preaching was, in fact, much more complex and contested than this view would suggest. In her invaluable overview of early modern debates about preaching, Shuger sets out two counter-traditions regarding theories of sacred rhetoric, identifying first a conservative tradition that, she suggests, sought to sever the link between language and affect, locating the power of the discourse in 'extra-linguistic factors, primarily the holiness, sincerity, and passion of the preacher himself' (Shuger 1993: 123). This tradition, Shuger argues, dominated English vernacular rhetorics and mutated after the Civil War to a rationalist variant, emphasising argumentative, rather than passionate, plainness. Second, she delineates a liberal tradition reconnecting the theological and artistic aspects of sacred eloquence, reintroducing a concern with style to sacred discourse through its interest in how language created specific emotional and aesthetic effects (Shuger 1993: 125). Within Protestant liberal sacred rhetoric, Shuger suggests, the preacher was concerned to try to move the emotions not by rational analysis, but by amplification ('the extension of simple statement by all such devices as tend to increase its rhetorical effect' [*OED* 4]) and *hypotyposis* (the vivid description of a scene), since the understanding was that the will is 'moved more by sense than intellect' (Shuger 1993: 127). She quotes the German Reformed scholar Bartholomew Keckermann's recommendations to the preacher to dramatise biblical scenes and to place the subject before people's eyes 'surrounded with various striking details and circumstances [. . .] so that the listener, carried outside himself, seems to behold the event as if placed in its midst' (Shuger 1993: 127).

Examined within this framework, Quaker preaching strategy no longer seems to exist wholly beyond, or in opposition to, orthodox sacred rhetoric but becomes legible as a dimension of the so-called 'liberal' tradition, not because of any express interest in questions of style but because, as Shuger puts it, of its 'aesthetic of vividness, drama and expressivity' (Shuger 1993: 126). Those addressed by Fox and Waugh were, indeed, placed in the midst of an 'event', and listeners were, to Higginson's dismay, all too frequently 'carried outside' themselves. Whilst we have no record of the precise words spoken by Fox or Waugh on these occasions, we have countless other Quaker accounts that testify to the vividness and passion of Quaker public speaking. Margaret Killin (or Killam) and Barbara Patison, for example, published *A Warning from the Lord to the Teachers and People of Plimouth* (1655), and address their audience thus:

> Howle ye Rich men, for the misery which is coming upon you, for the rust of your Silver and Gold shall eat you thorow as a Canker, and shal rise up in judgement against you.
>
> Howle ye proud Priests, for the misery that is coming upon you, for ye shall run to and fro, as drunken men, and none shall be to pitie you [. . .] ye run and I never sent you, saith the Lord.
>
> (Killin and Patison 1655: 2)

In this striking instance of *hypotyposis*, Killin and Patison apostrophise rich men and priests, prophesying retributions appropriate to their social and spiritual misdemeanours: priests are to be reduced to undignified disorder and the rich consumed by the 'the rust of your Silver and Gold'. By setting forth the details of these punishments so graphically, the authors generate an intensely vivid and emotional address, clearly aiming to move not by rational argument but by passionate oratory. Reading early Quaker writing in relation to these two traditions of sacred rhetoric places the post-Restoration reaction against the excesses of the radical sects as, in part, a rationalist 'conservative' rejection of 'liberal' rhetorical enthusiasm. As Joseph Glanvill put it in his *Essay Concerning Preaching* (1678), preaching should be 'plain, practical, methodical, affectionate' (Glanvill 1678: 11); he continues,

> Much mischief is faln on Religion by reason of the transgression of this Rule: mysterious, notional preaching hath put many conceited people upon meddling with what they can never well understand, and so hath fill'd them with air, and vanity, and made them proud, phantastical, and troublesome; disobedient to their Governours, and contemptuous to their betters.
>
> (Glanvill 1678: 19–20)

The post-Restoration turn against radical religion was in part articulated as a refusal of particular modes of excessive and enthusiastic
discourse associated with the disruptions of the 1640s and 1650s. 'Fine
preaching' was understood as the rhetorical counterpart of fanatical
religion and social disorder.

If Quaker rhetoric can indeed be read as rhetorically coterminous
with other Protestant sacred discourse, then that prompts the question as to why critics such as Higginson were so profoundly disturbed
by the mode of address of the Quaker speaker. The answer is perhaps
to be found in the common ground that Shuger discerns between the
two (conservative and liberal) preaching traditions. She argues that,
despite their differing understandings of the nature and origin of
rhetorical power, both the conservative and the liberal analysis makes
a primary distinction not between plainness and eloquence, as might
be expected, but between ornament and passion. And this common-
ality, she suggests, is founded on another: '[i]n order to grasp the
project of the sacred rhetorics, one must [. . .] come to grips with
their consistent emphasis on the necessity of emotional power – an
emphasis not found in Classical rhetoric' (Shuger 1993: 131). Instead
of severing emotion from cognition, early modern sacred rhetorics
'relocate the theological virtues in the emotions' (Shuger 1993: 133).
Certainly, even advocates of plainness and opponents of rhetorical
excess such as Glanvill recognised that preaching could not comprise
an appeal purely to the intellect, but the 'affections' must be engaged;
otherwise, he said, religion 'hath no considerable hold' upon those
that hear it (Glanvill 1678: 54). If the debate is indeed framed between
the coordinates of ornament and passion (rather than plainness and
eloquence), this goes some way towards explaining an apparent incon-
sistency in Quaker aesthetic and discursive practice. The rhetorical
extravagance, even excesses, of writers like Killin and Patison might
initially seem to be at odds with the famous Quaker plain style, whether
in dress ('Quaker grey') or pronominal usage (the insistence on using
'thee' and 'thou' for the second-person singular). Yet, if the opposition is understood not to be between plainness and eloquence, but
between ornament and passion, then the apparent disparity dissolves,
as their rhetorical style can be said to eschew ornament – elegance
of style *for its own sake*, as an appeal *only* to the senses, rather than
in the service of Truth – in favour of discursive practices congruent
with Truth. And if 'plain style' in dress and speech was perceived as
one route to that Truth, so the passionate rhetorical exposition of
the forms and implications of ungodliness, in order to engage the
emotions and turn the hearer to the indwelling Christ, was another.

Underlying the emphasis on the emotions in sacred rhetorics, Shuger argues, was an attempt to find a solution to 'the ancient dilemma': the problem of finding 'a way to bring that which is remote and yet most worth knowing into some kind of relationship with what we can more accurately grasp' (Shuger 1993: 135). By this account, preaching comes to be seen as an attempt to quicken the emotions so that the mysteries of faith and the remoteness of God are brought nearer to the believer. To illustrate the point, Shuger discusses Donne's sermons, in which Christ is represented as a way of making the magnificence of God (which is remote) nearer to us, by putting it in our own, human, form:

> The visible body [of Christ] acts as the sign of the remote, excellent object, thus negotiating the poles of the ancient dilemma; *praesentia*, or spatial proximity (nearness), is thus convertible with 'bodiliness', or the ability to be seen. The equivalent to the Incarnation and sacrament in rhetorical theory is the verbal representation of this visible body, i.e., *hypotyposis*, imagery, metaphor, and the related techniques for making things seem close/visible generally grouped under *enargia* or vividness.
>
> (Shuger 1993: 135)

An equation is made here between '"bodiliness", or the ability to be seen' (that is, the way in which Christ's incarnation makes visible the divine), and 'the verbal representation of this visible body, i.e. *hypotyposis*, imagery, metaphor, and the related techniques'. A rhetorical strategy is thus not simply a strategy – an effective but ultimately arbitrary means by which to communicate a theological point. It is rather the rhetorical *equivalent*, or bodying forth in language, of that theology. The aptness of the relation is thus not only to be determined by its impact on hearers, but instead resides within a closer formal correspondence or equivalence – as homologue, rather than analogue – between medium and message, rhetoric and theology. Just as the incarnation and the sacrament make the divine present by making vivid that which is invisible or remote, so these rhetorical figures do likewise, and they do so by generating and appealing to emotion as well as to knowledge. Shuger summarises the point thus: 'The invisible things of God can only be known or loved by being made flesh' (Shuger 1993: 136), and they are made flesh by being rendered vivid by the figures of sacred rhetoric as much as by the sacraments. Language, at its most powerful and persuasive, elicits emotion 'by making the excellent but remote object present to the senses and imagination' (Shuger 1993: 136).

The final observation of Shuger's that relates to Quaker public discourse, and reinforces the importance of the idea of the 'bodying forth' of a theology, concerns the insistence within Protestant rhetorics (as in classical) that the vividness recommended is consistently and explicitly understood as 'theatrical'.[5] Keckermann advised the preacher to dramatise biblical scenes 'as in a theater', whilst others describe how the Bible brings a character 'in upon the stage speaking as if he were present', or compare the Bible with 'a comic drama beheld by the theater of the universe', and describe the second Psalm as 'a miniature play' (Shuger 1993: 137). It is perhaps this 'theatrical' dimension, and the possibilities afforded by embodied dimensions of the performance of the preacher – the modulation of register, pitch and pace, of posture and gesture – that lay behind the contemporary valuation of the sermon over the written text. As the Independent minister William Greenhill put it in the preface to a printed edition of his sermons:

> Reader, although these *Sermons* were taken by the Pen of a ready *Writer*, and printed as they were taken, yet look not for that Spirit, Power, and Life, was in them when Preached. The Press is a dead thing to the Pulpit. A Sermon from thence is like Meat from the Fire, and Milk from the Brest; but when it is in Ink and paper, it's only cold Meat and Milk, it hath lost its lively taste, though it may nourish and become a standing Dish, to feed upon daily.
>
> (Greenhill 1656: A4v).

The power inherent within the *performance* of the sermon, here commended by Greenhill, was precisely the element of Quaker preaching practice to which Higginson objected and which Fox deployed with such effect: 'And I set my eyes upon [one of their deacons] and spoke sharply to him in the power of the Lord; and he cried, "Don't pierce me so with thy eyes, keep thy eyes off me"' (Fox 1952: 157). The rhetorical impact of the speaker results in part from the words and the manner of their delivery, but as importantly from the emotion generated by the embodied presence of the speaker. This composite, embodied rhetorical power was understood by Quakers and non-Quakers alike as a potent force that needed to be directed aright.

Through this detailed exposition of Shuger's argument, we can begin to unravel the source of the disturbance felt by Higginson and others concerning Quaker rhetorical practice. At the core of her analysis of early modern sacred rhetorics is an argument concerning the importance and interrelation of three elements: first, the making present of that which is absent; second, the need to harness emotion in order that this approximation might be achieved; and third, a formal continuity between theological doctrine and rhetorical tropes and figures. All three of these, I suggest, are key to understanding early Quaker public discourse; all three pose a challenge that is rooted in enfleshment; and all three lie at the heart of the profound disturbance caused by Quaker public speaking. The Quaker doctrine of the indwelling, already returned Christ depended on a *literal* making present, or incorporation, of the absent; the emotion exemplified in and generated by Quaker preaching is manifested in the disturbingly embodied responses of the hearers; and Quaker practices of public speaking and their enactment of 'signs and wonders', in a range of situations that refused to recognise any absolute distinction between the sacred and non-sacred, constituted a kind of embodied rhetoric. And the focus on enfleshment, the bodily manifestations of the divine presence, was articulated in part through a rereading and reworking of the increasingly ambiguous gendered significations of that corporeal being. In the rest of this chapter, I shall examine the distinctive ways in which these elements are discernible in Quaker public discourse. How are the relatively commonplace and uncontentious rhetorical devices identified by Shuger pushed to new and troubling limits by Quaker preachers and prophets? What was it about Quaker discourse and practice that exceeded the bounds of 'vividness' endorsed by more orthodox theories of preaching? Moreover, to what extent might our understanding of these Quaker enactments call into question the very terms through which rhetoric is framed?

The figure at the core of most analysis of rhetoric, whether in a classical or a sacred, or indeed a contemporary, context, is the metaphor. Etymologically, the substitution, transfer or 'carrying over' of meaning from one thing to another, and theorised within linguistics and beyond as the most pervasive linguistic trope and the omnipresent principle of all languages, it is, in the context of this discussion of sacred rhetoric, perhaps the paradigmatic linguistic instance of the making present of that which is absent. If it is therefore unsurprising to find metaphor at the centre of Quaker rhetorical strategy, it is perhaps more striking to see the way in which it is persistently deployed in such a way as to draw attention to, and call into question, the boundary between the metaphorical and the literal. One example of early Quakers' play with this distinction in their public self-presentations and circumstantial interpretation can be found in Dorothy Waugh's account: when the Mayor of Carlisle asked from whence she came, she replied, 'out of Egypt, where thou lodgest'. Similarly, Besse records the following exchange in William Dewsbury's examination by Judge Hales in Northampton in 1654/5:

Judge *Hales. Art thou* Dewsberry?
W.D. Yea. I am so call'd.
Judge *Hales. Where dost thou live?*
W.D. I live in the Lord, and I have a Wife and three Children at *Wakefield* in *Yorkshire.*

(Besse 1753: I, 519)

Waugh and Dewsbury both offer strikingly metaphorical responses to their examiners' questions about where they come from: 'out of Egypt, where thou lodgest'; 'I live in the Lord, and I have a Wife and three Children at *Wakefield* in *Yorkshire*'. Both indicate a refusal to recognise a distinction between, on the one hand, different discursive registers – the spiritual/biblical and the legal – and, on the other, the metaphorical and the literal. Indeed, in that these questions allow only for a 'literal' answer (that is, an answer consonant with the social/civic domain over which their questioners hold jurisdiction), the speakers are in effect offering these metaphorical responses as 'literally' true. Similarly, when Fox wrote that he 'obeyed the Lord God and went and stood a-top of the cross in the middle of the market and there declared unto them that the day of the Lord was coming' (Fox 1952: 156–7), and Waugh notes that she was 'haled [. . .] off the cross', there is little doubt that they are both invoking a metaphorical equivalence between Christ's cross and the market cross, an equivalence underwritten by the Quaker insistence that Christ dwelt within each believer. This equivalence is in turn endorsed by the closing editorial comment to Waugh's text, which suggests that 'all these things are but a taste of the whole, inflicted upon the body of Christ in this nation' (Waugh 1656: 30). From a Quaker perspective, any event, any circumstance or location, can be read as a metaphor of spiritual wayfaring and warfaring.

There were of course strategically desirable outcomes to be achieved by such responses: Waugh and Dewsbury effectively withheld information about their places of habitation that would have left them open to charges of vagrancy, to which itinerant Friends were particularly vulnerable, while the analogy between the market cross and Christ's crucifixion served the purpose of suggesting innocent suffering and the godliness of the persecuted. More importantly, in terms of Quaker rhetoric and theology, however, this play with the proximity or over-lap of the literal and metaphorical, this insistence on the continuity between the one and the other, enacts the erasure of boundaries between the spiritual and the material that lay at the heart of Quaker doctrine and that has its primary expression in the notion of the indwelling Christ, such that the believer, whilst not him- or herself Christ, had that of Christ within. We see the consequences of this, for instance, in the account of Fox's trial at Lancaster Assizes in 1652, which concentrated on testing the blasphemy of this doctrine and was articulated through interrogating him on his breaches of the boundary between the spiritual and the carnal. He is charged with having affirmed 'that he had the divinity essentially in him', that 'he was equal with God' and 'as upright as Christ'. In each case, rather than simply confessing or denying it, he reframed the matter such that its terms of reference no longer applied. '[T]he saints', he said, 'are the temples of God and God doth dwell in them'; 'he that sanctifieth and they that are sanctified are all of one in the Father and the Son'; 'all teaching which is given forth by Christ is to bring the saints to perfection, even to the measure, stature, and fullness of Christ' (Fox 1952: 134–5). In each case, the answer suggests that to interpret Fox's words 'literally' as the justices were doing was a distortion of Quaker doctrine, but to take his words as metaphorical was also to misunderstand the 'literal' truth of the presence of the indwelling Christ. Friends thus inhabited a world where to draw a distinction between the metaphorical and the literal no longer made sense, pre-cisely because of the elisions of spiritual and material exemplified in this foundational belief. Dewsbury, Waugh and Fox are not simply engaged in language play for strategic ends; they are rather demon-strating how, having turned to the inward light, there is a continuity, a congruence, between their own selves and lives and those of Christ. The distinction which at first appears to be a rhetorical comparison between separate domains is dissolved in the recognition of the truth of the indwelling Christ. Metaphor is remade as no less than the literal truth.

This dissolution of the distinction between the metaphorical and the literal in Quaker rhetoric occurred not only in speech acts but also in other, often theatrical, embodied acts – the Quakers' performance of 'signs' as a critique of current political or religious malaise – which suggest the necessity of thinking about the significance of a rhetoric beyond language.[6] Fox's interruption of the church service in Carlisle, for instance, or his speaking in Kendal market, where he threw silver from his pocket out amongst the people and spoke against 'all deceitful merchandise and ways' (Fox 1952: 121), involved not only the denunciation of wrongdoing, but its enactment in locations, and on occasion with the use of props, that figured directly as part of the Truth to be communicated: his message was consonant with the sign and scene by which it was enacted. Waugh's text, too, turns on a vivid instance of *hypotyposis*, in the performance of what almost constitutes a piece of participatory street theatre. Waugh speaks her message in Carlisle marketplace; she is hauled off 'the cross' and relocated to Carlisle gaol, where she is remade, by the mayor, as a different kind of public spectacle, by placing the bridle on her. The disorderly woman thus seeks to appropriate the commercial space of the market and remake it as a sacred space in which people might turn to recognise the divine light within them. The mayor refuses this appropriation and forcibly transforms her into the figure of the silent (because silenced) woman, the bridle instating and enacting his triumph over the unruly woman. The mayor's bridled figure, furthermore, requires an audience as much as did the prophet in the marketplace – hence, in a further echo of the theatre, the charging of twopence for people to come in and see her.

Moreover, Quaker dramas such as these *themselves* play with, and confuse, the categories of the metaphorical and literal: Fox threw his silver into the streets as both a symbolic and a literal 'offering' to the people (Fox 1952: 121). We see this confusion most sharply, however, in the early Quaker practice of 'going naked as a sign'. Many Friends were moved to this particular form of symbolic enactment; Elizabeth Fletcher from Kendal, for example, was sixteen years old at the time of her mission to Oxford in 1654:

> Elizebeth ffletcher was a very modest, grave, yong woman, yet Contrary to her owne will or Jnclination, in obedience to ye Lord, went naked through ye Streets of that Citty, as a signe against that Hippocreticall profession they then made there, being then Presbeterians & Jndependants, wch profession she told them the Lord would strip them of, so that theire Nakedness should Appear, wch shortly after [. . .] was fullfilled upon them.
>
> (Penney 1907: 259)

Richard Bauman, analysing this practice, suggests that it ultimately failed as a rhetorical strategy because the public display of the naked (or near naked) body was so striking and shocking in its own right that it tended to engage the onlookers' attention so wholly at that level that they were prevented from looking beyond the literal fact for a metaphorical meaning. [. . .] [T]hey were not prepared to grant special power to going naked as a means of expressing verbal metaphor.

(Bauman 1983: 92)[7]

Similarly shocking was James Nayler's notorious entry into Bristol on horseback, preceded by a small group of Friends singing 'Holy, holy, holy, Lord God of Israel' and spreading garments before him. The interpretation offered by Nayler was that 'it pleased the Lord to set me up as a sign of the coming of the righteous One' (Braithwaite 1961: 254, 256); it was, however, read by the authorities on a literal level as blasphemy rather than as a sign or embodied metaphor. Whatever their relative success or failure as rhetorical strategies, both examples demonstrate a Quaker reliance on metaphor, and on the enactment of metaphor, whether on the level of telling the mayor that he dwelt in Egypt, or going naked as a sign, or Nayler's entry into Bristol. Waugh, Nayler and many others literally embodied the sign of their theology. Rather than being deployed at a discursive level as aspects of the theory of preaching, these acts constituted the literal enfleshment of Quaker doctrine. We might therefore, with regard to early Quaker practice, extend Shuger's analysis of the power of metaphor and the theatrical as the means of moving emotions in order to bring the remoteness of divinity into the realm of human experience. The theories of sacred rhetoric with which she was working in her essay understand rhetoric as residing wholly within the domain of the linguistic: the metaphor, clearly, is a figure of speech, but the 'theatrical' of which she writes is also understood on a linguistic level – indeed, at a metaphorical level – as concerning the vivid description of a scene, the dramatic delivery of a sermon, the analysis and representation of a biblical text. In no instance is there the suggestion that the 'theatrical' extends in a concrete form into religious practice or the metaphorical into the mode of engagement with a congregation or audience. In Quaker hands, however, this rhetorical ambition to bring the remote into closer approximation with that which is known is brought squarely into the realm of practice. Rather than the visible body of the historical Christ acting as a sign of a remote divinity, it is the visible bodies of Friends themselves that take on this function, as the doctrine of the indwelling Christ moves that sign into the present time and place. The theatricality recommended by theorists of sacred rhetoric is extended to the domain of bodily, as well as linguistic, performance and extends beyond the notion of performance as imitation of something other, something that literally is not, to become the enactment or embodiment of something that more truly is.

This enfleshment of Quaker rhetoric can be understood, in part, as relating to the broader Quaker analysis of language and silence. For Friends, human language was flawed and corrupt, a dimension of our postlapsarian state, and as such it was both an imperfect medium for the revelation of divine truths and a carnal distraction from the still, small voice within which all believers needed to strive to hear. Quaker meetings for worship enacted this distrust of human discourse – and in particular of priests with their 'trade of words' – in their rejection of formalised or ritualised speaking. Instead, they were structured around a condition of attentive silence, broken only when a Friend was confident of being spiritually moved to speak and whose speech led back to an enhanced state of silence. Quakerism is thus premised on a sense of the inadequacy, fallenness and carnality of language.[8] This in turn relates to Friends seeking lived modes of signification, *beyond* the linguistic, a desire articulated most succinctly in the famous phrase attributed to George Fox: 'Let your lives speak', but traceable in essence too to his *Journal* ('their lives and conversations did preach and reach to the witness of God in all people') and Epistles ('let your lives preach').[9] Speaking and preaching are thus functions of action as well as, or rather than, of language. Thus we see Quakers 'speaking' through their ceaseless itinerant missions, their appropriation of public spaces, their embracing of opposition, hostility and abuse. Quaker rhetoric extended the conventional preacherly reliance on metaphor and theatricality into the literal and concrete circumstances of their lives, performing the drama of their theology in the streets, gaols, marketplaces and steeplehouses and reading these dramas as divinely charged signs (rather than simply as metaphors) of the state of godliness in the nation, the corruption of carnal powers and of the progress of the Lamb's War.

It is this insistence on the physical and spatial, as well as linguistic, dimension of rhetorical practice that inescapably enmeshed Friends in the realm of the social; and this sociality and spatiality is perhaps nowhere more evident than in the gendering of its rhetorical enactments. As Michele Lise Tarter has argued, the long-standing gendered dualisms of body and soul, reason and passion, intellect and emotion, meant that 'the very corporeality of earliest Quaker prophesying instantly slated this sect as a "feminized" and deviant band of worshippers' (Tarter 2001: 146; see too Mack 1992: 172–83, 277–8). The embodied rhetoric of a practised theology thus met broader discursive genderings to produce the movement as a force representing a particular kind of social and spatial, as well as religious, disruption. Taking Waugh's detention in Carlisle gaol as an exemplar, the contested nature of the boundary between the literal and the metaphorical within Quaker rhetoric can be seen to be marked out through the contested meanings of social spaces in which gender propriety, and indeed class privilege, raised the legal stakes. If Waugh had not been a woman of low social rank, her treatment in the marketplace would doubtless have taken a different course. The occupation of the marketplace for the purposes of Quaker preaching was deemed a transgression of propriety in part because of the social identity of the speaker (female, a servant), in part because of her annexation of this civic space to her spiritual and political purposes, but also because of the way that these rhetorical challenges were fought out through the power to determine the meanings of her performance. It is this contest in which the mayor was engaging when he had Waugh hauled off the market cross, imprisoned, bridled and whipped out of town. He was refusing the interpretation by Waugh of the circumstances in which she had placed herself and instead seeking to impose his own metaphorisation of her unruly body by relocating it from marketplace to gaol, from oppositional speech to imposed silence, in order to make it serve as a warning to those that paid their money to come and see her. By extending their sacred rhetorics into spatial and social dimensions, rather than limiting them to the linguistic, Quakers found themselves confronting head on the dominant civic and political interpretations of those dimensions, made sharply evident here by the mayor's remaking of the public spectacle of the unruly woman speaking into the equally public spectacle of the woman restrained and silenced by the bridle. Characteristically, however, the mayor's apparent triumph is in turn 'remade' by Waugh in her published account. Here she seeks to resecure this sequence of events to her own rhetorical ends, such that the spectacle of the silenced woman becomes yet another means to 'tender' the hearts of the potentially regenerate for, Waugh writes, 'the people to see me so violently abused were broken into teares' (1656: 30). Waugh and the mayor struggle over the interpretation of this series of events, both of them seeking to fix its meanings to serve their own ends. In publishing her account, Waugh demonstrates the inadequacy of the power of the bridle to silence her; she thereby shows too that

the mayor's victory had been a hollow one, his attempt to harness
the power of the spectacle in fact serving only to further Friends'
progress. Her published account ensures that she has the last, rather
triumphalist, word.[10]

Whilst Tarter's claim that the Quaker movement was a highly
gendered one is crucial to an understanding of the way that the
enfleshment of its rhetoric figured within the reception of the early
movement, it is also important to consider the meaning of this claim
within the contested significance of the gendered categories used
to discredit Quakerism at the time. In other words, rather than
identifying a fixed and straightforwardly pejorative feminisation of
the early movement, we might instead think of the gendering of
Quakerism as integral to the continuous rhetorical battles concerning
the meaning and the reach of spirituality. To take one indicative
instance that particularly aggravated Francis Higginson, we see a
Quaker refusal of gender distinction both at a conceptual and practical
level. Under the heading 'Of the Wicked Practises of the Quakers',
Higginson included the fact that 'Girles' were vocal in meetings for
worship (Higginson 1653: 10, 11), and he also recounted the following
anecdote:

> One *Williamsons* Wife [. . .] said in the hearing of divers there
> [. . .] that she was the Eternall Son of God; And when the men
> that heard her, told her that she was a woman, and therefore
> could not be the Son of God; She said, no, you are women, but I
> am a man.
>
> (Higginson 1653: 3–4)

Higginson glosses this as 'impious' and 'absurd', but '*Williamsons*
Wife' is taking a position not uncommon among early Quakers and
making the same point made by Priscilla Cotton and Mary Cole in
1655 when they argued that the persecuting priests were 'women'
because of their weakness, whilst they, because of their godliness,
were not.[11] This refusal of fixed meanings to gendered categories,
precisely because of their social significations, and the explicit and
audacious redeployment of those categories was, at this early moment
in the movement's history, already a commonplace Quaker rhetorical
strategy. The category 'woman', just like the marketplace or the gaol,
could be appropriated and remade, ascribed new and often contrary meanings (and thereby metaphorised), but those new meanings
themselves undo the process of metaphorisation itself by insisting on
the literal and divinely originating Truth (rather than the partiality of

human truth) of these newly revealed meanings forged in the light. The remaking of gender itself is an integral and indicative dimension of the rhetorical enactment of Quaker doctrine.

Such strategies with regard to gender might be challenged according to the same criteria that Bauman applied in his criticism of the act of going naked as sign: just as the publicly naked body was too saturated with social meaning for its symbolic significance to be easily remade by Quaker enactments, so too the social meanings of gendered categories – and in particular their status as fixed, natural and God-given – made them particularly resistant to appropriation and recasting. The doctrine of the indwelling Christ, through the 'celestial flesh' of those who had turned to the inward light, sanctioned the 'ungendering' of not only the soul, but also the spiritualised body, even as it inhabited the still fallen and imperfect social domain.[12] On the one hand, the aggravation expressed by Higginson and others could be said to result from the audacious scope of Friends' rhetorical resources and devices, reversing previous significations and refusing conventional linguistic and social boundaries and conventions. On the other hand, their ambitious refusals of spiritual and social convention also demonstrated the limits to what might be achieved through these rhetorical acts through sheer force of spiritual conviction, no matter how strongly those acts might be endorsed by a congruency with their theological underpinnings. Thus, the moments of encounter with legal, civic or religious sanction demonstrated precisely the limits on the Quakers of transforming social meanings with the urgency and rapidity they desired. Perhaps in their insistence on taking their rhetoric into an embodied domain beyond language and into practices whereby the comparative security of metaphor was called into question through the assertion of a literal truth value, they demonstrated the sociality of language and its resistance to the immediacy of willed transformation.

In conclusion, we might extend the critical evaluation of this problematic from a focus on the gendering of the movement to a discussion of Quaker public discourse more generally: Friends' rhetorical practices are not only indicative of audacity, ambition and conviction, but also, and more importantly, are a discursive embodiment of the doctrine of early Friends. In other words, the rhetorical disturbance caused by the early movement was also, and inseparably, a doctrinal disturbance and a proper recognition of the challenge posed to more orthodox theological positions. If 'bodiliness', or the making visible of that which was absent, is, as Shuger argued, the key rhetorical strategy for the closing of the gap between the divine and the human, then early Quaker practice might be said to encapsulate all the possibilities and all the pitfalls of that position taken to its limit. It is for this reason that Quaker public discourse is both legible as operating within the same rhetorical framework as more orthodox preaching practice, but also as profoundly challenging to it. Quaker rhetoric shares with the more conventional sacred rhetoric of Protestantism an understanding of the need to 'convince' through engaging the emotions of the listener with the vivid bodying forth of the mysteries of the gospel, but it does so not primarily through linguistic means, but by enacting those mysteries in and through Friends' own 'celestial flesh'. As a rhetorical practice this is distinctive by virtue of its negotiation of, and play with, ideas of proximity and distance, between the literal and the metaphorical as between the divine and the human, the spiritual and the social. Friends thereby went beyond a rhetorical *equivalence* of the doctrine they preached and moved instead into its rhetorical embodiment.

For Quakers, this embodiment and inhabiting of their doctrine extended the domain of preaching into the rhetorical performance of their theology in the cities, streets, churches, gaols and fields in which they lived and moved. By embodying, making visible, the foundational doctrine of the indwelling Christ in this way, and thereby living in a world remade and reinterpreted by their doctrine, they provoked the ire of the civic, religious and political authorities they confronted. Living and enacting their theology in the social spaces of the towns and villages to which its preachers and prophets travelled was, by their own lights, only to act on the belief that 'the steeplehouse and the ground on which it stood were no more holy than that mountain' (Fox 1952: 109). It was also, however, to make claims for the jurisdiction of their theology that proved intolerable to those whose positions, authorities and beliefs were challenged by such a lived rhetoric. Quakers did not so much *let* their lives preach, as *make* them preach, in a rhetoric whose unbounded reach refused to give ground to, or leave space for, any claims that countered their own.

Notes

1. Higginson had been instrumental in the arrest of James Nayler and Francis Howgill in Kirkby Stephen in November 1652, which resulted in their trial for blasphemy in Appleby in January 1653; see Peters (2005: 185, 181–90 *passim*).
2. On accusations of witchcraft and Roman Catholicism, see Prynne (1655), Fox (1952: 142), and Mack (1992: 249–50).

3. On the differing relations of the radical sects to Calvinism and predestination, see Tolmie (1977) and Wallace (1982).
4. On the use of the bridle, see Underdown (1985).
5. Cicero considered *actio* (delivery) as 'the dominant factor in oratory', and both he and Quintilian emphasised the performative dimensions of oratorical delivery. See Cicero (1996: 3.55.213 ff), Quintilian (1921: 11.2.51 ff). For an overview of the debate about oratory and acting see Rhodes (1992: 12–19). Many thanks to Alison Thorne for providing these references and for clarifying the correspondence between classical and sacred rhetoric on this issue.
6. See Carroll (1978) for a delineation and discussion of the different kinds of Quaker 'signs'.
7. On 'going naked as a sign', see Penney (1907: 364–9), Carroll (1978), Bauman (1983: 84–94).
8. On the relative importance of speech and silence in early Quakerism, see Bauman (1983), especially Chapters 2 and 8.
9. Despite the phrase 'let your lives speak' frequently being attributed to Fox, I have been unable to identify a precise source for it. The closest I have found are cited here: the phrase from the *Journal* can be found in Fox (1952: 169) (see too 1952: 263: 'that your carriage and life may preach among all sorts of people'), and the one from the epistles from Epistle 200 (see Tuke 1825: 115).
10. For fuller discussion of this point with regard to the spatialised politics of sectarian discourse in the 1650s, see Hinds (2004).
11. A fuller discussion of this aspect of Cotton and Cole's text can be found in Hinds (1996: 192–9).
12. The phrase 'celestial flesh' is Richard Bailey's but is also cited by Tarter in order to indicate Quaker conceptions of the body that are transformed by a recognition and acceptance of the indwelling Christ; see Bailey (1992: 38–40), Tarter (2001: 148, 159 n.9).

11 Afterword

Neil Rhodes

In the first general account of rhetoric to be published in English, Thomas Wilson expounded the figure of 'Comprehension' with the following illustration: 'What becometh a woman best, and first of al? Silence. What seconde? Silence. What third? Silence. What fourth? Silence. Yea, if a man should aske me til dowmes day, I would stil crie, silence, silence, without the whiche no woman hath any good gift' (1982: 400–1). Scholars have not in fact been completely silent on the subject of women and early modern rhetoric, as Jennifer Richards and Alison Thorne show in their introduction to this book, but it is true that the field was long regarded as distinctively masculine territory. Wilson's prescription with regard to female silence is, of course, a pastiche of the famous story about Demosthenes, much quoted in the early modern period, in which he was asked what the most important part of oratory was and replied, 'Action'; and the second? 'Action'; and so on. Wilson himself produced the first English translations of Demosthenes, whom he described (following Quintilian) as 'almost the verye lawe of eloquence' (Demosthenes 1570: I3r), so this was a story he would have taken to heart. The twist that he gives to it reminds us that, while Demosthenes was referring specifically to delivery, the fifth part of rhetoric, the art of rhetoric more generally was directed towards action in the real world. Wilson also tells us at the very start of *The Arte of Rhetorique* that Pyrrhus had employed a pupil of Demosthenes called Cineas to win countries and cities for him through the power of his eloquence. This ancient perception of rhetoric as one of the martial arts was reinforced in the modern era by scholars such as Walter Ong, who emphasised its associations with masculine courage (Ong 1971: 14). Rhetoric was a tool of the male ego, an extension of war by other means. The woman's role was to remain silent, or to supplicate.

But the historical masculinisation of rhetoric makes it clear that gender was an issue from the start. The *ars rhetorica* may have been gendered male, but Rhetorica itself, as early modern iconography shows, was gendered female through its associations with *copia*, verbal abundance. The need to stake out rhetoric as male territory derived from anxieties about *copia* that Ong himself recognised: 'Our fears of it resemble our fears of the Great Mother who swallows her children' (Ong 1971: 14). It was this aspect of rhetoric that enabled Patricia Parker to reclaim the subject from its masculine straitjacket in her ground-breaking book *Literary Fat Ladies* (Parker 1987). At the heart of Parker's book lay the perception that the language of rhetoric and the language of the body were intimately connected and that the body in question was female. The early modern quest for *copia*, in which Erasmus's textbook *De copia* played a central role, operated on a principle of dilation and amplification, following the biblical injunction to go forth and multiply – for all its masculine ethos rhetoric was essentially a *matrix* of verbal generation. Consequently, much of Parker's discussion focused on rhetorical and sexual 'opening'. But at the same time, her lifting the lid on the Pandora's box of early modern *copia* (as it would have appeared to the male viewer) naturally raised questions of closure and control. Wilson's imperatives for female silence derive from a cluster of familiar anxieties about female loquacity and the uncontrollability of the tongue – the propensity towards looseness and errancy – which ultimately find physiological expression in the concept of the wandering womb. The woman's 'speaking out' is a dangerous inversion of the social order and its regulation becomes an issue in the preservation of civil society. In rhetorical terms, the unruly dilations of female *copia* become subject to the masculine compartmentalisation of the *ars rhetorica* with its reliance on disposition, partition and distribution as mechanisms of control.

Parker's extraordinarily rich and suggestive work not only transformed the story of early modern rhetoric itself but also enabled it to reoccupy some of the central ground in early modern cultural studies more generally. The tropes and figures were no longer rusting pieces of machinery but the nerves and sinews of a poetics that brought gender, politics and the body into creative alignment. The 'nervous' was, in fact, the keyword of a later study which complemented *Literary Fat Ladies*. Here, just as copia and dilation had been associated with the female body, the principles of a virile style were constructed in terms of metaphors drawn from the male body where the attribute *nervosus* (sinewy) was paramount (Parker 1996: 201–22). This manly, 'nervous' discourse, labelled 'Attic', was advocated in preference to the soft,

Asiatic effeminacy of decadent Ciceronianism. The implications of this work, together with the analysis of sexually charged figures such as *hysteron proteron* (the preposterous), are extended in the characteristically dense and brilliant essay in the present volume. Here Parker analyses the relationship between backward writing, palindromes and sexuality, focusing in particular on the gendered and sexual nuances of that highly suggestive figure.

Many of Parker's themes might also direct us towards a text which is especially responsive to an investigation of early modern rhetoric and gender, Jonson's *Epicoene: or The Silent Woman*. Its alternative titles, in fact, deliberately mesh those subjects and produce an ironic take on Thomas Wilson's strictures regarding female silence: the silent woman would be an aberration of nature, a hybrid creature like the otters, centaurs and other 'monsters' that crowd the play. But this is much more than a thin joke. *Epicoene* also links rhetoric, gender and politics because it illustrates so many of Jonson's deeply held beliefs about the relationship between language and society that he recorded in *Discoveries*: that style may be manly or effeminate; that it imitates the composition of the body; that it is an indicator of personal integrity, or the lack of it; and that it reflects the health of the society that produces it. No English writer of the period was more aware of the social dimension of language. This is why the play's ultimate satirical target is less the delinquent female than the anti-social male. The real 'monster' is neither the silent woman nor, for that matter, the loquacious woman – and there are plenty of those – but the man whose hatred of noise is so extreme that he is willing to neuter himself, declare himself to be 'no man', in order to avoid marriage to a woman who can speak. Communication and copulation, Jonson implies, are both fundamental to the social order.

This is another way of saying that Jonson's play, like most comedies, is concerned with marriage, though it climaxes, with deliberate perversity, in a desperate search for divorce. It was Jonson too who speculated pruriently on the most famous non-marriage of the period, that of Elizabeth I. 'She had a membrana on her which made her uncapable of men' (Jonson 1985: 602), he gossiped to Drummond of Hawthornden. Rather more probably this was a deliberate personal and political choice which, as Helen Hackett shows, enabled Elizabeth to manipulate the symbolism of wife and mother in relation to her own subjects. Paradoxically, Hackett argues, as Elizabeth's virginity was assimilated into her iconic status and her lack of issue became an accepted fact, so her poets piled on the cornucopian imagery. The symbolic project was an extraordinary rhetorical feat, fusing the themes of the present book in a unique act of collusion between monarch and subjects. It also forces us to confront other paradoxes. However much we repeat the conventional wisdom about rhetoric and action or rhetoric and power as being specifically male territory, we cannot escape the fact that the single most powerful individual in the entire period from the Reformation to the Civil War was a woman. Her words mattered. We can read her speeches in the excellent Chicago edition, including those on the subject of her marriage.[1] And here is a further paradox. One of the most famous sixteenth-century school rhetorical exercises was the *suasoria* on the pros and cons of marriage – a composition exercise for boys, of course, not girls. Erasmus wrote a model encomium on marriage for his pupil William Blount, which Wilson inserted into his *Arte of Rhetorique*. This percolated down to the arguments for marriage in Shakespeare's Sonnets. But while countless schoolboys would have rehearsed the benefits (and perils) of matrimony, and an even greater number of later readers absorbed Shakespeare's persuasions to the Young Man, by far the most politically significant choice of whether or not to marry was made by a woman (Mack 2002: 196–201).

During Elizabeth's last decade, while Lyly and Spenser composed elaborate images of fruitfulness as the possibility of issue dried up, in other quarters republican theories of government began to be seriously entertained. An early contribution to that debate came from Shakespeare in the narrative poem which concludes with the founding of the Roman republic, *The Rape of Lucrece*. The story about the rape and suicide of an aristocratic Roman wife, and the subsequent overthrow of a tyrannical monarchy, puts a woman at the centre of one of the core foundation myths in history. Yet it was published under a female monarch. Recent discussion of the poem has characterised Lucrece as the English body politic, abused by monarchical possession but increasingly vocal in the articulation of its political rights (Hadfield 2005: 152). Here Huw Griffiths argues that Shakespeare identifies his own voice with the experience of the silenced woman, a point that would underline the poem's complementarity with *Venus and Adonis* (also dedicated to Southampton) where Shakespeare gives Venus much of the pro-marriage rhetoric that he was to use in the Sonnets. But in *Lucrece*, Griffiths shows, the key rhetorical figure is that of *adynaton* (inexpressibility), and Lucrece's silence can be read as a commentary on the absence of a masculine public sphere in which republican politics could be articulated in the last years of Elizabeth's reign. Griffiths' political reading of *Lucrece* may remind us that if the foundation myth centres on female silence, republican Rome itself traditionally represents the classic period in the history of rhetoric, the period where eloquence is nurtured by political freedom and supported by a set of specifically masculine values. Yet *Lucrece* also points us to other early modern texts that place the female very much at the centre of their engagement with the Roman republic. The climax of *Coriolanus* is the scene where the rampant male ego is subdued by an overwhelming female eloquence, prompting the remarkable stage direction, 'He holds her by the hand, silent'. (Not surprisingly, in the eighteenth and nineteenth centuries the play was performed with the title *Coriolanus; or The Roman Matron*.) In Jonson's *Sejanus*, where 'free speech' and 'virtue' act as talismanic republican terms, the Germanican faction is presided over by a woman, Agrippina. Even if early modern texts imply some political tension between English queens and Roman matrons, together they provide a powerful challenge to the assumption that the female rhetorical role was confined to the private sphere.

It remains true, of course, that Elizabeth's position was unique and that any account of rhetoric, gender and politics in early modern England must also address the issue of public and private, or domestic, spheres of activity. This is a point that takes us back to Lucrece because it concerns the media of communication. What Lucrece cannot utter she is able to express in writing, and it is through the silent and private act of letter-writing that she is initially able to communicate with her husband. The composition of letters, as James Daybell points out, was regarded by Erasmus as the fourth category of rhetoric and one that was particularly suited to women in that it lacked the dimension of 'action'. But while the letter did not involve a woman in speaking out in public, it did enable her to engage in political activity. We know about the male humanist networks of friendship constructed through the medium of letters, notably by Erasmus himself, but women too were able to create networks of both friendship and patronage through this medium. Daybell's essay looks closely at letters of recommendation written by upper-class women in order to illustrate an ethos of 'friendship' as political alliance. The persona they adopt is that of patron, which lends a tone of self-assurance to the writing, but the silent medium also helps to obviate the need for the development of a humility topos. These women are in quiet control.

The formal letter may constitute a distinctive rhetorical category, but it also overlaps with other kinds of rhetoric. A letter of recommendation must to some extent be epideictic; when it moves towards supplication it inclines to the forensic. Daybell's letter writers enjoy the power of patronage, but their role also falls into the characteristically female one of intercession. Supplication and intercession are the themes of Rachel Heard's essay, which also takes us into the realm of drama, and she begins by recalling that women were not allowed to plead in court in the early modern period. There were no historical Portias. There were, however, many suppliant women both in history and fiction from Greek tragedy (one thinks of Euripides' *Suppliant Women*) through the exemplary collections such as the 'Tradition of Women Worthies', which Heard discusses, to the plays of Shakespeare. The only contemporary illustration of a scene from a Shakespearian performance shows us Tamora in *Titus Andronicus* kneeling to plead for the life of her son. In these situations the kind of persuasive eloquence that will win cities and countries is not quite what is called for, nor is virile style. The central problem that Heard's essay explores is how a woman can be rhetorically effective without being fired up in the way that Quintilian and others recommend. If a woman has to avoid seeming impassioned in order to avoid seeming unfeminine, can she ever be persuasive? Is there an unimpassioned eloquence? Heard answers this by focusing on *philophrenesis*, or gentleness of speech, showing that this 'winning kinde of Rhetoricke', in Richard Brathwait's phrase, worked essentially through the principle of moderation. On the model of Medina in *The Faerie Queene* II, the role of female speakers was 'to temper and quench, not kindle' the emotions of their audience, to be propitiatory and to intercede between men. This 'mild oratory', which Cicero himself refers to, is the positive female antithesis of the negatively labelled effeminate styles so deplored by the advocates of manly Attic.

More ambiguous is the figure of Echo, which Danielle Clarke discusses. Indeed, the term 'figure' here is itself ambiguous, since Echo is both a mythological character and (almost) a figure in the rhetorical sense through her function of duplication and replication. As Clarke points out, she represents the potential for copious female discourse, but also the impossibility of its ever being realised, as the principle of creative imitation dwindles into empty repetition. One might say that Echo is not so much a literary fat lady as the original thin lady, wasted into mere voice by hopeless longing. In this respect she is herself echoed by Milton's Eve who, without Adam, would have 'pined with vain desire' (*Paradise Lost*, 4.466). But Eve is, of course, far from being an ineffectual wraith, and in pursuing the connection between Eve and Echo Clarke reminds us that God has left the command not to eat the fruit 'Sole daughter of his voice' (9.653). It is a phrase packed with irony. Eve's own speech here is adventurous and transgressive, while her description of the divine prohibition reduces it to the status of female subsidiarity, a version of Echo. Although this may indeed contribute to Eve's inscription within a culture of misogyny, from a rhetorical point of view it is a moment of breathtaking reversal.

One thing that is obvious from the essays in this book is the number of different ways in which the subject can be approached. It is important that we do not conflate these too readily, since they raise different kinds of issue. We can begin with action and silence. We can talk about rhetoric in terms of gender categories and in doing so we can recognise the political implications of this categorisation. We can also talk about female oratory, speeches *by* women, where the most obvious instance would be Elizabeth I herself. We can extend the dimension of rhetoric to cover letter-writing as well as speaking and we can extend the dimension of the political to cover the private as well as the public sphere. We can return to women's speech to identify a persuasive rhetoric based on a female but not an effeminate ethos. And we must remain constantly aware of the distinction, as well as the negotiation, between fictional representation and historical fact. Women did not really dress up as advocates in order to practise their skills in forensic rhetoric in the law courts, not in early modern England, at any rate. Yet there is one early modern genre that provides us with a rich source of information on women, rhetoric and politics which completely ignores the boundaries between fact and fiction. This is the literature of example. '[N]o kinde of argument in all the Oratorie craft, doth better perswade and more universally satisfie then example', Puttenham wrote (1936: 39). Plutarch's well-known essay on how literature should most profitably be read stipulated that you extract the matter from it, and women provided a great deal of 'matter'. Despite the proverbial association of men with deeds and women with words, the multitude of women in early modern exemplary collections represented *res* rather than *verba*.

This is the subject of Susan Wiseman's essay, which asks the pertinent question, 'Why hasn't example been considered as one of the significant ways in which politics was gendered in the period?' Wiseman shows how different female examples can be spun for different effects and different moral messages. Esther can be presented either as a story of transgressive female supplication forgiven or as a more conventional story of supplication. The figure of Lucretia – Shakespeare's Lucrece – was even more malleable, at least in the hands of Machiavelli, who presented her as a figure of chastity in the *Discorsi* and of adulterous desire in the *Mandragola*. One source of female exemplarity that Wiseman mentions is especially significant in the present context. Thomas Heywood's *Gunaikeion: Nine Bookes of History Concerninge Women* (1624) is the closest thing that we have to an encyclopedia of women in early modern England, a massive storehouse of examples designed (so Heywood claims) to display the many and varied virtues of the sex. Here are English queens and Roman matrons, women orators, witches, Amazons, women who have died strange deaths, women excellent in poetry and women who have changed their sex, all arranged in categories presided over by one of the nine muses (Crook and Rhodes 2000: 135–48). It was certainly a popular book and in one instance treated as a companion to Shakespeare. In January 1639 Mrs Ann Merricke wrote to her friend Mrs Lydall from the country, complaining that without the theatre for entertainment she had to make do 'with the studie of Shakespeare, and the historie of woemen' (Ingleby 1909: 443). *The Generall History of Women* was the title given to Heywood's book when it was reissued in 1657. This edition came with a new preface by Edward Phillips, Milton's nephew and amanuensis, written roughly at the time when composition of *Paradise Lost* was getting under way. So it is a book with some intriguing associations, but also an extraordinarily rich rhetorical source for women as *exempla*.

Heywood's voluminous collection of female exemplarity was anything but transgressive, but between his death in 1641 and the reissue of the book in 1657 England experienced extremes of political and religious dissent. Wholly new forms of expression for the female voice appeared, one of which was Quakerism, discussed here by Hilary Hinds. As a form of worship that sought unmediated access to divine truth, Quakerism valued silence, since human language was a distraction from the inner voice of conscience, but also encouraged spontaneous and impassioned public speaking by women as well as men. Overcome by spiritual emotion, women and children were particularly prone to 'quaking' fits, which disapproving male commentators took to be evidence of their innate irrationality. Civic authorities were anxious to censure transgressive female speech and Hinds tells the story of Dorothy Waugh, a servant and early Quaker convert, who spoke out in the marketplace at Carlisle and was imprisoned and made to wear a scold's bridle, the most extreme manifestation of the male imposition on women of the rule of silence. In fact, Quaker rhetoric probably provides the most interesting example of a gendered reconstruction of action and silence in the early modern period. Waugh's silencing was a punishment, yet also a chosen state within her faith. Moreover, Quaker doctrine emphasised the physical reality of divine truths by conflating the literal and the metaphorical in a rhetoric of enfleshment. In striking fulfilment of this, Hinds recounts, another young woman, Elizabeth Fletcher, took the the symbolic action of walking naked through the streets of Oxford. Although we might see points of tension in Quaker thinking between the principle of silence and the rhetoric of enfleshment, this particular example of *actio* seems wholly appropriate. Nakedness and silence are equally states where the soul bares all.

While Dorothy Waugh and Elizabeth Fletcher subscribed to a particular religious faith, the speaking out in public, the subsequent silencing and the symbolic action of 'going naked' belong to a wider rhetorical tradition in which women have always played a major role: this is the rhetoric of anti-rhetoric, plain-dealing, truth-telling. The silence urged upon all women by Thomas Wilson and valued as the medium of truth by the Quakers, often speaks volumes. This is the silence of Cordelia. But truth-telling can take forms other than silence, as we see from both Kent and the Fool in *King Lear* (and perhaps we should add Lear himself, stripping off on the heath), as well as from female characters such as Paulina in *The Winter's Tale*. Paulina is an interesting figure because she has some underlying characteristics of the shrew or scold which are completely transformed by the dramatic situation into the virtues of integrity, loyalty and conscience. This is a play where a female voice articulates the crimes of the king and goes unpunished. The use of a female persona for the purposes of truth-telling is the subject of Martin Dzelzainis's subtle reading of Marvell's *The Third Advice to a Painter*. Dzelzainis links Marvell's political satire to the figure of *parrhesia* (freedom of speech) voiced in this case through the person of the Duchess of Albemarle. As in the case of Paulina or the characters in *King Lear*, it is a matter of 'telling truth to power'. But he also explains that, while *parrhesia* implies sincerity, a straightforward speaking from the heart, it was frequently associated with dissimulation. It is, after all, a rhetorical figure, and insincerity is the oldest charge against rhetoric. The strategy Marvell adopts to guarantee the truthfulness of his speaker, Dzelzainis argues, is to emphasise her coarseness: she is in both senses a plain speaker, the female counterpart, perhaps, to Cromwell's advice to a painter to include (in traditional phrasing) the 'warts and all'.

With Marvell we enter the Restoration and with the Restoration changing conditions for rhetoric in England. French influence was significant here, as well as on the stage. New rhetorics from Rollin and Lamy were to create the concept of belles-lettres which developed during the eighteenth century, promoting the more passive and feminine activities of reading and conversation. The principles of conversation, in particular, were discussed at length by Addison and Steele in the pages of *The Spectator* and by Swift in his *Polite Conversation,* contributing to what was widely regarded as a feminisation of culture in the early eighteenth century (Clery 2004). A new class of professional writers began to produce anthologies aimed at educating literary taste and that audience certainly included women. Books such as *The Agreeable Variety* (1717) 'by a lady', or Daniel Bellamy's *The Young Ladies Miscellany* (1723), also provide striking illustrations of the feminisation of rhetoric itself. Bellamy tackles the objection that 'the Art of Pronunciation is no Female Accomplishment' by pointing out that 'Homer's Stentor was never admitted amongst the Number of his fine Speakers', adding that 'The Young Lady, that can pronounce her Words with a firm, strong, articulate Voice, is by Nature qualify'd for speaking well in Publick, and wants nothing but Art to direct her Judgement' (Bellamy 1723: A4r–v). In the conversible world, women could set a standard of social eloquence by combining firm ariculation with gentleness of expression. By 1762 Adam Smith was telling his Glaswegian students, perhaps rather optimistically, that 'the conversation of Ladies is the best Standard of Language, as there is a certain delicacy and agreeableness in their behaviour and adress' (Smith 1983: 4). So we might see the essays in the present collection as a prequel to the feminisation of rhetoric in the eighteenth century as cultural values shifted from the old masculine ideal of political oratory to the more genteel social virtues of conversation and belles-lettres. The principles of conversation were in many respects the opposite of those of rhetoric: deference, accommodation, self-effacement – agreement and yielding, not winning the argument. Its rules extend the 'mild oratory' and 'gentleness of speech' so well described by Rachel Heard into a social virtue. As Fielding put it, conversation is 'the Art of pleasing' (Fielding 1972: 123).

That cultural shift did not go unchallenged. During the 1730s a political discourse of republicanism was revived, shorn of its associations with Lucretia and other Roman matrons and inspired by distinctly masculine values. Ancient eloquence was held to embody those values and there were calls for its revival, notably from David Hume. Like Thomas Wilson before him, Hume saw Demosthenes as the very pinnacle of eloquence, a man who was 'the most celebrated Spectacle of the World' and who combined 'Vehemence of Thought and Expression' with 'Vehemence of action' (Hume 1742: 13, 15). But for all his apparent enthusiasm for Greek oratory, Hume's views on rhetoric, gender and politics were decidedly ambiguous. Immediately before the essay 'Of Eloquence' in the second volume of the 1742 *Essays* we find a very different piece called, simply, 'Of Essay-Writing', which sets out the bellelettrist and feminised agenda of reading and conversation encouraged by Addison, Steele and Swift. Here Hume refers to women as 'the Sovereigns of the Empire of Conversation' and claims that 'Women of Sense and Education [. . .] are much better Judges of all polite Writing than Men of the same Degree of Understanding' (Hume 1742: 5–6). Hume's two essays neatly divide British cultural values in the first half of the eighteenth century in gendered terms.

What happens in the second half of the century takes us back to early modernity and forward into the modern era. The flagship of English eloquence moved from parliament to the theatre and is represented, supremely, by Shakespeare, a male author but one who had the woman's voice. Earlier, Ann Merricke had written privately to her friend about her country reading, and Margaret Cavendish had spoken out in the first published critical essay on Shakespeare, praising his natural representation of the passions and his ability to move readers to tears. Nobody, however, spoke out more boldly in defence of Shakespeare than Elizabeth Montagu whose work was denounced by Voltaire in the daunting arena of the Académie Française where she was in attendance with the British ambassador.[2] The confrontation represented a battle between French and English cultural values for dominance in Europe, and it was Voltaire who lost. While Voltaire tried to defend French neo-classical taste against the supposed vulgarity and barbarisms of the English writer, Montagu attacked his 'misrepresentations' and argued that, unlike French drama, Shakespeare's characters 'speak with human voices, are actuated by human passions' ([Montagu] 1769: 81). The debate was ostensibly about 'nature', but it was also about rhetoric because it was closely connected to the development in eighteenth-century Britain of a new kind of rhetoric that was much more closely attuned to the psychology and socialisation of the passions.[3] Shakespeare's plays are very important in this respect, but so are women. That the central writer of the early modern period should become a vehicle for the feminisation of rhetoric in the century following is just one of many ways in which the important issues raised by this book respond to later cultural change.

Notes

1 For Elizabeth's speeches in response to the Commons' petition that she marry see Elizabeth I (2000: 56–60, 70–7).
2 For Cavendish see Thompson and Roberts (1997).
3 For a fuller context for this see Rhodes (2004: 208–26).

Bibliography

Ahl, F. M. (1976) *Lucan: An Introduction*, Ithaca, NY, and London: Cornell University Press.

Amussen, Susan Dwyer (1988) *An Ordered Society: Gender and Class in Early Modern England*, New York and Oxford: Blackwell.

—— (1999) 'The Family and the Household', in David Scott Kastan (ed.), *A Companion to Shakespeare*, Oxford: Blackwell, pp. 85–99.

Anderson, R. C. (ed.) (1921) *Letters of the Fifteenth and Sixteenth Centuries From the Archives of Southampton*, Publications of the Southampton Record Society, 22, Southampton: Cox & Sharland.

Aristotle (1991) *On Rhetoric*, trans. G. A. Kennedy, Oxford: Oxford University Press.

Astell, M. (1696) *An Essay in Defence of the Female Sex*, London.

Aubrey, J. (1999) *Aubrey's Brief Lives*, ed. O. L. Dick, Boston, Mass.: Nonpareil.

Aughterson, K. (ed.) (1995) *Renaissance Woman: Constructions of Femininity in England, A Sourcebook*, London: Routledge.

Aylmer, J. (1559) *An Harborowe for Faithfull and Trewe Subjectes*, London.

Bacon, F. (1994) *The Essays*, ed. M. J. Hawkins, London: J. M. Dent.

Bailey, R. (1992) *New Light on George Fox and Early Quakerism: The Making and Unmaking of a God*, San Francisco, Calif.: Mellen Research University Press.

Bale, John (1548) *A Comedy Concernynge Thre Lawes of Nature, Moses, and Christ, Corrupted by the Sodomytes, Pharisees & Papystes Most Wycked*, Wesel.

—— (1550) *The Apology of Iohan Bale agaynste a Ranke Papist*, London.

—— (1551) *The First Two Partes of the Actes or Vnchast Examples of the Englysh Votaryes*, London.

—— (1562), *A New Comedy or Enterlude concerning thre Lawes of Nature, Moises, and Christ, Corrupted by the Sodomytes, Pharysies, and Papistes*, London.

Barker, E. (1660) *A Sermon Preached at the Funerall of [. . .] Lady Elizabeth Capell*, London.

Barry, L. (1952) *Ram-alley; or Merrie-trickes, A Comedy by Lording Barry*, ed. Claude E. Jones, Louvain: Librairie Universitaire.

Bate, J. (1994) *Shakespeare and Ovid*, Oxford: Oxford University Press.

Bates, C. (1992) *The Rhetoric of Courtship in Elizabethan Language and Literature*, Cambridge: Cambridge University Press.

Bauman, R. (1983) *Let Your Words Be Few: Symbolism of Speaking and Silence among Seventeenth-Century Quakers*, Cambridge: Cambridge University Press.

Baxter, R. (1673) *A Christian Directory*, London.

—— (1682) *A Breviate of the Life of Margaret[. . .] Late Wife of Richard Baxter*, London.

Beaumont, F. and Fletcher, J. (1966–96) *The Dramatic Works in the Beaumont and Fletcher Canon*, 10 vols, gen. ed. F. Bowers, Cambridge: Cambridge University Press.

Beilin, E. V. (1990) 'Writing Public Poetry: Humanism and the Woman Writer', *Modern Language Quarterly* 51: 249–71.

Bellamy, D. (1723) *The Young Ladies Miscellany*, London.

Belsey, C. (1985) *The Subject of Tragedy*, London and New York: Methuen.

Bennett, L. (2004) *Women Writing of Divinest Things: Rhetoric and the Poetry of Pembroke, Wroth and Lanyer*, Pittsburgh, Pa.: Duquesne University Press.

Bentley, T. (1582) *The Monument of Matrones*, 3 vols, London.

Berger, A. (1996) 'The Latest Word from Echo', *New Literary History*, 27: 621–40.

Besse, J. (1753) *A Collection of the Sufferings of the People Called Quakers; for the Testimony of a Good Conscience from [. . .] 1650 to [. . .] 1689*, 2 vols, London.

Blondel, D. (1661) *A Treatise of the Sibyls, So Highly Celebrated, As well by the Antient Heathens, as the Holy Fathers of the Church*, trans. J. Davies, London.

Boreman, R. (1669) *A Mirrour of True Christianity and a Miracle of Charity*, London.

Boys, J. (1660) *Æneas His Descent into Hell: As it is Inimitably Described by the Prince of Poets in the Sixth of his Æneis*, London.

Braithwaite, W. C. (1961) *The Beginnings of Quakerism*, Cambridge: Cambridge University Press.

Brathwait, R. (1618) *The Good Wife: or, A Rare One Amongst Women*, London.

—— (1620) *Essaies upon the Five Senses*, London.

—— (1631) *The English Gentlewoman, Drawne out to the Full Body*, London.

—— (1640) *Ar't Asleepe Husband? A Boulster Lecture*, London.

Bray, A. (1990) 'Homosexuality and the Signs of Male Friendship in Elizabethan England', *History Workshop Journal*, 29: 3–8.

Breton, N. (1616) *Crossing of Proverbs*, London.

Bruto, G. M. (1598) *The Necessarie, Fit, and Convenient Education of a Yong Gentlewoman*, London.

Bulwer, J. (1644) *Chironomia; Or, the Art of Manuall Rhetorique*, London.

Burrow, C. (ed.) (2002) *Complete Sonnets and Poems by W. Shakespeare*, Oxford: Oxford University Press.

Burrows, J. (2005) 'Andrew Marvell and the "Painter Satires": A Computational Approach to their Authorship', *Modern Language Review* 100: 281–97.

Byng, T. (1603) *Sorrowes Ioy. Or, A Lamentation for our Late Deceased Soveraigne Elizabeth, with a Triumph for the Prosperous Succession of our Gratious King, Iames*, Cambridge.

Byrne, M. St Clare (ed.) (1981–) *The Lisle Letters*, 6 vols, Chicago, Ill.: University of Chicago Press.

Calvin, J. (1980) *Letters of John Calvin Selected from the Bonnet Edition*, Edinburgh: Banner of Truth Trust.

Campbell, W. G. (1995) 'The Figure of Pilate's Wife in Aemilia Lanyer's *Salve Deus Rex Judaeorum*', in G. W. Williams and B. J. Baines (eds) *Renaissance Papers*, Southeastern Renaissance Conference, pp. 1–13.

Capp, B. (1996) 'Separate Domains? Women and Authority in Early Modern England', in P. Griffiths, A. Fox and S. Hindle (eds) *The Experience of Authority in Early Modern England*, Basingstoke: Macmillan, pp. 117–45.

Carrington, L. (1997) 'Women, Rhetoric and Letter Writing: Marguerite d'Alençon's Correspondence with Bishop Briçonnet of Meaux', in M. Meijer Wertheimer (ed.) *Listening to Their Voices: The Rhetorical Activities of Historical Women*, Columbia, SC: University of South Carolina Press, pp. 215–32.

Carroll, K. C. (1978) 'Early Quakers and "Going Naked as a Sign"', *Quaker History* 67: 69–87.

Castiglione, B. (1994) *The Book of the Courtier*, ed. V. Cox and trans. T. Hoby, London: J. M. Dent.

Cave, T. (1979) *The Cornucopian Text: Problems of Writing in the French Renaissance*, Oxford: Oxford University Press.

Chapman, G. (1987) *The Plays of George Chapman: The Tragedies*, ed. A. Holaday (assisted by G. Blakemore Evans and T. L. Berger), Cambridge: D. S. Brewer.

—— (1964) *Bussy D'Ambois*, ed. Nicholas Brooke, London: Methuen.

—— (1965) *Bussy D'Ambois*, ed. Maurice Evans, London: Ernest Benn.

Chaucer, Geoffrey (1957) *The Poetical Works of Chaucer*, ed. F. N. Robinson, London: Oxford University Press.

Cicero (1996) *De oratore*, trans. E. W. Sutton and H. Rackham, Cambridge, Mass.: Harvard University Press.

Clark, S. (1997) *Thinking with Demons: The Idea of Witchcraft in Early Modern Europe*, Oxford: Clarendon.

Clarke, D. (2000a) '"Form'd into Words by Your Divided Lips": Women, Rhetoric and the Ovidian Tradition', in D. Clarke and E. Clarke (eds) *'This Double Voice': Gendered Writing in Early Modern England*, Basingstoke: Macmillan, pp. 61–87.

—— (2000b) '"In Sort as She it Sung": Spenser's "Doleful Lay" and the Construction of Female Authorship', *Criticism* 42: 451–68.

—— (2001) *The Politics of Early Modern Women's Writing*, London: Longman.

Clarke, D. and Clarke, E. (eds) (2000) *'This Double Voice': Gendered Writing in Early Modern England*, Basingstoke: Macmillan.

Clery, E. J. (2004) *The Feminization Debate in Eighteenth-Century England: Literature, Commerce, Luxury*, Basingstoke: Palgrave Macmillan.

Coch, C. (2003) '"Mother of My Contreye": Elizabeth I and Tudor Constructions of Motherhood', in K. Farrell and K. Swain (eds) *The Mysteries of Elizabeth I: Selections from 'English Literary Renaissance'*, Amherst, Mass.: University of Massachusetts Press, pp. 134–61.

Coiro, A. B. (1993) 'Writing in Service: Sexual Politics and Class Position in the Poetry of Aemilia Lanyer and Ben Jonson', *Criticism* 35: 357–76

Colclough, D. (1999) '*Parrhesia*: The Rhetoric of Free Speech in Early Modern England', *Rhetorica* 17: 177–212.

Connor, S. (2000) *Dumbstruck: A Cultural History of Ventriloquism*, Oxford: Oxford University Press.

Coole, D. (1988) *Women in Political Theory*, Brighton: Harvester.

Cotgrave, J. (1655) *The English Treasury of Wit and Language*, London.

Coverdale, Miles (trans.) (1549) 'The paraphrase vpon the epistle of the Apostle sainct Paule to the Galathians' in *The Seconde Tome or Volume of the Paraphrase of Erasmus upon the Newe Testament: Conteyning the Epistles of S. Paul and the other Apostles*, London.

Crawford, P. (1996) *Women and Religion in England 1500–1720*, 2nd edn, London and New York: Routledge.

Crook, N. and N. Rhodes (2000) 'The Daughters of Memory: Thomas Heywood's *Gunaikeion* and the Female Computer' in N. Rhodes and J. Sawday (eds) *The Renaissance Computer: Knowledge Technology in the First Age of Print*, London: Routledge, pp. 135–48.

Darcie, A. (1622) *The Honour of Ladies*, London.

Davies, J. (1975) *The Poems of Sir John Davies*, ed. R. Krueger, Oxford: Clarendon.

Davis, N. Z. (1976) '"Women's History" in Transition: The European Case', *Feminist Studies* 3: 83–103.

—— (1987) *Fiction in the Archives: Pardon Tales and Their Tellers in Sixteenth-Century France*, Stanford, Calif.: Stanford University Press.

Day, A. (1586) *The English Secretorie*, London.

Daybell, J. (ed.) (2004) *Women and Politics in Early Modern England, 1450–1700*, Aldershot: Ashgate.

—— (2006a) 'Scripting a Female Voice: Women's Epistolary Rhetoric in Sixteenth-Century Letters of Petition', *Women's Writing. Special Issue: Epistolarity to 1900* 13: 3–20.

—— (2006b) *Women Letter Writers in Tudor England*, Oxford: Oxford University Press.

de Lille, Alain (1980) *The Plaint of Nature*, trans. James E. Sheridan, Toronto: Toronto Pontifical Institute of Medieval Studies.

Demosthenes (1570) *The Three Orations of Demosthenes*, trans. T. Wilson, London.

Derrida, J. (1977) *Of Grammatology*, trans. G. Chakravorty Spivak, Baltimore, Md.: Johns Hopkins University Press.

Dick, B. F. (1965) 'The Role of the Oracle in Lucan's *de Bello Civili*', *Hermes* 93: 460–6.

DiGangi, M. (1997) *The Homoerotics of Early Modern Drama*, Cambridge: Cambridge University Press.

Dixon, P. (1971) *Rhetoric*, London: Methuen.

Dod, J. and Cleaver, R. (1612) *A Godlie Forme of Householde Government*, London.

Dollimore, J. (1984) *Radical Tragedy: Religion, Ideology and Power in the Drama of Shakespeare and his Contemporaries*, Brighton: Harvester.

Donaldson, I. (1982) *The Rapes of Lucretia*, Oxford: Clarendon.

Donawerth, J. (1995) 'The Politics of Renaissance Rhetorical Theory by Women', in C. Levin and P. A. Sullivan (eds) *Political Rhetoric, Power, and Renaissance Women*, Albany, NY: State University of New York Press, pp. 257–72.

—— (ed.) (2002) *Rhetorical Theory by Women before 1900: An Anthology*, Lanham, Md.: Rowman & Littlefield.

Donovan, J. (1980) 'The Silence Is Broken', in Sally McConnell-Ginet, Ruth Borker and Nelly Furman (eds) *Women and Language in Literature and Society*, New York: Praeger, pp. 205–18.

Doran, S. (1996) *Monarchy and Matrimony: The Courtships of Elizabeth I*, London and New York: Routledge.

Drake, J. (1696) *An Essay in Defence of the Female Sex*, London.

Drayton, M. (1941) *The Works of Michael Drayton*, 5 vols, ed. J. W. Hebel, Oxford: Blackwell.

Drew-Bear, A. (1994) *Painted Faces on the Renaissance Stage*, Lewisburg, Pa.: Bucknell University Press.

Earle, J. (1628) *Micro-cosmographie. Or, A Peece of the World Discovered; in Essayes and Characters*, London.

Elizabeth I (2000) *Collected Works*, ed. L. S. Marcus, J. Mueller and M. B. Rose, Chicago, Ill.: University of Chicago Press.

Elyot, T. (1940), *Sir Thomas Elyot's 'The Defence of Good Women'*, ed. E. J. Howard, Oxford, Ohio: The Anchor Press.

Enterline, L. (2000) *The Rhetoric of the Body from Ovid to Shakespeare*, Cambridge: Cambridge University Press.

Erasmus, D. (1978) *De copia verborum*, ed. C. R. Thompson, *The Collected Works of Erasmus*, Vol. XXIV, Toronto: University of Toronto Press.

—— (1985) *De conscribendis epistolis*, ed. J. K. Sowards, *The Collected Works of Erasmus*, Vol. XXV, Toronto: University of Toronto Press.

Eskin, C. R. (1999) 'The Rei(g)ning of Women's Tongues in English Books of Instruction and Rhetorics', in B. J. Whitehead (ed.) *Women's Education in Early Modern Europe: A History, 1500–1800*, New York and London: Garland Publishing, pp. 100–32.

Farnaby, T. (1647) *M. Val. Martialis epigrammaton libri animadversi, emendati & commentariolis iuculenter explicati*, Geneva.

Fellowes, E. H. (1967) *English Madrigal Verse 1588–1632*, eds F. W. Sternfeld and D. Greer, Oxford: Oxford University Press.

Ferguson, M. (2003) *Dido's Daughters: Literacy, Gender and Empire in Early Modern England and France*, Chicago, Ill.: University of Chicago Press.

Fielding, H. (1972) 'An Essay on Conversation' in *Miscellanies*, Vol. I, ed. H. K. Miller, Oxford: Clarendon.

Fleming, J. (1994) 'Dictionary English and the Female Tongue', in Richard Burt and John Michael Archer (eds) *Enclosure Acts: Sexuality, Property, and Culture in Early Modern England*, Ithaca, NY: Cornell University Press, pp. 290–325.

Fletcher, A. J. (1995) *Gender, Sex and Subordination in England 1500–1800*, New Haven, Conn.: Yale University Press.

Florio, J. (1598) *A Worlde of Wordes*, London.

Foucault, M. (2001) *Fearless Speech*, ed. J. Pearson, Los Angeles, Calif.: Semiotext(e).

Fox, A. (1995) 'The Complaint of Poetry for the Death of Liberality: The Decline of Literary Patronage in the 1590s', in J. Guy (ed.) *The Reign of Elizabeth I: Court and Culture in the Last Decade*, Cambridge: Cambridge University Press, pp. 229–57.

Fox, G. (1952) *The Journal of George Fox*, ed. J. L. Nickalls, Cambridge: Cambridge University Press.

Frye, S. and Robertson, K. (eds) (1999) *Maids and Mistresses, Cousins and Queens: Women's Alliances in Early Modern England*, Oxford: Oxford University Press.

Fuller, W. (1628) *The Mourning of Mount Libanon: Or, The Temples Teares*, London.

Fulwood, W. (1568) *Enemie of Idlenesse*, London.

Gardiner, D. (1929) *English Girlhood at School: A Study of Women's Education through Twelve Centuries*, Oxford: Oxford University Press.

Garrard, M. D. (1989) *Artemesia Gentilischi: The Image of the Female Hero in Baroque Art*, Princeton, NJ: Princeton University Press.

Garter, B. (1578) *The Ioyfull Receyving of the Queenes most Excellent Maiestie into hir Highnesse Citie of Norwich*, London.

Gélis, J. (1991) *History of Childbirth: Fertility, Pregnancy and Birth in Early Modern England*, trans. R. Morris, Cambridge: Polity.

Gibson, A. (1599) *A Womans Woorth, Defended Against All the Men in the World*, London.

Gibson, J. (2000) 'Letters', in M. Hattaway (ed.) *A Companion to English Renaissance Literature and Culture*, Oxford: Blackwell, pp. 615–19.

Gillespie, K. (2004) *Domesticity and Dissent in the Seventeenth Century: English Women Writers and the Public Sphere*, Cambridge: Cambridge University Press.

Glanvill, J. (1678) *An Essay Concerning Preaching: Written for the Direction of A Young Divine; and Useful also for the People, in Order to Profitable Hearing*, London.

Glenn, C. (1997) *Rhetoric Retold: Regendering the Tradition from Antiquity through the Renaissance*, Carbondale, Ill.: Southern Illinois University Press.

Goldberg, J. (1986) *Voice, Terminal, Echo: Postmodernism and English Renaissance Texts*, New York: Methuen.

—— (1990) *Writing Matter: From the Hands of the English Renaissance*, Stanford, Calif.: Stanford University Press.

—— (1997) *Desiring Women's Writing: English Renaissance Examples*, Stanford, Calif.: Stanford University Press.

Gouge, W. (1976) *Of Domesticall Duties*, Amsterdam: Walter J. Johnson, Theatrum Orbis Terrarum.

Gowing, L. (1996) *Domestic Dangers: Women, Words and Sex in Early Modern London*, Oxford: Oxford University Press.

Graf, F. (1991) 'Gestures and Conventions: The Gestures of Roman Actors and Orators', in J. Bremmer and H. Roodenburg (eds) *A Cultural History of Gesture: From Antiquity to the Present Day*, Cambridge: Polity Press, pp. 36–58.

Graham, K. J. E. (1994) *The Performance of Conviction: Plainness and Rhetoric in the Early English Renaissance*, Ithaca, NY: Cornell University Press.

Greene, T. (1982) *The Light in Troy: Imitation and Discovery in Renaissance Poetry*, New Haven, Conn.: Yale University Press.

Greenhill, W. (1656) *Sermons of Christ*, London.

Greer, G. (2000) *John Wilmot, Earl of Rochester*, Horndon: Northcote House.

Guillén, C. (1986) 'Notes toward the Study of the Renaissance Letter', in B. K. Lewalski (ed.) *Renaissance Genres: Essays on Theory, History and Interpretation*, Cambridge, Mass.: Harvard University Press, pp. 70–101.

Guillory, J. (1993) *Cultural Capital: The Problem of Literary Canon Formation*, Chicago, Ill.: University of Chicago Press.

Guy, J. (ed.) (1995a) *The Reign of Elizabeth I: Court and Culture in the Last Decade*, Cambridge: Cambridge University Press.

—— (1995b) 'Introduction: The 1590s: The Second Reign of Elizabeth I?' in J. Guy (ed.) *The Reign of Elizabeth I: Court and Culture in the Last Decade*, Cambridge: Cambridge University Press, pp. 1–19.

Habermas, J. (1989) *The Structural Transformation of the Public Sphere: An Inquiry into a Category of Bourgeois Society*, trans. T. Burger, Cambridge, Mass.: MIT Press.

Hackett, H. (1995) *Virgin Mother, Maiden Queen: Elizabeth I and the Cult of the Virgin Mary*, Basingstoke: Macmillan.

—— (2003) '*A Midsummer Night's Dream*', in J. Howard and R. Dutton (eds) *A Companion to Shakespeare's Works, Vol. 3: The Comedies*, Oxford: Blackwell, pp. 338–57.

Hadfield, A. (1994) *Literature, Politics and National Identity: Reformation to Renaissance*, Cambridge: Cambridge University Press.

—— (1997) *Spenser's Irish Experience: Wilde Fruit and Savage Soyl*, Oxford: Oxford University Press.

—— (1998) *Literature, Travel, and Colonial Writing in the English Renaissance*, Oxford: Oxford University Press.

—— (2005) *Shakespeare and Republicanism*, Cambridge: Cambridge University Press.

Haigh, C. (1988) *Elizabeth I*, London and New York: Longman.

Halliwell, J O. (ed.) (1841) *Rara Mathematica, or a Collection of Treatises on the Mathematics and Subjects Connected with Them*, London.

Halpern, R. (1991) *The Poetics of Primitive Accumulation: English Renaissance Culture and the Genealogy of Capital*, Ithaca, NY: Cornell University Press.

Hammer, P. (1999) *The Polarisation of Elizabethan Politics: The Political Career of Robert Devereux, Earl of Essex 1585–1597*, Cambridge: Cambridge University Press.

Hampton, T. (1990) *Writing From History: The Rhetoric of Exemplarity in Renaissance Literature*, Ithaca, NY: Cornell University Press.

Hardie, P. (ed.) (2002) *The Cambridge Companion to Ovid*, Cambridge: Cambridge University Press.

Harris, B. J. (1990) 'Women and Politics in Early Tudor England', *Historical Journal* 33: 259–81.

—— (2002) *English Aristocratic Women, 1450–1550: Marriage and Family, Property and Careers*, Oxford: Oxford University Press.

—— (2004) 'Sisterhood, Friendship and the Power of English Aristocratic Women, 1450–1550', in J. Daybell (ed.) *Women and Politics in Early Modern England, 1450–1700*, Aldershot: Ashgate, pp. 21–50.

Hart, J. (1569) *An Orthographie*, London.

Hartley, T. E. (1981) *Proceedings in the Parliaments of Elizabeth I*, Vol. I, Leicester: Leicester University Press.

Harvey, E. D. (1992) *Ventriloquized Voices: Feminist Theory and English Renaissance Texts*, London: Routledge.

Harvey, G. (1577) *Rhetor, or a Two-Day Speech on Nature, Art, & Practice*, trans. M. Reynolds, London. Available on-line at <http://comp.uark.edu/~mreynold/rhetor/html>.

Haskell, F. (1989) 'Charles I's Collection of Pictures', in A. MacGregor (ed.) *The Late King's Goods: Collections, Possessions and Patronage of Charles I in the Light of the Commonwealth Sale Inventories*, London and Oxford: Alistair McAlpine in association with Oxford University Press, pp. 203–31.

Hassig, D. (1995) *Medieval Bestiaries*, Cambridge: Cambridge University Press.

Hawkes, T. (1985) 'Telmah', in P. Parker and G. Hartman (eds) *Shakespeare and the Question of Theory*, London and New York: Methuen, pp. 310–32.

Henderson, J. R. (1983) 'Defining the Genre of the Letter: Juan Luis Vives' *De Conscribendis Epistolis*' in *Renaissance and Reformation* 7(19): 89–105.

—— (1993) 'On Reading the Rhetoric of the Renaissance Letter' in H. F. Plett (ed.) *Renaissance-Rhetorik/Renaissance Rhetoric*, Berlin and New York: Walter de Gruyter, 143–62.

Henderson, K. U. and McManus, B. F. (eds) (1985) *Half Humankind: Contexts and Texts of the Controversy about Women in England, 1540–1640*, Chicago, Ill.: University of Illinois Press.

Heywood, T. (1637) *A Curtaine Lecture*, London.

—— (1640) *The Exemplary Lives and Memorable Acts of Nine the Most Worthy Women of the World*, London.

—— (1657) *The Generall Historie of Women*, London.

Heywood, T. and Brome, R. (1979) *An Edition of The Late Lancashire Witches by Thomas Heywood and Richard Brome*, ed. L. H. Barber, New York and London: Garland Publishing.

Higgins, P. (1973) 'The Reactions of Women, with Special Reference to Women Petitioners', in B. Manning (ed.) *Politics, Religion and the English Civil War*, London: Edward Arnold, pp. 178–222.

Higginson, F. (1653) *A Brief Relation of The Irreligion of the Northern Quakers*, London.

Hinds, H. (1996) *God's Englishwomen: Seventeenth-Century Radical Sectarian Writing and Feminist Criticism*, Manchester: Manchester University Press.

—— (2004) 'Sectarian Spaces: the Politics of Place and Gender in Seventeenth-Century Prophetic Writing', *Literature and History*, 13(2): 1–25.

Hobbes, T. (1991) *Leviathan*, ed. Richard Tuck, Cambridge: Cambridge University Press.

Hoby, M. (1998) *The Private Life of an Elizabethan Lady: The Diary of Lady Margaret Hoby 1599–1605*, ed. Joanna Moody, Stroud: Sutton Publishing.

Hollander, J. (1981) *The Figure of Echo: A Mode of Allusion in Milton and After*, Berkeley, Calif.: University of California Press.

Hornbeak, K. G. (1934) *The Complete Letter-Writer in English 1568–1800*, Northampton, Mass.: Smith College.

Horneck, P. (1699) *A Sermon on the Death of the Right Honourable Lady Guilford*, London.

H[owell], T. (1560) *The Fable of Ovid Treting of Narcissus*, London.

Hudson, Anne (ed.) (1997) *Selections from English Wycliffite Writings*, Toronto: University of Toronto Press.

Hughes, A. (1995) 'Gender and Politics in Leveller Literature' in S. D. Amussen and M. A. Kishlansky (eds) *Political Culture and Cultural Politics in Early Modern England: Essays Presented to David Underdown*, Manchester: Manchester University Press, pp. 162–88.

Hughes, D. O. (1986) 'Distinguishing Signs: Ear-Rings, Jews and Franciscan Rhetoric in the Italian Renaissance City', *Past and Present* 112: 3–59.

Hull, S. W. (1982) *Chaste, Silent and Obedient: English Books for Women, 1475–1640*, San Marino, Calif.: Huntington Library.

Huloet, R. (1970) *Abecedarium anglico-latinum, 1552*, Menston: Scolar Press.

Hume, A. (1865) *Of the Orthographie and Congruitie of the Britan Tongue*, ed. Henry B. Wheatley, London: Trübner & Co. for the Early English Text Society.

Hume, D. (1742) *Essays, Moral and Political*, Vol. II, Edinburgh.

Humiliata, S. M. (1949–50) 'Standards of Taste Advocated for Feminine Letter Writing, 1640–1797', *Huntington Library Quarterly* 13: 261–77.

Hutchinson, L. (1817) *On the Principles of Christian Religion*, London: Longman.

Hutson, L. (1992) 'Why the Lady's Eyes are Nothing Like the Sun', in C. Brant and D. Purkiss (eds) *Women, Texts and Histories*, London: Routledge, pp. 13–38.

—— (1994) *The Usurer's Daughter: Male Friendship and Fictions of Women in Sixteenth-Century England*, London: Routledge.

Hutton, R. (2004) 'Monck, George, First Duke of Albemarle (1608–1670)', *Oxford Dictionary of National Biography*, Oxford: Oxford University Press.

232   *Bibliography*

Ingleby, C. M. (1909) *The Shakspere Allusion-Book*, rev. John Munro, London: New Shakspere Society.

Irigaray, L. (1991) 'The Power of Discourse and the Subordination of the Feminine', in M. Whitford (ed.) *The Irigaray Reader*, Oxford: Blackwell, pp. 118–39.

Jacobson, H. (1974) *Ovid's Heroides*, Princeton, NJ: Princeton University Press.

James VI and I (1597) *Daemonologie in Forme of a Dialogue*, Edinburgh.

—— (1971) *Basilicon Doron, or His Majesties Instructions to His Dearest Sonne, Henry the Prince*, in *The Workes* [1616], Hildesheim and New York: Georg Olms Verlag.

James, M. (1986) *Society, Politics and Culture: Studies in Early Modern England*, Cambridge: Cambridge University Press.

Jardine, L. (1983) *Still Harping on Daughters: Women and Drama in the Age of Shakespeare*, Hemel Hempstead: Harvester Wheatsheaf.

Jeanneret, M. (1998) 'The Vagaries of Exemplarity: Distortion or Dismissal?', *Journal of the History of Ideas* 59: 565–79.

Jones, A. R. (1987) 'Nets and Bridles: Early Modern Conduct Books and Sixteenth-Century Women's Lyrics', in N. Armstrong and L. Tennenhouse (eds) *The Ideology of Conduct: Essays on Literature and the History of Sexuality*, London and New York: Methuen.

Jonson, B. (1925–52) *Ben Jonson: Works*, 11 vols, eds C. H. Herford, P. Simpson and E. Simpson, Oxford: Oxford University Press.

—— (1985) *Ben Jonson*, ed. I. Donaldson, Oxford: Oxford University Press.

Jordan, C. (1990) *Renaissance Feminism: Literary Texts and Political Models*, Ithaca, NY and London: Cornell University Press.

Justinus, M. J. (1564) *The Abridgment of the Histories of Trogus Pompeius, Collected and Wrytten in the Laten Tonge, by the Famous Historiographer Iustine, and Translated into English by Arthur Goldyng*, London.

Kahn, V. (1985) *Rhetoric, Prudence, and Skepticism in the Renaissance*, Ithaca, NY: Cornell University Press.

—— (2004) *Wayward Contracts: The Crisis of Political Obligation in England, 1640–1740*, Princeton, NJ: Princeton University Press.

Kantorowicz, Ernst H. (1957) *The King's Two Bodies: A Study in Mediaeval Political Theology*, Princeton, NJ: Princeton University Press.

Kelly, J. (1999) 'Did Women have a Renaissance?', in L. Hutson (ed.) *Feminism and Renaissance Studies*, Oxford: Oxford University Press, pp. 21–47.

Kerrigan, J. (ed.) (1991) *Motives of Woe: Shakespeare and 'Female Complaint': A Critical Anthology*, Oxford: Clarendon.

Kettering, S. (1989) 'The Patronage Power of Early Modern French Noblewomen', *Historical Journal* 32: 817–41.

Kilgour, M. (2005) '"Thy perfect image viewing": Poetic Creation and Ovid's Narcissus in *Paradise Lost*', *Studies in Philology* 102: 307–39.

Killin, M. and Patison, B. (1655) *A Warning from the Lord to the Teachers & People of Plimouth*, London.

Krontiris T. (1992) *Oppositional Voices: Women as Writers and Translators of Literature in the English Renaissance*, London and New York: Routledge.

Lanham, R. A. (1976) *The Motives of Eloquence: Literary Rhetoric in the Renaissance*, New Haven, Conn.: Yale University Press.

—— (1991) *A Handlist of Rhetorical Terms*, Berkeley, Calif.: University of California Press.

Lanyer, A. (1993) *The Poems of Aemilia Lanyer, Salve Deus Rex Judaeorum*, ed. S. Woods, New York and Oxford: Oxford University Press.

Laqueur, T. (1990) *Making Sex: Body and Gender from the Greeks to Freud*, Cambridge, Mass.: Harvard University Press.

Larminie, V. (1995) *Wealth, Kinship and Culture: The Seventeenth-Century Newdigates of Arbury and Their World*, Woodbridge: Boydell.

Lefkowitz, M. (1983) 'Influential Women', in A. Cameron and A. Kuhrt (eds) *Images of Women in Antiquity*, Canberra and London: Croom Helm, pp. 49–64.

Lemay, H. R. (1992) *Women's Secrets: A Translation of Pseudo-Albertus Magnus's 'De Secretis Mulierum' with Commentaries*, Albany, NY: State University of New York Press.

Leupin, Alexandre (1989) *Barbarolexis: Medieval Writing and Sexuality*, trans. K. M. Cooper, Cambridge, Mass.: Harvard University Press.

Levey, S. M. (1998) *An Elizabethan Inheritance: The Hardwick Hall Textiles*, London: National Trust.

Lévi-Strauss, C. (1969) *The Elementary Structures of Kinship*, trans. J. Harle Bell and J. R. von Sturmer, ed. R. Needham, Boston, Mass.: Beacon Press.

Lewalski, B. K. (1993) *Writing Women in Jacobean England*, Cambridge, Mass. and London: Harvard University Press.

—— (1998) 'Seizing Discourses and Reinventing Genres', in M. Grossman (ed.) *Aemilia Lanyer: Gender, Genre and the Canon*, Lexington, Ky.: University Press of Kentucky, pp. 49–59.

Livy, T. (1971) *The Early History of Rome*, trans. A. de Selincourt, Harmondsworth: Penguin.

Lloyd, G. (1996) 'The Man of Reason', in A. Garry and M. Pearsall (eds) *Women, Knowledge, and Reality: Explorations in Feminist Philosophy*, London: Routledge, pp. 149–65.

Locke, J. (1975) *Essay Concerning Human Understanding*, ed. P. H. Nidditch, Oxford: Clarendon.

Lord, George de F. (gen. ed.) (1963–75) *Poems on Affairs of State: Augustan Satirical Verse, 1660–1714*, 7 vols, New Haven, Conn.: Yale University Press.

Love, H. (1998) *The Culture and Commerce of Texts: Scribal Publication in Seventeenth-Century England*, Amherst, Mass.: University of Massachusetts Press.

Lucan (1631) *Lucans Pharsalia: Or The Civill Warres of Rome, betweene Pompey the great, and Ivlius Cæsar. The whole tenne Bookes, Englished by Thomas May*, London.

Luckyj, C. (2002) '*A Moving Rhetoricke*': *Gender and Silence in Early Modern England*, Manchester: Manchester University Press.

Lunsford, A. A. (ed.) (1995) *Reclaiming Rhetorica: Women in the Rhetorical Tradition*, Pittsburgh, Pa.: University of Pittsburgh Press.

Lyall, R. (1996) 'The Construction of a Rhetorical Voice in Sixteenth-Century Scottish Letters', in A. Gilroy and W. M. Verhoeven (eds) *Prose Studies: Correspondences: A Special Issue on Letters* 19, pp. 127–35.

Lyly, J. (1902) *Euphues and his England*, in R. W. Bond (ed.) *The Complete Works of John Lyly*, 3 vols, Oxford: Clarendon.

—— (1996) *Endymion*, ed. D. Bevington, Manchester: Manchester University Press.

Lyne, R. (2001) *Ovid's Changing Worlds: English Metamorphoses 1567–1632*, Oxford: Oxford University Press.

Lyons, J. D. (1989) *Exemplum: the Rhetoric of Example in Early Modern France and Italy*, Princeton, NJ: Princeton University Press

MacCaffrey, W. T. (1991) 'Patronage and Politics Under the Tudors', in L. Levy Peck (ed.) *The Mental World of the Jacobean Court*, Cambridge: Cambridge University Press, pp. 21–35.

Machiavelli, N. (1979a) *The Discourses*, trans. L. J. Walker, ed. B. Crick and rev. B. Richardson, Harmondsworth: Penguin.

—— (1979b) *La Mandragola* in *Machiavelli*, trans. and ed. P. Bondella and M. Musa, Harmondsworth: Penguin.

Mack, Patricia (1992) *Visionary Women: Ecstatic Prophecy in Seventeenth-Century England*, Berkeley, Calif.: University of California Press.

Mack, Peter (2002) *Elizabethan Rhetoric: Theory and Practice*, Cambridge: Cambridge University Press.

—— (2005) 'Rhetoric, Ethics and Reading in the Renaissance', *Renaissance Studies* 19: 1–21.

Maclean, I. (1980) *The Renaissance Notion of Woman*, Cambridge: Cambridge University Press.

McLeod, R. (1984) 'Spellbound', in G. B. Shand and R. C. Shady (eds) *Play-Texts in Old Spelling: Papers from the Glendon Conference*, New York: AMS Press, pp. 81–96.

McRae, A. (2004) *Literature, Satire and the Early Stuart State*, Cambridge: Cambridge University Press.

Magnusson, L. (1999) *Shakespeare and Social Dialogue: Dramatic Language and Elizabethan Letters*, Cambridge: Cambridge University Press.

—— (2001) 'Widowhood and Linguistic Capital: The Rhetoric and Reception of Anne Bacon's Epistolary Advice', *English Literary Renaissance* 31: 3–33.

—— (2004) 'A Rhetoric of Requests: Genre and Linguistic Scripts in Elizabethan Women's Suitors' Letters', in J. Daybell (ed.) *Women and Politics in Early Modern England, 1450–1700*, Aldershot: Ashgate, pp. 51–66.

Makin, B. (1673) *An Essay to Revive the Antient Education of Gentlewomen*, London.

Maltzahn, N. von (2005) *An Andrew Marvell Chronology*, Basingstoke: Palgrave Macmillan.

Marston, J. (1986) *The Selected Plays of John Marston (Plays by Renaissance & Restoration Dramatists)* (eds.) MacDonald P. Jackson and Michael Neill, Cambridge: Cambridge University Press.

Martial (1993) *Epigrams*, 3 vols, ed. and trans. D. R. Shackleton Bailey, Cambridge, Mass.: Harvard University Press.

Martindale, C. (ed.) (1988) *Ovid Renewed: Ovidian Influences on Literature and Art from the Middle Ages to the Twentieth Century*, Cambridge: Cambridge University Press.

Martindale, C. and Martindale, M. (eds) (1990) *Shakespeare and the Uses of Antiquity*, London: Routledge.

Marvell, A. (1971) *The Poems and Letters of Andrew Marvell*, 2 vols, ed. H. M. Margoliouth, rev. P. Legouis with the assistance of E. E. Duncan Jones, Oxford: Clarendon.

—— (2003a) *The Poems of Andrew Marvell*, ed. Nigel Smith, Harlow: Pearson Longman.

—— (2003b) *The Prose Works of Andrew Marvell*, 2 vols, ed. M. Dzelzainis and A. Patterson, New Haven, Conn., and London: Yale University Press.

Masten, J. (1997) 'Pressing Subjects Or, the Secret Lives of Shakespeare's Compositors', in J. Masten, P. Stallybrass and N. Vickers (eds) *Language Machines: Technologies of Literary and Cultural Production*, New York: Routledge, pp. 75–107.

Matthes, M. M. (2000) *The Rape of Lucretia and the Founding of Republics*, Pennsylvania, Pa.: University of Pennsylvania Press.

Maus, K. (1993) 'A Womb of His Own: Male Renaissance Poets in the Female Body', in J. G. Turner (ed.) *Sexuality and Gender in Early Modern Europe: Institutions, Texts, Images*, Cambridge: Cambridge University Press, pp. 266–89.

Mauss, M. (1969) *The Gift: Forms and Functions of Exchange in Archaic Societies*, trans. I. Cunnison, London: Cohen & West.

Maximus, Q. V. (1684) *His Collection of the Most Memorable Acts and Saying of Orators*, London.

Mellinkoff, R. (1973) 'Riding Backwards: Theme of Humiliation and Symbol of Evil', in *Viator: Medieval and Renaissance Studies*, 4: 153–76.

—— (1991) *Outcasts: Signs of Otherness in Northern European Art of the Late Middle Ages*, 2 vols, Berkeley, Calif.: University of California Press.

Mendelson, S. and Crawford, P. (1998) *Women in Early Modern England*, Oxford: Oxford University Press.

Menninger, K. (1969) *Number Words and Number Symbols: A Cultural History of Numbers*, trans. Paul Broneer, Cambridge, Mass.: MIT Press.

Merlin, P. (1599) *A Most Plaine and Profitable Exposition of the Booke of Ester, Delivered in 26 Sermons*, London.

Middleton, T. (1966) *A Game at Chess*, ed. J. W. Harper, New York: Hill & Wang.

Milton, J. (1953–82) *The Complete Prose Works of John Milton*, 8 vols, ed. D. M. Wolfe et al., New Haven, Conn.: Yale University Press.

——— (1971) *Paradise Lost*, ed. A. Fowler, London: Macmillan.

Minsheu, J. (1617) *Ductor in Linguas; or Guide unto the Tongues*, London.

Mitchell, L. C. (2003) 'Entertainment and Instruction: Women's Roles in the English Epistolary Tradition', *Huntington Library Quarterly* 66: 331–47.

Momigliano, A. (1973) 'Freedom of Speech in Antiquity', in Philip Wiener (ed.) *Dictionary of the History of Ideas*, 6 vols, New York: Scribner, pp. 252–63.

[Montagu, E.] (1769) *An Essay on the Writings and Genius of Shakespear*, London.

Montaigne, M. de (1910) *The Essayes of Michael Lord of Montaigne*, Vol. II, trans. John Florio, London: J. M. Dent.

——— (1993) *The Complete Essays of Michel de Montaigne*, ed. M. A. Screech, Harmondsworth: Penguin.

More, T. (1528) *A Dialogue Concernynge Heresyes & Matters of Religion*, London.

——— (1533) *The Second Parte of the Co[n]futacion of Tyndals Answere*, London.

Mulcaster, R. (1581) *Positions Wherin Those Primitive Circvmstances Be Examined, Which Are Necessarie For The Training Vp Of Children*, London.

——— (1970) *The First Part of the Elementary, 1582*, Menston: Scolar Press.

Nashe, T. (1600) *Prologue to Summers Last Will and Testament*, London.

——— (1958) *The Works of Thomas Nashe*, 5 vols, ed. R. B. McKerrow, Oxford: Blackwell.

Neale, J. E. (1957) *Elizabeth I and her Parliaments*, 2 vols, London: Cape.

——— (1960) *Queen Elizabeth I*, Harmondsworth: Penguin.

Newall, V. (1973) 'The Jew as a Witch Figure', in V. Newall (ed.) *The Witch Figure*, Boston, Mass. and London: Routledge & Kegan Paul, pp. 95–124.

Newman, K. (1991) *Fashioning Femininity and English Renaissance Drama*, Chicago, Ill.: Chicago University Press.

Nichols J. (ed.) (1823) *The Progresses and Public Processions of Elizabeth I*, London.

Norbrook, D. (1994) 'Rhetoric, Ideology, and the Elizabethan World Picture', in P. Mack (ed.) *Renaissance Rhetoric*, Basingstoke: Macmillan, pp. 140–64.

——— (1999) *Writing the English Republic: Poetry, Rhetoric and Politics 1627–1660*, Cambridge: Cambridge University Press.

——— (2002) *Poetry and Politics in the English Renaissance*, Oxford: Oxford University Press.

——— (2004) 'Women, the Republic of Letters, and the Public Sphere in the Mid-Seventeenth Century', *Criticism* 46: 223–40.

Norbrook, D. and Woudhuysen, H. (eds) (1992) *The Penguin Book of Renaissance Verse, 1509–1659*, London: Allen Lane/Penguin.

O'Callaghan, M. (2000) *The 'Shepheards Nation': Jacobean Spenserians and Early Stuart Political Culture 1612–1625*, Oxford: Oxford University Press.

O'Day, R. (1982) *Education and Society 1500–1800: The Social Foundations of Early Modern Britain*, London: Longman.

O'Hara, D. (1991) '"Ruled by my friends": Aspects of Marriage in the Diocese of Canterbury, c. 1540–1570', *Continuity and Change* 6: 9–41.

Oiken, S. M. (1979) *Women in Western Political Thought*, Princeton, NJ: Princeton University Press.

Ong, W. J. (1971) *Rhetoric, Romance and Technology: Studies in the Interaction of Expression and Culture*, Ithaca, NY: Cornell University Press.

Orgel, S. (1965) *The Jonsonian Masque*, New York: Columbia University Press.

—— (1989) 'Nobody's Perfect: Or Why Did the English Stage Take Boys for Women?', *South Atlantic Quarterly* 88: 7–29.

—— (1994) 'The Comedian as the Character C', in M. Cordner, P. Holland and J. Kerrigan (eds) *English Comedy*, Cambridge: Cambridge University Press.

Orlin, L. C. (1995) 'The Fictional Families of Elizabeth I', in C. Levin and P. A. Sullivan (eds) *Political Rhetoric, Power, and Renaissance Women*, Albany, NY: State University of New York Press.

Ostashevsky, E. (2004) 'Crooked Figures: Zero and Hindu-Arabic Notation in Shakespeare's *Henry V*', in D. Glimp and M. R. Warren (eds) *Arts of Calculation: Quantifying Thought in Early Modern Europe*, New York: Palgrave Macmillan, pp. 205–28.

Ovid (1977) *Heroides, Amores*, trans. G Showerman and G. P. Goold, Cambridge, Mass.: Harvard University Press.

—— (1993) *The Metamorphoses of Ovid*, trans. A. Mandelbaum, London: Harcourt.

—— (2002) *Ovid's Metamorphoses Translated by Arthur Golding*, ed. M. Forey, Harmondsworth: Penguin.

Palmer, Thomas (1988) *The Emblems of Thomas Palmer: Two Hundred Poosees*, ed. John Manning, New York: AMS Press.

Parke, H. W. (1988) *Sibyls and Sibylline Prophecy in Classical Antiquity*, ed. B. C. McGing, London: Routledge.

Parker, P. (1987) *Literary Fat Ladies: Rhetoric, Gender, Property*, London: Methuen.

—— (1989) 'On the Tongue: Cross-Gendering, Effeminacy and the Art of Words', *Style* 23: 445–65.

—— (1996) 'Virile Style', in L. Fradenburg and C. Freccero (eds) *Premodern Sexualities*, London: Routledge, pp. 201–22.

Paster, G. K. (1993) *The Body Embarrassed: Drama and the Disciplines of Shame in Early Modern England*, Ithaca, NY: Cornell University Press.

Pateman, C. (1988) *The Sexual Contract*, Cambridge: Polity Press.

—— (1991) '"God Hath Ordained to Man a Helper": Hobbes, Patriarchy and Conjugal Right', in M. Lyndon Shanley and C. Pateman (eds) *Feminist Interpretations and Political Theory*, Cambridge: Polity Press, pp. 53–73.

Patterson, A. (1978) *Marvell and the Civic Crown*, Princeton, NJ: Princeton University Press.

—— (2000a) *Marvell: The Writer in Public Life*, Harlow: Longman.

—— (2000b) 'Lady State's First Two Sittings: Marvell's Satiric Canon', *Studies in English Literature* 40: 395–411.

Payne, H. (2002) 'The Cecil Women at Court', in P. Croft (ed.) *Patronage, Culture and Power: The Early Cecils 1558–1612*, New Haven, Conn.: Yale University Press, pp. 265–81.

Peacham, H. (1593) *The Garden of Eloquence*, London.

Peele, G. (1952–70) *The Life and Works of George Peele*, 3 vols, ed. C. T. Prouty, New Haven, Conn.: Yale University Press.

Peltonen, M. (1995) *Classical Humanism and Republicanism in English Politicial Thought 1570–1640*, Cambridge: Cambridge University Press.

Penney, N. (ed.) (1907) *First Publishers of Truth: Being Early Records, now First Printed, of the Introduction of Quakerism into the Counties of England and Wales*, London: Friends' Historical Society.

Peters, K. (2005) *Print Culture and the Early Quakers*, Cambridge: Cambridge University Press.

Petronius (1925) *Petronius*, trans. M. Heseltine, London: William Heinemann.

Pigman, G. (1980) 'Versions of Imitation in the Renaissance', *Renaissance Quarterly*, 33: 1–32.

Plutarch (1936) *Plutarch's Moralia*, 14 vols, trans. F. Cole Babbitt, London: William Heinemann.

Pocock, J. G. A. (1975) *The Machiavellian Moment: Florentine Political Thought and the Atlantic Republican Tradition*, Princeton, NJ: Princeton University Press.

Pomeroy, Sarah B. (1994) *Goddesses, Whores, Wives and Slaves: Women in Classical Antiquity*, London: Pimlico.

Provoste, J. (1698) *A Sermon on the Occasion of the Death of the Right Honourable Elizabeth Lady Cutts*, London.

Prynne, W. (1655) *The Quakers Unmasked, And Clearly Detected to be but the Spawn of Romish Frogs, Jesuites, and Franciscan Fryers*, London.

Purkiss, D. (1992) 'Material Girls: The Seventeenth-Century Woman Debate', in C. Brant and D. Purkiss (eds) *Women, Texts and Histories 1575–1760*, London: Routledge, pp. 69–101

Puttenham, G. (1579) *Partheniades* (BL MS Cotton Vesp. E.viii).

—— (1936) *The Arte of English Poesie* ed. G. Doidge Willcock and A. Walker, Cambridge: Cambridge University Press.

Quilligan, M. (1990) 'The Constant Subject: Instability and Authority in Wroth's *Urania* Poems', in E. Harvey and K. Maus (eds) *Soliciting Interpretation: Literary Theory and Seventeenth-Century Poetry*, Chicago, Ill.: University of Chicago Press, pp. 307–35

Quintilian (1921) *Institutio Oratoria*, 4 vols, trans. H. E. Butler, London: Heinemann.

Rabil, Jr., A. (ed. and trans.) (1996) H.C. Agrippa von Nettesheim, *Declamation on the Nobility and Preeminence of the Female Sex*, Chicago, Ill.: University of Chicago Press.

Rackin, P. (1993) 'Historical Difference/Sexual Difference', in J. R. Brink (ed.) *Privileging Gender in Early Modern England*, Kirksville, Mo.: Sixteenth Century Journal Publishers, pp. 37–64.

Rainbowe, E. (1647) *Sermon on [. . .] Susanna, Countess of Suffolke*, London.

—— (1677) *Sermon [. . .] on Anne, Countess of Pembroke*, London.

Ray, J. (1670) *A Collection of English Proverbs*, Cambridge.

Read, C. (1960) *Lord Burghley and Queen Elizabeth*, London: Jonathan Cape.

Rebhorn, W. A. (1995) *The Emperor of Men's Minds: Literature and the Renaissance Discourse of Rhetoric*, Ithaca, NY: Cornell University Press.

Record, R. (1969) *The Grounde of Artes*, New York and Amsterdam: Da Capo Press.

Rhodes, N. (1992) *The Power of Eloquence and English Renaissance Literature*, Hemel Hempstead: Harvester Wheatsheaf.

—— (2004) *Shakespeare and the Origins of English*, Oxford: Oxford University Press.

Rich, B. (1613) *The Excellency of Good Women*, London.

Richards, J. (2003) *Rhetoric and Courtliness in Early Modern Literature*, Cambridge: Cambridge University Press.

—— (2007) *Rhetoric: the New Critical Idiom*, London: Routledge.

Robertson, J. (1942) *The Art of Letter-Writing: An Essay on the Handbooks Published in England During the Sixteenth and Seventeenth Centuries*, London: Liverpool University Press.

Roesslin, E. (1598) *The Birth of Mankynde Otherwyse Named the Womans Booke*, trans. T. Raynalde, London.

Rotman, B. (1987) *Signifying Nothing: The Semiotics of Zero*, New York: St Martin's Press.

Rousseau, G. S. (1993) '"A Strange Pathology": Hysteria in the Early Modern World 1500–1800', in S. L. Gilman (ed.) *Hysteria beyond Freud*, Berkeley, Calif.: University of California Press, pp. 91–224.

Rubin, G. (1975) 'The Traffic in Women: Notes on the Political Economy of Sex', in R. R. Reiter (ed.) *Towards an Anthropology of Women*, New York: Monthly Review Press, pp. 157–210.

Rueff, J. (1673) *The Expert Midwife*, London.

Sacks, P. (1985) *The English Elegy: Studies in the Genre from Spenser to Yeats*, Baltimore, Md.: Johns Hopkins University Press.

Sadler, J. (1636) *The Sicke Womans Private Looking-Glasse wherein methodically are handled all uterine affects, or diseases arising from the Wombe*, London.

Salmon, J. H. M. (1991) 'Seneca and Tacitus in Jacobean England', in L. Levy Peck (ed.) *The Mental World of the Jacobean Court*, Cambridge: Cambridge University Press, pp. 169–88.

Salter, T. (1579) *The Mirrhor of Modestie*, London.

Sandys, G. (1626) *Ovid's Metamorphoses Englished*, London.

—— (1632) *Ovid's Metamorphoses Englished*, Oxford.

Schochet, G. J. (1988) *The Authoritarian Family and Political Attitudes in Seventeenth-Century England*, New Brunswick, NJ: Transaction.

Schoenfeldt, M. (1999) *Bodies and Selves in Early Modern England: Physiology and Inwardness in Spenser, Shakespeare, Herbert, and Milton*, Cambridge: Cambridge University Press.

Schwartz, R. (1988) *Remembering and Repeating: Biblical Creation in 'Paradise Lost'*, Cambridge: Cambridge University Press.

Schwoerer, L. G. (1998) 'Women's Public Political Voice in England: 1640–

1740', in H. L. Smith (ed.) *Women Writers and the Early Modern British Political Tradition*, Cambridge: Cambridge University Press pp. 56–74.

Scodel, J. (2002) *Excess and the Mean in Early Modern English Literature*, Oxford and Princeton, NJ: Princeton University Press.

Screech, M. (ed.) (1993) *The Complete Essays of Michel de Montaigne*, Harmondsworth: Penguin.

Sedgwick, E. K. (1985) *Between Men: English Literature and Male Homosocial Desire*, New York: Columbia University Press.

Shakespeare, W. (1968) *The Norton Facsimile: The First Folio of Shakespeare*, prepared by Charlton Hinman, London: Paul Hamlyn.

—— (1974) *The Riverside Shakespeare*, ed. G. Blakemore Evans et al., Boston, Mass.: Houghton Mifflin.

—— (2003) *Much Ado About Nothing*, ed. F. H. Mares, Cambridge: University of Cambridge Press.

Shakespeare, W. and Quarles, J. (1655) *The Rape of Lucrece, Committed by Tarquin the Sixt; and the Remarkable Judgments that Befel him for it. [. . .]. Whereunto is Annexed, The Banishment of Tarquin; Or, the Reward of Lust by J. Quarles*, London.

Shapiro, M. (1996) *Shakespeare and the Jews*, New York: Columbia University Press.

Shirley, J. (1686) *An Illustrious History of Women*, London.

Shuger, D. (1993) 'Sacred Rhetoric in the Renaissance', in H. F. Plett (ed.) *Renaissance Rhetoric*, Berlin and New York: Walter de Gruyter, pp. 121–42.

Sidney, P. (1973) 'A Letter to Queen Elizabeth', in K. Duncan-Jones and J. van Dorsten (eds) *Miscellaneous Prose*, Oxford: Clarendon.

—— (1985) *The Old Arcadia*, ed. K. Duncan-Jones, Oxford: Oxford University Press.

—— (1989) 'A Defence of Poesy', in K. Duncan-Jones (ed.) *Sir Philip Sidney*, Oxford: Oxford University Press.

Skinner, Q. (1978) *The Foundations of Modern Political Thought*, 2 vols, Cambridge: Cambridge University Press.

—— (1996) *Reason and Rhetoric in the Philosophy of Hobbes*, Cambridge: Cambridge University Press.

Skinner, Q. and Phillipson, N. (eds) (1993) *Political Discourse in Early Modern Britain*, Cambridge: Cambridge University Press.

Smith, A. (1983) *Lectures on Rhetoric and Belles Lettres*, ed. J. C. Bryce, Oxford: Clarendon.

Smith, H. L. (1998) *Women Writers and the Early Modern British Political Tradition*, Cambridge: Cambridge University Press.

Smith, T. (1583) *De Republica Anglorum: The Maner of Government or Policie of the Realme of England*, London.

Smith, T. S. (2004) '*The Lady's Rhetorick*: The Tip of the Iceberg of Women's Rhetorical Education in Enlightenment France and Britain', *Rhetorica* 22: 349–73.

Sondergard, S. L. (2002) *Sharpening Her Pen: Strategies of Rhetorical Violence by*

Early Modern English Women Writers, Selinsgrove, Pa.: Susquehanna University Press.

Sowernam, E. (1617) *Ester Hath Hang'd Haman: Or An Answer to a Lewd Pamphlet, Entituled, The Arraignment of Women*, London.

Spenser E. (1999) *The Shorter Poems*, ed. R. A. McCabe, Harmondsworth: Penguin.

Steele, R. (ed.) (1992) *The Earliest Arithmetics in English*, Oxford: Oxford University Press.

Stevenson, J. (2005) *Women Latin Poets*, Oxford: Oxford University Press.

Stewart, A. (1997) *Close Readers: Humanism and Sodomy in Early Modern England*, Princeton, NJ: Princeton University Press.

Stone, I. F. (1988) *The Trial of Socrates*, London: Jonathan Cape.

Strabo (1961) *The Geography of Strabo*, 8 vols, trans. H. L. Jones, London: William Heinemann.

Stretton, T. (1998) *Women Waging Law in Elizabethan England*, Cambridge: Cambridge University Press.

Stubbs, J. (1968) *'Gaping Gulf' with Letters and other Relevant Documents*, ed. L. E. Berry, Charlottesville, Va.: University of Virginia Press.

Sutherland, C. M and Sutcliffe, R. (eds) (1999) *The Changing Tradition: Women in the History of Rhetoric*, Calgary: University of Calgary Press.

Tadmor, N. (2001) *Family and Friends in Eighteenth-Century England: Household, Kinship, and Patronage*, Cambridge: Cambridge University Press.

Tarter, M. L. (2001) 'Quaking in the Light: The Politics of Quaker Women's Corporeal Prophecy in the Seventeenth-Century Transatlantic World', in J. M. Lindman and M. L. Tarter (eds) *A Centre of Wonders: the Body in Early America*, Ithaca, NY: Cornell University Press, pp. 145–62.

Thompson, A. and Roberts, S. (1997) *Women Reading Shakespeare, 1660–1900: An Anthology of Criticism*, Manchester: Manchester University Press.

Thorne, A. (2006) 'Women's Petitionary Letters and Early Seventeenth-Century Treason Trials', *Women's Writing: Special Issue: Epistolarity to 1900* 13: 23–43.

Tilley, M. (1950) *A Dictionary of the Proverbs in England in the Sixteenth and Seventeenth Centuries*, Ann Arbor, Mich.: University of Michigan Press.

Tilney, E. (1573) *A Briefe and Pleasant Discourse of Duties in Mariage, Called the Flower of Friendshippe*, London.

Tolmie, M. (1977) *The Triumph of the Saints: The Separate Churches of London, 1616–1649*, Cambridge: Cambridge University Press.

Torshell, S. (1620) *The Womans Glorie*, London.

Trachtenberg, J. (1943) *The Devil and the Jews: the Medieval Conception of the Jew and its Relation to Modern Antisemitism*, New Haven, Conn.: Yale University Press.

Trapnel, A. (1654) *Anna Trapnel's Report and Plea, or, a Narrative of her Journey From London into Cornwall*, London.

Tuke, S. (ed.) (1825) *Selections from the Epistles, &c. of George Fox*, York: W. Alexander & Son.

Tuke, T. (1616) *A Treatise Against Painting and Tincturing of Men and Women*, London.

Turner, W. (1562) *The Seconde Parte of William Turners Herball*, London.

Tuvil, D. (1616) *Asylum Veneris, or a Sanctuary for Ladies*, London.

Underdown, D. E. (1985) 'The Taming of the Scold: The Enforcement of Patriarchal Authority in Early Modern England', in A. J. Fletcher and J. Stevenson (eds) *Order and Disorder in Early Modern England*, Cambridge: Cambridge University Press, pp. 116–36.

Valesio, P. (1980) *Novantiqua: Rhetorics as a Contemporary Theory*, Bloomington, Ind.: Indiana University Press.

Van Houdt, T. et al. (eds) (2002) *Self-Presentation and Social Identification: the Rhetoric and Pragmatics of Letter Writing in Early Modern Times*, Leuven: Brill.

Vickers, B. (1989) *In Defence of Rhetoric*, Oxford: Clarendon.

Virgil (1668) *The Works of Publius Virgilius Maro Translated, Adorned with Sculpture, And Illustrated with Annotations, By John Ogilby*, London.

Wall, A. D. (2001) 'Deference and Defiance in Women's Letters of the Thynne Family: The Rhetoric of Relationships', in J. Daybell (ed.) *Women's Letters and Letter-Writing in England, 1450–1700*, Basingstoke: Palgrave, pp. 77–93.

Wall, W. (1993) *The Imprint of Gender: Authorship and Publication in the English Renaissance*, Ithaca, NY: Cornell University Press.

Wallace, D. D., Jr. (1982) *Puritans and Predestination: Grace in English Protestant Theology, 1525–1695*, Chapel Hill, NC: University of North Carolina Press.

Wallace, J. M. (1968) *Destiny His Choice: The Loyalism of Andrew Marvell*, Cambridge: Cambridge University Press.

Watson, F. (1912) *Vives and the Renascence Education of Women*, London: Edward Arnold.

Waugh, D. (1656) 'A Relation Concerning Dorothy Waughs Cruell Usage by the Mayor of Carlile', in Anon., *The Lambs Defence Against Lyes*, London.

Wayne, V. (1987) 'Zenobia in Medieval and Renaissance Literature', in C. Levin and J. Watson (eds) *Ambiguous Realities: Women in the Middle Ages and Renaissance*, Detroit, Mich.: Wayne State University Press, pp. 48–65.

Webbe, William (1870) *A Discourse of English Poetrie* (1586), repr. in *English Reprints*, ed. Edward Arber, London.

Webster, J. (1975) *Three Plays*, ed. D. Gunby, Harmondsworth: Penguin.

Weil, R. (1999) *Political Passions: Gender, the Family and Political Argument in England 1680–1714*, Manchester: Manchester University Press.

Wells-Cole, A. (1997) *Art and Decoration in Elizabethan and Jacobean England*, New Haven, Conn., and London: Yale University Press for Paul Mellon Centre for British Art.

Wentworth, P. (1598) *A Pithy Exhortation to her Majesty for Establishing her Successor*, London.

Wertheimer, M. Meijer (ed.) (1997) *Listening to Their Voices: The Rhetorical Activities of Historical Women*, Columbia, SC: University of South Carolina Press.

Whately, W. (1619) *A Bride-Bush: Or A Direction for Married Persons*, London.

Whigham, F. (1981) 'The Rhetoric of Elizabethan Suitors' Letters', *Publications of the Modern Language Association* 96: 864–82.

Williams, G. (1994) *A Dictionary of Sexual Language and Imagery in Shakespearean and Stuart Literature*, 3 vols, London and Atlantic Highlands, NJ: Athlone Press.

Wills, G. (1995) *Witches and Jesuits: Shakespeare's 'Macbeth'*, Oxford: Oxford University Press.

Wilson, J. (1980) *Entertainments for Elizabeth I*, Woodbridge: D. S. Brewer

Wilson, T. (1982) *Arte of Rhetorique*, ed. T. J. Derrick, London and New York: Garland Publishing.

Withington, P. (2005) *The Politics of Commonwealth: Citizens and Freemen in Early Modern England*, Cambridge: Cambridge University Press.

Wolcomb, R. (1606) *The State of the Godly Both in this Life, and in the Life to Come*, London.

Woodbridge, L. (1984) *Women and the English Renaissance: Literature and the Nature of Womankind, 1540–1620*, Brighton: Harvester Press.

Woods, S. (1999) *Lanyer: A Renaissance Woman Poet*, Oxford: Oxford University Press.

Woodward W. H. (1905) *Vittorino da Feltre and other Humanist Educators: Essays and Versions*, Cambridge: Cambridge University Press.

Worden, B. (1996) *The Sound of Virtue: Philip Sidney's 'Arcadia' and Elizabethan Politics*, New Haven, Conn.: Yale University Press.

Wright, P. (1987) 'A Change in Direction: The Ramifications of a Female Household, 1558–1603', in D. Starkey (ed.) *The English Court From the Wars of the Roses to the Civil War*, Harlow: Longman, pp. 147–72.

Wroth, M. (1983) *The Poems of Lady Mary Wroth*, ed. J. Roberts, Baton Rouge, La.: Louisiana State University Press.

Yates, F. A. (1947) 'Queen Elizabeth I as *Astraea*', *Journal of the Warburg and Courtauld Institutes*, 10: 27–82.

Zaret, D. (2000) *Origins of Democratic Culture: Printing, Petitions and the Public Sphere in Early Modern England*, Princeton, NJ: Princeton University Press.

Ziolkowski, J. (1985) *Alan of Lille's Grammar of Sex: The Meaning of Grammar to a Twelfth-Century Intellectual*, Cambridge, Mass.: The Medieval Academy of America.

Zitner, S. P. (1975) '*King Lear* and its Language', in Rosalie L. Colie and F. T. Flahiff (eds) *Some Facets of 'King Lear': Essays in Prismatic Criticism*, Toronto and Buffalo, NY: University of Toronto Press, pp. 3–22.

Zwicker, S. N. (1987) 'Lines of Authority: Politics and Literary Culture in the Restoration', in Kevin Sharpe and Steven N. Zwicker (eds) *Politics of Discourse: The Literature and History of Seventeenth-Century England*, Berkeley, Calif.: University of California Press, pp. 230–70.

Index